Listen to the voices of the past,
catch the scent of memory.
Closer here to god than you may ever be
I bide my time, I wait to see…

This is me behind the mask of years,
still here although my voice is faint
and eyes awash with age's tears…

Others tiptoe restlessly —
each an island in their own white bed,
rehearsing just how it will be
when their time comes.

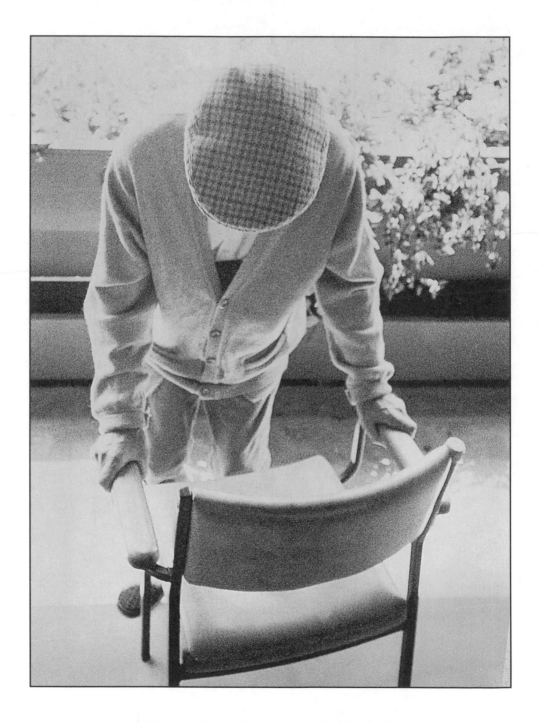

We shared a sadness at your lonely death,
both wishing you had chosen closeness,
had given us just some small sign, invited us to stay —
but you had sent us both away.

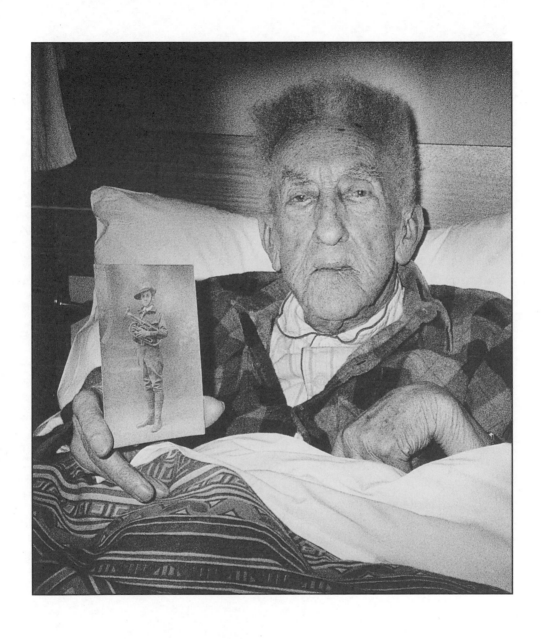

And old men pass quietly through,
without so much as a hint
as to who they might have been.

The death of the other is a loss which affects my own life . . .
(Jüngel, *Death*)

Oh, what a work it was to die! — to shake off a body that had no more
worth left in it than a snake's cast skin, Mary could imagine him saying of
himself. — Not so she. She clung jealously to each day on which she still had
him with her . . . and at length . . . there was nothing to be done but to sit
and watch him die.
(Henry Handel Richardson, *The Fortunes of Richard Mahony*)

We all labour against our own cure; for death is the cure of all diseases.
(Sir Thomas Browne, *Religio Medici*)

Like pilgrims to th' appointed place we tread,
The world's an inn, and death the journey's end.
(John Dryden, *Palamon and Arcite*)

I said, 'No, the last thing I need is an ambulance. But maybe you could bring
me some hot milk and brandy'.
(May Sarton, *After the Stroke: a Journal*)

Living, Dying, Caring

Other titles published by Ausmed Publications

Renal Nursing – a guide to practice
Bobbee Terrill

Infectious Diseases in Children
Tara Walker

Ageing at Home: Practical Approaches to Community Care
Edited by Theresa Cluning

Complementary Therapies for Nurses and Midwives — from vision to practice
Edited by Pauline McCabe

Keeping in Touch with someone who has Alzheimer's
Jane Crisp

Geriatric Medicine, 2nd edn
Len Gray, Michael Woodward, Ron Scholes, David Fonda and Wendy Busby

The Midwife and the Bereaved Family
Jane Warland

Living in a New Country: Understanding Migrants' Health
Edited by Pranee Liamputtong Rice

Palliative Care Nursing: A Guide to Practice
Edited by Sanchia Aranda and Margaret O'Connor

Caring for the Person with Faecal Incontinence
Karen Cavarra, Andrea Prentice and Cynthea Wellings
Revised by Janette Williams

Practical Approaches to Infection Control in Residential Aged Care
Kevin J. Kendall

Promoting Men's Health
Edited by Tom Laws

Nursing the Person with Cancer
Edited by Gordon Poulton

Nursing Documentation: writing what we do
Edited by Jennifer Richmond

Spirituality: The Heart of Nursing
Edited by Professor Susan Ronaldson

Rethinking Dementia — an Australian approach
Edited by Sally Garratt and Elery Hamilton-Smith

Thinking Management: Focusing on People
Edited by Jean Anderson

Caring for People with Problem Behaviours, 2nd edn
Bernadette Keane and Carolyn Dixon

Asian Mothers, Western Birth
Edited by Pranee Liamputtong Rice

Unique and Ordinary
Rosalie Hudson and Jennifer Richmond

Living, Dying, Caring:

life and death in a nursing home

ROSALIE HUDSON
and
JENNIFER RICHMOND

Foreword by ALAN PEARSON

AUSMED PUBLICATIONS

Melbourne

Australasian Health Education Systems Pty Ltd
(ACN 005 611 626)
trading as
Ausmed Publications
277 Mount Alexander Road
Ascot Vale, Victoria 3032, Australia

First published June 1994 (as *Unique and Ordinary: Reflections on living and dying in a nursing home*)
Reprinted September 1996
Second edition published October 2000 (as *Living, Dying, Caring: life and death in a nursing home*)

Further copies of this book and of all other Ausmed publications are available from the Distribution Manager, Ausmed Publications, PO Box 4086, Melbourne University, Victoria 3010, Australia.
Telephone +61 3 9375 7311.
Fax +61 3 9375 7299.
E-mail ausmed@ausmed.com.au
Home page www.ausmed.com.au

National Library of Australia Cataloguing-in-Publication data:
Hudson, Rosalie, 1938–
Living, Dying, Caring: life and death in a nursing home.

Bibliography.
Includes index.
ISBN 0 9577988 6 5
1. Nursing home care - Australia. 2. Nursing home patients - Care - Australia. 3. Aged - Institutional care - Australia. I. Richmond, Jennifer, 1953– . II. Title.

362.160994
Edited by Julie Domanski and Robyn Whiteley
Text set in 11/14 Adobe Garamond
Cover, design, typesetting and printing by Hyde Park Press, 4 Deacon Avenue, Richmond, South Australia 5033, telephone (08) 8234 2044, fax (08) 8234 1887, e-mail hpp@olis.net.au

ACKNOWLEDGEMENTS
On page 267, the three lines from 'Do Not Go Gentle into That Good Night' by Dylan Thomas from *Collected Poems* published by JM Dent are used by permission of David Higham Associates.

DISCLAIMER
While the stories in the publication are based on factual situations, real names and other details have been altered to protect the identity of the persons concerned. Resemblance to any particular person is therefore purely coincidental.
Neither the photographs nor the poems are intended to reflect any particular person depicted in the stories.
Photographs of deceased residents are used with permission of next of kin.

FOREWORD

As Australia moves into the 21st century, new strategies are needed to provide services that keep pace with the rapidly rising ageing population. Not only will there be a larger number of Australians over age 65, this age group will constitute a greater proportion of the total population (from 10 per cent in the late 1990s to 11.7 per cent — 2.33 million people — by the year 2001). The number of people 80 years or older will double during the next two decades and many will require nursing home or domiciliary care.

Nursing homes provide supportive accommodation and nursing for people who need assistance to reach their own aspirations in their daily lives. Although only 4.4 per cent of all Australians reside in nursing homes, the deleterious effects on older people living in institutional settings has been well documented. Commonwealth governments have instigated a series of reforms over the past 20 years, all aiming to provide quality care and to promote resident rights. Early measures focused on demedicalising nursing homes and providing a more home-like environment. There is now much less emphasis placed on the treatment of physical problems and more attention is directed to providing holistic care and improving quality of life.

Caring, intelligent, sensitive and creative nursing is central to quality care in the nursing home setting; it embodies the values identified, assembled and preserved by countless numbers of nurses throughout the ages; and it has touched the lives of a large proportion of the world's population at some time or other. Nursing's very essence, though dependent upon a thorough understanding of the physical and social sciences, lies in the nurse's ability to reach out to another in a very human, practical way and to 'be there' as a caring other. It is this very essence that nurses, doctors, health service managers and planners, governments and the general population find so difficult to describe or define, and it is the most difficult to pass on to those who are learning to become nurses. Most significantly, all of us who are nurses have experienced difficulty in holding onto the essence of nursing in the hurly-burly, ever-changing reality of contemporary health care.

This book skilfully and elegantly exposes the essence or core of nursing that is so highly valued by society as a whole and by nursing home residents in particular. Beautifully written, the practical wisdom of the authors and their ability to articulate complex concepts shines throughout this important text. Living and dying in a nursing home can be a positive, affirming experience for older people and their relatives and friends and this book offers a solid foundation on which nurses and care workers can create possibilities to ensure that such an experience takes place. I congratulate the authors on this illuminating work and commend it to health policy makers, managers, nurses, medical practitioners, allied health workers and care workers in aged care.

Alan Pearson
RN, ONC, DipNEd, DANS, MSc, PhD, FCN(NSW), FINA, FRCNA, FRCN
Professor of Nursing at La Trobe University, Melbourne, Victoria, Australia

Melbourne
November 2000

CONTENTS

INTRODUCTION

This book is based on our 1994 publication *Unique and Ordinary: Reflections on living and dying in a nursing home* When considering a second edition, we realised there were many changes required and more stories to tell. These changes and stories are more significant than mere amendments, so they find themselves in a new book. However, the basic theme of death and dying is common to all humans, and those readers familiar with our first title will recognise this piece of wisdom in our carrying forward into the new book so many of the old stories that have endured and maintained their relevance.

The experience of death is unique to those who are dying. The residents are, therefore, our teachers. This philosophy translates into practice when care is individualised and continuously evaluated. In this way the residents help us to build on previous learning. These stories have caused us to pause and reflect on the nature of each resident's unique life and death and what it is that stimulates us to improve their care. In action–reflection mode, this book recalls the stories of residents who have lived and died in our nursing home, and draws implications for enhanced practice. We have discovered that, while there is much in our practice to be commended, there is also much that could be improved. These are ordinary stories reflecting the lives and deaths of ordinary nursing home residents. However, although there are some common threads, there is no general prescription of care which may be applied to every situation.

The stories also bear the stamp of the staff; of the organisational culture and the philosophy of partnership that guides all our care. These are our stories; they are not intended to convey any distinctions of quality. Your stories may reflect similar or quite different facets of care. There is no intrinsic 'rightness' about our illustrations; they do not reflect perfect care. However, many issues are raised which may provoke deeper thought, different educational emphases and attitudinal changes in carers. Our aim in publishing these reflections is to invite discussion aimed at promoting best practice in the care of nursing home residents.

In bringing these stories to you, we acknowledge that they are both extraordinary and ordinary; extraordinary in their individuality, yet ordinary in the sense that residents die in nursing homes every day. We confess to a degree of sadness in changing deceased residents' names to protect confidentiality; for their names and personalities

1

remain fresh in our memory. In a society which favours youth over old age, where institutionalisation often signifies loss of uniqueness, we acknowledge that, in writing of former residents in this way, we too have lost some of their identity.

The book is not merely about end-of-life care; we believe that, from the moment of placing their name on the waiting list, residents and families will have questions, fears and anxieties; acknowledging that for most residents this will be their last home. What reassurance may be offered at this point, so that when death is imminent, the resident feels secure? It will be shown throughout the book that security and trust are not automatically or instantly conveyed. As many of the stories show, thoughtful, compassionate and sensitive care throughout the resident's life in the nursing home lays the foundation for security and dignity at the time of death.

We also raise the question of outcomes; how is the quality of death and dying measured? How is each episode of care evaluated? In reflecting on practice, we emphasise the constant challenge raised by these questions and conclude that quality outcomes are determined by an agreed goal of care, which may differ in each situation. In other words, the foundation for responsive care is laid by careful assessment and continuous review.

In bringing this material together, we acknowledge our professional growth since we first started writing 10 years ago. If there is some variation in style, tone or writing skill between the old and new material, it is hoped that may be an encouraging sign of the exciting process of human development that continues until life's end, as the stories of the residents who contributed to this book will attest. From data collected over a period of 10 years, we have selected the case histories of approximately 40 residents. Woven into the factual material are our own reflections, documented through personal journalling at the time of the resident's death. The written and verbal reflections of others are also included, adding to the richness of the data. Perceptions, impressions, joys and sadness are revealed as elements in the grieving and growing process surrounding death. This means the stories are told in a variety of ways, reflecting the unique nature of each resident's death and the variety of inter-relationships throughout their life in the nursing home. While the stories are of ordinary lives of ordinary residents in an ordinary nursing home, each life and death is revealed in its uniqueness. In many respects, therefore, this book will have relevance for those concerned with issues of death and dying as they affect older people in any care setting.

We aim to place in broad context the comprehensive clinical skills and palliative care principles central to the care of dying residents. We believe that, by reflecting on these stories, we also are affected. The life and death of each resident reminds us that our own life is transient, making its mark and taking its place within a broad historical context. This broader understanding of death reminds us that we do not remain isolated from and unaffected by the death of another person, for death is part of the human condition. Our reflections are influenced by classical and contemporary literature and other creative modes of expression. Hence, the many faces of death are represented through photography and poetry as well as anecdote and analysis. These reflections are intended to convey something of death's elusive mystery; for ultimately, death may not be fully captured either by imagination or scientific scrutiny.

The reflections following each story are intended to draw out implications for practice. We discuss the meaning of the lived experience associated with each story, delving more deeply than a mere analysis of the facts. In this new book, we have identified quality issues for enhanced practice in the stories and the reflections presented. These issues have been divided into three sections for quick reference; the gerontic nurse, management and indirect carers. We acknowledge the wide variety in terminology for those involved in aged care and offer a brief explanation of these terms. Gerontic nurse signifies a professional registered nurse with postgraduate qualifications or relevant experience, who understands the complexities and challenges of caring for frail residents until death. In many facilities, a gerontic nurse will be selected as the nurse in charge of a group of residents (charge nurse, unit manager or other designation). Management refers to the person with overall responsibility for the nursing home and usually applies to the director of nursing and/or other administrative staff accountable to the government for the outcome of all care. Indirect carers are those who (usually on a part-time basis) are not involved in direct personal care of the resident, but who play a vital role in the residents' holistic care. The term 'indirect carers' includes all non-nursing staff, such as food and domestic services staff, clerical staff, maintenance persons, chaplains, hairdressers, podiatrists, allied health professionals (music therapy, occupational therapy, leisure activities, physiotherapy, complementary therapy) and volunteers. This list is indicative of the range of indirect carers but is not exhaustive. The term 'indirect' is not intended to convey a secondary role to that of the nursing/personal care workers. Many of the stories show the far-reaching effects of the death of one resident not only on the whole nursing home community but also on the wider community.

We are not merely spectators of human activity, but agents of change. In reflecting on our practice we have the potential to change the way things are for the ultimate benefit of the residents in our care. We have made several references to the value of research into the area of death and dying; the field is wide open for the kind of research that will influence practice and enrich the lives of dying residents and their carers. We have also made the point that, while factors of statistics, documentation, research and continuous quality improvement have a significant place, at best they are only a guide to care and not a guarantee of dignified death. Such objective data can be effectively applied only by means of sensitive, reflective interpretation. Many of the stories and their reflections signify the importance of attitudes. When there is an attitudinal change away from the notion of custodial care to that of empathy and advocacy, then nursing home residents will flourish.

We gratefully acknowledge the unique contribution of our primary sources: residents past and present, staff, volunteers, visiting doctors and other health professionals, pastoral visitors, relatives and friends of the nursing home. Their experiences form the substance of this book.

Rosalie Hudson and Jennifer Richmond
November 2000

CHAPTER ONE

⁓⁂⁓

GOALS OF CARE: IDEAL AND REALITY

Ageism, or a stereotypical attitude towards older people, is such a part of our culture that we don't notice it. Ageism can be discerned in pejorative language that refers to an older person as an 'oldie', a 'dirty old man' or 'such a sweet old thing'. Ageism is evident in the cult of youth which would prefer to see ageing abolished. It is also evident in economic descriptions of the ageing population as 'a tidal wave which will swamp us all', or in the mind of the market where persons are valued only for their productivity. Ageism is apparent in architecture that makes access to buildings difficult for older persons, and in advertising which projects the perfect body image. It may also be discerned in funding constraints which deny nursing home residents access to the highest quality palliative care and in inadequate resource allocation which prevents proprietors from adequately improving accommodation standards. All these attitudes perpetuate the community's perception of nursing homes as places to be avoided at all costs. The 'out of sight out of mind' attitude signifies a denial of death, protecting the public from their own fears of ageing — and of death.

The increasing frailty of residents admitted to nursing homes means staff are familiar with death. Although there is increased understanding of the dying residents' needs on the part of professionals educated in palliative care, the rhetoric of holistic care and dignified death is not always apparent in practice. A continuing gap between theory and practice means many miss out on optimum care at the point of death. How may the ideal be achieved — that is, the provision of skilled care which addresses the dying resident's physical, spiritual, psychological and emotional needs, practised within a homelike environment?

The increasing availability of hospice/palliative care services for patients who are terminally ill (who have a medical diagnosis likely to result in death within months) is laudable; the philosophy of their care is well recognised and respected. Yet there is a puzzling lack of resources specific to the unique situation of the nursing home resident who is dying. Hospice/palliative care services set standards for what may often be a younger group of patients managed at home with family support in the clearly defined, final stages of terminal illness. Yet there is a clear disparity between these services and the provision of palliative care to nursing home residents who are dying.

Palliative care aims to enable persons with terminal illness to live in dignity, peace and comfort for the duration of their illness. Its focus is on control and alleviation of symptoms and on maintenance of quality of life, rather than cure of disease. For this reason, palliative care is often best provided in the patient's home rather than in a hospital.

When the nursing home is regarded as the patient's home the environment readily exists for the application of high-quality palliative care. However, some palliative practices exclude the nursing home resident whose terminal illness is not clearly defined, being a combination of acute and chronic degenerative disorders that may or may not include cancer. Palliative care guidelines acknowledge the increasing number of deaths in nursing homes and the demographic trends which indicate the increase of cancer as a cause of death. Complicating chronic disorders and imprecise diagnosis should not deny a nursing home resident access to high-quality palliative care.

To provide excellent care for nursing home residents who are dying, palliative care policies and procedures need to be formulated, using these objectives as a framework:
- to meet the physical, emotional, spiritual, cultural and social needs of people with a terminal illness
- to protect the rights and dignity of people with a terminal illness
- to ensure continuity of care as each person's circumstances change
- to support the residents, their families and carers as a unit
- to enable bereavement and follow-up counselling.

More specifically, palliative care is a specialist discipline requiring:
- knowledge of pain management and symptom control
- access to pastoral and spiritual services
- understanding of and commitment to patient advocacy
- culturally sensitive care
- a care team drawn from diverse disciplines.

Palliative care continues after the death of the patient when support and counselling for the family/carer are offered.

In any field, specialist care is expensive, and palliative care is no exception. Despite an increasing number of deaths in nursing homes each year, a wide gap remains between the theoretical formula for palliation and the resources available for its practice in aged care. There are no guidelines available on how to make an already lean budget stretch further. Considering other criteria are met, this economic disadvantage leads us to describe current nursing home care of the dying as 'palliative care — without the budget'.

Consequently, the reality of death in a nursing home may be less than the ideal. However, as the following chapters unfold, it will be evident that one readily available resource, and one which is often under-rated, is the commitment of nursing home staff. Already skilled and experienced in caring for older people who are frail and dying, these carers have the potential for developing greater expertise in palliative care. In practice, however, reaching the ideal without appropriate funding is often at the staff's personal cost. Consider, for example, the following ideals and realities:

1. **Palliative care has as its goal the delivery of high-quality care to people in the terminal phase of their illness. The focus is on controlling and alleviating symptoms, rather than effecting a cure.**

Bob's pain was getting worse. The doctor thought it was liver cancer, but perhaps wisely, decided not to subject Bob to hospital investigations. Because Bob was aphasic following a stroke he couldn't describe his pain verbally nor was he able to make sense of a visual analogue scale. The nurses who had cared for him continuously for three years were skilled at interpreting his body language and suggested a narcotic analgesic be ordered. The doctor, who was reluctant to prescribe morphine, seemed unaware of any other treatment for Bob's symptoms as described by the nurses. Knowing he had not read widely in this area the doctor suspected that the nurses were more knowledgeable. Resenting this, he became angry when they raised the matter again. Meanwhile Bob was quietly dying — in pain.

2. **All persons have the right to informed decision making about their care.**

It is sometimes difficult to define when active treatment stops and symptom management begins; it is not clear at what point Bob ceases to be an elderly person with a chronic illness and becomes an elderly person with a terminal illness requiring palliative care. In residential aged care, where diagnostic procedures may either be unavailable or inappropriate, it is not easy to discern when the focus of care should change from active treatment to palliation.

It was only in hindsight that we realised many decisions were based on our attitudes rather than Bob's needs. ('Come on Bob, it will do you good to go to music group with your friends!' Or, 'You must eat or you'll fade away to a shadow.') What choices may have been given to Bob had his place on the path to death been clear? Bob had been given no information about the metastatic spread of his cancer, and therefore no options were presented to him concerning symptom control. Even if he suspected he was dying there was no opportunity to make his own decisions about his care.

3. Palliative care needs are best met within the context of an interdisciplinary team.

A community palliative care team is drawn from many different disciplines and it is acknowledged that such team building requires time. A team framework promotes optimum practice, particularly when a diverse group of health professionals is moulded into a cohesive whole. In the aged-care setting, however, the funding model is reductionist rather than holistic, rewarding each separate health professional for discipline-specific focus on the resident's deficits. Furthermore, when tasks pertaining to the resident's functional deficits are weighted for funding purposes, the resident is again divided into parts, and holistic care is compromised. Busy staff concentrate on specific interventions but the team may not have an overall view.

It seems that holistic, interdisciplinary care falls into the area of unfunded luxury dependent on the goodwill of staff. For example:
- *The chef knows Bob's food preferences and prepares special menus for him, but only when she has time.*
- *A nurse accompanies Bob to his outpatients appointment in her own time.*
- *When Bob can't hold the newspaper any more the cleaner spends his morning tea break reading the sports pages to him.*
- *The charge nurse and allied health staff discuss Bob's special needs in a hasty after-work meeting.*
- *The evening charge nurse discusses a delicate situation with the relatives after the morning charge nurse phones from home to convey her concern.*
- *The music therapist calls at the library on his way home to borrow music tapes he hopes will soothe Bob's restlessness.*
- *Bob's family are unable to visit frequently so the staff organise themselves into an (unpaid) roster in order to sit with Bob in his last hours.*

Another important area not always covered in nursing homes is the dying resident's spiritual care needs. Chaplaincy services are not considered an important funding issue, resulting in ad hoc arrangements rather than planned interventions based on thorough assessment. Where there is a chaplain or pastoral care worker available, they are seldom considered part of the team; issues of accountability, reporting and documentation are not always clearly defined.

While the semblance of a team is evident, palliative care in nursing homes lacks the professional cohesion and budget resources to provide the best outcome for all concerned.

4. There must be appropriate access to consultants in palliative care.

The matter of referral to a palliative care consultant remains a complex and sensitive issue. Many general practitioners are reluctant to refer, believing they have sufficient resources to deal with complex symptom control and pain relief. Families are not always sure of their rights to seek a second opinion and nursing staff are concerned about alienating local doctors by advocating the services of a consultant. In the hospital system the lines of communication between oncologist, surgeon, physician and palliative care consultant are not always clear.

Bob was the third resident within six weeks to need the services of a consultant oncologist or physician who would consider referral to a palliative care consultant. Even if the local doctor agrees to make the referral, few specialists will make a 'home visit' to a pensioner in a nursing home. 'Get an ambulance and send him in to the clinic', is a common response to such a request. However, it is not quite so simple. Who would accompany Bob? Who would speak for him and allay his anxiety? On that day it was not possible to provide an escort for him, and his family were unable to assist. The charge nurse's comprehensive letter was returned unopened and when she telephoned all she heard was, 'No, I'm afraid it's not possible for the doctor to come to the phone'. When the consultant finally saw Bob, he sent him back to the nursing home, the letter of advice to the local doctor arriving three weeks later. Bob spent six hours in the hospital transit lounge waiting for someone to notice him, waiting for the ambulance to arrive for his return trip. Was it his age which determined his low priority?

The consultant had suggested dietary advice for Bob. A dietitian would visit, but not for about 10 days because she was so busy. That visit would cost the nursing home a significant amount; the community dietitian, who used to provide a free service, had been retrenched due to restructuring.

5. Staff are encouraged, educated and supported.

Good staff morale is dependent on encouragement, education and support. This in turn, benefits the care of residents. However, when death occurs, nurses may find it very hard to let go, or to say goodbye. Hospice/palliative care manuals acknowledge the importance of debriefing, of providing the opportunity for staff and family to vent their feelings after a death has occurred. This also provides an opportunity for the team to evaluate all the care, identifying positive aspects and learning from errors and omissions. In the nursing home where there is no funding for such meetings, staff still deserve to be debriefed, encouraged, educated and supported.

There was a difference of opinion about whether Bob should be in hospital or remain in the nursing home. 'But didn't you see his face when he came back from outpatients! We couldn't send him back, this is his home.' A review meeting was called, three staff offering to cover other resident care so the most appropriate staff could attend. The doctor's opinion was sought and when a revised plan of care was established, the charge nurse wrote it up carefully at home. Now the goal of care was clearly spelled out and the staff were no longer in a situation of conflict.

It was agreed that Bob should have a low dose of morphine, administered regularly. There were several new staff members since the last in-service education session on the use of narcotics; hence, some misguided opinions were still circulating. Several brief discussions ensued until all staff were acquainted with the issues. Bob died only a few minutes after an injection of morphine, given reluctantly by a newly appointed registered nurse. 'I knew he shouldn't have had another dose,' said the uninformed staff member. Although it was 7 p.m. and the director of nursing had only just arrived home, she returned to support the staff and to share her own grief, for she too had become very fond of Bob. No time for any comprehensive debriefing, only a quick calling together of all available staff for a stand-up 'meeting' before they resumed their busy evening's work. Consensus was reached about necessary phone calls; there were certain staff and volunteers who would like to know immediately. This time-consuming task was shared in order to minimise the overtime. In the absence of family ('We've said our goodbyes' they had told us), staff were encouraged to say their goodbyes to Bob in their own individual and private way.

Staff support is usually confined to the period immediately after the resident's death, for the incoming resident requires full attention. What happens to the accumulated grief, especially if there are several deaths in a short space of time? Some staff seem to get by, but some find difficulty in expressing their feelings.

What encouragement was due to staff who had given so much of their energy and affection to Bob over three years? A sincere word of thanks to the staff from nursing administration goes a long way. When a person dies in the hospice setting, there are often family members and friends to offer positive feedback to staff, providing ongoing encouragement and praise. However, in the nursing home, families themselves are quite often elderly and frail, their focus necessarily drawn towards their own welfare. The source of praise and encouragement must, therefore, come from elsewhere. Often this word is spoken but not passed on. Staff meeting minutes and notes of commendation are all important avenues for communicating positive feedback. These extra tasks impose an extra burden on administration staff usually busy with the processes of arranging admission of another resident.

Some weeks after Bob's death a call from his son prompted a senior nurse to visit Bob's elderly widow after work. Bob's widow wanted to be discreet. She was relieved that her son had called the nursing home, but embarrassed too. She was fond of all the nurses; after knowing them for three years some strong attachments had formed. She had her favourites, mostly the nurses Bob liked best. One of the not-so-favoured nurses, it transpired, had been phoning and calling in frequently and, in a most insensitive and intrusive way, off-loading her own sadness onto Bob's widow who just couldn't take it any more. She didn't want to get the nurse into trouble but she really did not want to see this nurse ever again.

Within the hospice/palliative care framework of formal interdisciplinary team meetings, issues of role boundaries and staff needs are regularly examined. Supervision is made available for staff who may be stressed by a particular death and bereavement follow-up is coordinated by qualified staff. As we have seen, in the nursing home there is no framework for such a formal team. Staff who give that 'something extra' to provide good care may be in danger of overstepping role boundaries so that inappropriate involvement becomes accepted practice. In the absence of education, evaluation, support and supervision, close relationships with residents may easily cross the barrier between professional and unprofessional conduct.

6. Terminal illness experience is individual, calling for dynamic, flexible and responsive care.

Many aspects of a resident's care needs may change rapidly when death is near. Flexibility, ingenuity and goodwill often take the place of a formalised response.

The charge nurse may be an hour late leaving work or come in on her day off to attend a meeting. The director of nursing may not leave the nursing home until late, there being no-one else to record and type up the result of the case conference which contains important information for the night staff. Another nurse felt 'not right' going off duty while Bob was dying, so he stayed on for an extra half-hour. Night staff varied their time-bound routine in order to give Bob a warm bath just when he needed it because they had learned that it soothed his pain and encouraged sleep. It was hard to catch up, and other residents were anxious about their routine being changed. A member of the domestic staff sat in the foyer with Bob's wife when she should have been on her round with the tea trolley. They seemed to understand each other and Bob's wife wanted to talk to this mature and friendly woman in a way 'those young girls wouldn't understand'.

Thus, dynamic, flexible and responsive care is given, but without the matching resources.

7. Skilled staff are appropriately selected.

Many staff still perceive a stigma attached to working in a nursing home. It is ironic that skilled palliative care nurses, while awaiting a position in a recognised palliative care service, will often work in the acute-care setting and risk becoming de-skilled, rather than work in aged care where their skills in palliative care nursing would be greatly valued. An increasing number of community palliative care services are offering their expertise to nursing homes on a consultancy basis. However, this service often lacks coordination within the nursing home.

Bob's nursing needs became increasingly complex in the last weeks of his life. On some days he was cared for by a nurse with palliative care skills; on other days he was in the hands of casual or unqualified staff who lacked the relevant experience. As far as Bob was concerned, he wanted to be cared for by the nurses he knew.

The key to this dilemma is continuity. While increasing emphasis is being given to employing nursing home staff with appropriate qualifications, the ideal is far from being realised. The opposite agenda is also at work, where some government departments and some proprietors consider the cost of employing qualified staff too burdensome. However, when the plan of care is well formulated and communicated by those with the necessary educational preparation, the resident will benefit. When a significant proportion of nursing home staff have minimal educational preparation, resident care may be greatly enhanced when guided by those with particular expertise in palliative care. In reality, the nurse with palliative care qualifications seldom has time for teaching those who would benefit most.

8. Family/carer must be included as part of the unit of care.

Palliative care principles appear at times to fit more neatly with a cultural lifestyle which presupposes articulate, English-speaking, assertive family members with problem-solving skills. In reality, many close family members of nursing home residents do not fit that pattern. That is not to say they should be precluded from the unit of care, but that added skills are required on the part of nursing home staff and adequate time is needed to spend with family members. The ideal assumes the plan, objectives and goals of care will include the family. In reality, it is often the staff who become the family.

Bob's wife was fairly frail and years of visiting hospitals had made her defer to all the important decision-makers in the health team. She felt it was not her place to ask questions. Noticing her increasing difficulty in coping with regular visits to the nursing home, the staff wanted to protect her and she, in her own way, was grateful for their consideration. Bob's son was unwilling to step in and take control, believing the place at Bob's bedside rightfully belonged to his mother. Neither the wife nor the son initiated any communication nor offered any suggestions about Bob's care, so the nursing staff took on the added role of advocate.

Care planning is a sophisticated process requiring formal education. While in an increasingly consumer-oriented society more relatives are aware of their rights in respect to palliative care, Bob's family were unacquainted with the concept. Staff require additional skills and sensitivity in guiding families without imposing their own opinions or disempowering the resident and family. It remains a significant challenge for all in the health-care team to adapt the care plan to the unique needs of every resident within the context of their unique circumstances.

OTHER ISSUES

Within the constraints of this chapter, it is not possible to include a full discussion of such important factors as pain management, pastoral and spiritual care, cultural care and bereavement support. Government recommendations for developing a protocol for palliative care in nursing homes indicate that all these factors should be considered. Many of these issues are taken up in other chapters, demonstrating that, in reality, palliative care is provided for nursing home residents without being defined as such or without being confined to the last hours or weeks of the resident's life.

It is clear that many nursing homes are endeavouring to provide the kind of comprehensive service expected of them. However, in terms of a desirable outcome for the resident who is dying, the real cost of delivering the appropriate service needs to be measured. Regrettably, residents' needs for palliative care are not matched by available resources and, short of placing further demands on caring staff, it is not clear how the gap is to be filled.

QUALITY ISSUES FOR ENHANCED PRACTICE

The gerontic nurse

- Relevant palliative care goals for the particular resident must be stated clearly on the care plan and communicated to all care staff.
- Include medical personnel, allied health staff and the chaplain (where appropriate) when planning a resident's palliative care.
- Involve family members in identifying palliative care goals for their relative.
- Assist and empower nurses with less theoretical knowledge by alerting them to symptoms they should watch for, for example, the side effects of morphine.

Management

- Consider employing at least one palliative care nurse or establishing a consultancy arrangement.
- Provide regular in-service education to ensure staff understand the meaning of palliative care.
- Communication to doctors must be comprehensive, and referred to in procedures that are accessible to direct care staff.
- Ensure access to a palliative care medical specialist.

Indirect carers

- Protocols need to be established to make clear the role of indirect carers in palliative care, for example, their role in documentation, their availability and their involvement in team meetings and care planning.

CHAPTER TWO

This chapter focuses on the resident's lived experience in its complexity; encompassing cultural, temporal and social relationship factors.

CONFLICT OF INTEREST: COMFORT MEASURES ONLY

How is a realistic goal of care developed; one that acknowledges the needs of the family as well as the needs of the resident? This story traces the short-term residency of Mrs Peterson, transferred from acute care where it was determined 'nothing more can be done'. The family were angry, defiant, guilty, shocked and determined to 'buy' the best care for their mother. They expected a miracle recovery and at first demanded intensive rehabilitation. What factors come into play when nursing home staff and the visiting doctor are placed under such pressure? When finally the family were able to understand their mother's prognosis, they attempted to modify their expectations from rehabilitation and cure to the mutually agreed goal of 'maximum comfort'.

'She's definitely a Category One!' asserted Mrs Peterson's daughter, Chris, as she negotiated a place for her mother on our priority waiting list. Astonished to find that according to hospital criteria her seriously ill mother was no longer considered 'acute', Chris had quickly used every available professional contact to find out about nursing home admission. Sounding triumphant, she acknowledged the mutual benefit for her mother and the nursing home in having her mother's name placed at the top of our waiting list, knowing her Category One status would attract the highest funding.

The family, with a brash arrogance signifying their underlying fear and anxiety, were seeking understanding — a sympathetic forum in which to air their guilt at not taking their mother home. They were shocked to see their 70-year-old mother, a health and fitness fanatic, whose only previous illness was appendicitis, lying comatose following what the medical report recorded as a 'major right hemisphere stroke…suggesting a poor prognosis…requiring nursing home care if she survives'.

Attempts by the nursing home to gain a comprehensive discharge plan from the hospital were fruitless. The hospital's care plan appeared to be lacking in direction; no rationale was given for the nasogastric tube still being in place when Mrs Peterson came to us and there was no mention of the complex family dynamics.

Chris was the family's spokesperson regarding their mother's quality of life in a nursing home. 'I see her dispirited. I only want her to regain some of her dignity.' 'Dying with dignity' is an often-heard phrase, but who measures dignity? 'Spirit' is open to many interpretations; as well as catering for Mrs Peterson's physical needs, how could staff address her 'dispiritedness'?

The family's profound sense of loss was apparent. Following the initial shock of their mother's sudden stroke, they had a resurgence of hope. 'What can we do to rehabilitate her? I want all measures taken to aid her recovery. What about speech therapy, physiotherapy? I will come in for two hours each day and talk to her, to try and bring her back. I know she recognises me and I'm sure she tried to speak yesterday. And please make sure her TV is tuned to the current affairs programs each night. She never misses those.' Then followed rage and anger when Mrs Peterson was discovered one morning to be slightly uncovered and in a wet bed. Increasing frustration was evident in Chris as she found herself at times unable to bear the pain of visiting. 'I can't believe this has happened to her. I want to remember her as she was.'

The doctor was made anxious by repeated calls from the family. 'I want every effort made towards rehabilitation. She can move her right hand'. Staff were on tenterhooks — no word of thanks forthcoming for all the skilled and careful nursing, only complaints when the slightest imperfection was detected. (These discoveries were made by investigating under the bedclothes for any sign of dampness, wrinkles in the sheets or redness of skin.)

Nutrition and hydration were, of course, important items in the plan of care. After repeated attempts to re-insert the nasogastric tube that Mrs Peterson had deftly removed five times that day, staff were seeking direction. The hospital deemed Mrs Peterson's prognosis to be short, so the option of a tube directly into the stomach was deemed 'not worth all the trouble'. The need for a case conference was recognised, as a means by which the goal of care could be discussed. The atmosphere was tense: the daughter angry, guilty, demanding; the doctor impatient, defensive and frustrated; the charge nurse focusing on the documentation, seeking mutual goals; the director of nursing mediating, clarifying expectations.

A significant shift occurred in the first 10 minutes of the meeting when it became clear the purpose was to develop a comprehensive plan of care for Mrs Peterson. The family became less defensive and, during open discussion, more willing to trust. Where the family's emphasis had been on rehabilitation, there was now a shift to palliation. 'We want no resuscitation,' they decided. Another significant shift occurred in the doctor's response from an initial, 'I cannot decide in advance what I will do, but my duty is to preserve life', to a broader consideration of options. The conversation centred on the goal of care, with the nurse's repeated reassurance, 'When Dr Friedrickson states there is nothing more he can do for your mother medically, that is when we move in! There is a lot more we can do.' Together, a plan of care was developed which listed 12 specific needs to be addressed. Chris was overwhelmed to see the final plan with detailed objectives, lists of interventions, planned evaluation and date for review.

As the conference continued, nutrition and hydration emerged again as significant factors. Medical explanation was given to the family that, in the absence of a nasogastric tube, oral feeding would not be sufficient to sustain their mother's normal nutritional needs, but would be sufficient in these circumstances for her comfort. A suggestion by the charge nurse to seek opinion from the consultant speech pathologist, who would test Mrs Peterson's swallowing reflex in the presence of the daughter, was met with surprised appreciation: 'They would never have done that in the hospital. I never knew what tests were done and I was certainly not permitted to be present!'

In response to the family's stated wish for 'no heroics', the doctor explained infections such as pneumonia may develop, which, if untreated, may hasten their mother's death. It was also agreed that insertion of a urinary catheter would be an unwelcome intrusion and invasion of her dignity. 'She would hate it,' Chris stated. Nursing measures would prevent the development of pressure sores and, the doctor continued, urinary output would diminish as death became imminent.

Chris's anger subsided as she heard the positive steps listed for her mother's care; however, her expectations remained unrealistic. Her guilt was somewhat dissipated as the options for care, including home care, were explored and found to be impractical. When Chris interposed that 'money was no problem' it was suggested the family may find the services of a 24-hour private nurse in their own home, or accommodation in a private hospital would meet their needs more appropriately. The doctor's position changed from defensiveness to advocacy for the nursing home staff as he outlined these alternatives. His impatience was evident as he reminded the family that a nursing home was not a private hospital and they ought to be aware of the difference between realistic and unrealistic expectations. Chris had made up her mind. 'I was not the slightest bit impressed with the private hospital she was in. I'd like her to stay here, please.'

The site of care confirmed, frank discussion about the demanding nature of Chris's communication with staff resulted in some compromises. Other unrealistic expectations were further explored. 'You may sometimes find your mother in a wet bed. We have many other incontinent residents to care for and we cannot promise perfection.' A spirit of cooperation was sought rather than the continued confrontation which, it was agreed, was not in Mrs Peterson's best interests. However, agreement was reached only after lengthy and repeated discussion, testing the patience and tolerance of all present.

Doctors are busy people. This discussion was clearly not part of his normal daily routine and his impatience was showing. However, his defensive stance softened when it was clear the family would not take litigious steps against him for failing to preserve life at any cost. His frustration eased when the goal of care was agreed: to palliate rather than to cure. The doctor's entry in the clinical record became a source of authority and reassurance:

> Comfort measures only. Discussed with family the patient's compromised ability in terms of nutrition and hydration. Reassured family that frequent small offerings of fluids would suffice. Agreed there was no need for further medical intervention. Advised nursing staff that morphine would be ordered should the patient appear to be in pain.

As predicted, Mrs Peterson grew calmer when she no longer had to fight the nasogastric tube. Continuing to have a 'mind of her own' (why is surprise expressed when the seemingly passive resident exhibits this phenomenon!) Mrs Peterson would, on some days, eat and drink the small amounts offered but, on other days, simply clamp her mouth shut. Through skilled nursing, Mrs Peterson's mouth was kept moist and clean, her skin remained intact, her pain was alleviated and her dignity maintained until her death two weeks later.

As is often the case, throughout the complex daily interactions regarding Mrs Peterson's care, the nurse was in the middle. Acting as resident advocate, yet being aware of the crucial part played by the doctor, knowing the staff's level of frustration in the face of continued criticism, the charge nurse adopted the mediating role. Skilfully weighing all these factors, she welded together a team of doctor, staff and family to achieve the optimum level of care for Mrs Peterson.

And what of Mrs Peterson's 'dispiritedness'? Was her 'spirit' revived by allowing her to choose her own way of dying? She seemed to be saying, 'No tubes, thank you, and I'll eat and drink when I'm ready. What's life worth anyway when I can't do my exercises any more, or even make myself a glass of carrot juice when I fancy? And I do wish Chris would stop making such a fuss about everything!'

In evaluating Mrs Peterson's care, it seemed an appropriate for the nurse to write, 'Died peacefully and with dignity, all comfort measures having been well attended. Relatives comforted'.

ON REFLECTION...

Family in shock

By the time Mrs Peterson had reached our care she looked as we expected her to — semi-conscious, face distorted by the stroke, unable to answer questions, incontinent, body all awry on the stretcher. Accustomed to these factors, we are not always prepared to ask who this person was before the stroke. We don't have a picture of her former life. To consider the shock sustained by a family whose mother is active and independent one minute and a 'nursing home placement problem' the next, is to see things from a different perspective. Educational resources, literature, explanation and repeated reassurance are some issues in family-centred care which may be overlooked when the focus of care is only on the resident. Acknowledgment by staff of the family's profound sense of loss and a greater understanding of their frustration, anger and guilt may have encouraged Mrs Peterson's family towards earlier acceptance of the situation.

Clinical record reflecting physical care only

Residents' physical deficits in respect of hygiene, elimination, skin care, and mobility are usually well documented and prominent in the care plan. Issues such as loss and grief, family dynamics, or comfort measures required, do not fit the task approach and are, therefore, often neglected areas in the recorded history of care. This is not to say that such care is not given. However, because it is difficult to quantify, it is often not recorded. It is much easier to record respiration rate or quantity of urine passed. What of the resident's fears, responses, attitudes? What is recorded of the resident's spiritual needs? What is signified by the resident's dying process? Where are the entries which demonstrate the solace given to resident and family by many staff? What kind of entries are made at the point of death? Furthermore, what is written in the outcome section of the care plan?

Care of the doctor who cares for the resident

Mrs Peterson's file included a copy of a letter from the charge nurse to the doctor thanking him for his support. It was acknowledged that Mrs Peterson's family were not the easiest people to deal with and heavy demands were made on the doctor's time and patience. It appeared that a team approach provided the necessary support for the doctor to clarify goals of care. On the doctor's part, words of encouragement such as 'You're doing a good job' were not perceived as patronising, but as appropriate recognition by one health professional towards another. The doctor's thoughtful entry in the clinical record provided clear communication to family and staff that the most delicate issues had indeed been discussed. Furthermore, although Mrs Peterson did not require the morphine, the fact that it appeared in the notes as an option provided staff and family with confidence that the care was planned ahead.

Why not show the family the plan of care?

While certain medico-legal constraints and other local factors may apply to the resident's clinical record, the plan of care requires resident and family involvement where possible. In this instance, encouraging the Peterson family to read all the details of care was a reassuring exercise. Issues of trust and confidence were evident in the nurse taking pride in the documented plan and the family acknowledging these were not mere words on a page, but a plan of care for their mother.

Time factors

'Case conferences are all very well, but we don't have the time — and anyway, the doctor wouldn't come.' Economical use of time is of critical importance in all health care. Time set aside for a 30–45 minute case conference needs to be weighed against time spent on all those unofficial and informal conversations which take place round the nurses' desk or in multiple telephone calls to and from the family. These informal interactions do not necessarily explore or discuss in depth all the issues involved. Neither are they always recorded. For all concerned with Mrs Peterson's care, a printed record of the case conference provided an important guide. Yes, it's time consuming, but in most cases the benefit outweighs the burden.

Comfort measures only

Rather than signifying a hopeless situation in which nothing more could be done, the comfort measures given to Mrs Peterson occupied four pages of the care plan. Both family and staff were constantly reminded that palliative measures do not denote a withdrawal of care but a long list of physical, emotional, social and spiritual interventions.

Hospital to nursing home

Economic and political factors do not necessarily allow for a thorough case conference before the resident is transferred from the acute-care setting. From Mrs Peterson's perspective, and that of her family, a significant life change had occurred. In moving to a new 'home', where security of accommodation was to be expected for the duration of her life, it would seem an important consideration to ensure thorough communication before Mrs Peterson was discharged from hospital. For example, the issue of nasogastric feeding may have been resolved before she was transferred if sufficient attention had been given to the goal of care and a thorough assessment of the implications of removing the tube had been made. The family indicated that little information was given about the nature of the stroke and the likely prognosis. Implications for the nursing home are evident from this narrative, where the family were left frustrated and in ignorance — factors which then had to be addressed within the nursing home. Issues such as denial and shock need also to be considered when checking the family's perception of the situation.

Financial factors

Families are sometimes reassured by contributing financially to extra care such as providing luxury items of equipment outside the scope of the nursing home budget. In considering the question, 'What more can be done for our mother's comfort?', this family were prepared to consider such suggestions. Advantages and disadvantages of families who wish to pay for extra care may be factors to consider according to individual circumstances. It was particularly important in this situation to identify expectations and to clarify the difference between a nursing home and a private hospital.

After the death

Not all matters regarding Mrs Peterson's care were resolved in one brief case conference. Because ongoing expressions of guilt were still evident in Chris's communication, the family were encouraged to visit the nursing home after their mother's death to discuss any unresolved matters. An unexpected consequence of this invitation was the rather poignant and spontaneous approach made by Chris in which this businesslike, matter-of-fact daughter put her arms around a nurse and sobbed inconsolably. A further consequence came by way of the family's appreciation expressed in a substantial donation earmarked specifically 'for a staff night out'. In other words, a clear direction was given that 'management must not get their hands on it'. A general perception exists in nursing homes that rewards are few and far between. This tangible reward added significantly to staff morale.

'She's definitely a Category One!'

When funding arrangements are tied to the index of care requirements it is becoming increasingly common to refer to residents by their funding category or classification number rather than by a more personalised reference to their specific needs. In the case of Mrs Peterson, many attitudes and perceptions were evident. Chris implied that we should be grateful to admit a Category One resident; she had done her homework and knew this category attracted the highest funding. Some staff realised the benefits accruing to the nursing home of the extra funding attracted by a resident with high dependency needs, while others felt that no monetary reward would compensate for the trouble her admission caused.

Mrs Peterson's spirit

It is more common to think of 'spirit' as the chaplain's province than to focus on the unity of body, mind, spirit as an essential factor in comprehensive care of the whole person. It was clear from careful listening to the family's description of their mother, that Mrs Peterson's 'spirit' was located in her fierce determination and jealously guarded independence. To ignore this would be to artificially separate a vital part of her being; to concentrate exclusively on physical characteristics would be to deny her wholeness. She was not, according to her family, a religious person; yet she yearned for someone to acknowledge her 'spirit'.

QUALITY ISSUES FOR ENHANCED PRACTICE

The gerontic nurse

- The gerontic nurse encourages all staff to record family relationship factors and other non-physical needs in the documented care plan.
- Guidance may be required for some staff in documenting complex family factors in an objective manner which acknowledges the uniqueness of each situation.
- Nurses have every reason to be proud of a carefully documented care plan; when it matches the care actually given it becomes a powerful reminder to families of the nature of palliative care.
- Assessment of spiritual factors requires sensitivity and insight; these vital factors need to be incorporated into the total plan of care.

Management

- Management support and assistance in adopting a flexible approach to resident care (rather than repeating daily care routines) may assist all carers involved in a complex situation.
- Roster review may be needed in order to provide for a family case conference when complex problems are identified.
- Sensitive listening by management may forestall formal complaints when resident care is perceived as inadequate.
- Where resources allow, involvement at the hospital discharge planning meeting may help to smooth the transition from acute care and help to clarify immediate goals.
- Where there is no comprehensive 'spiritual assessment' tool in operation, such a tool may be formulated in collaboration with staff, or adapted from assessment packages used by other aged-care facilities.

Indirect carers

- Qualified counselling support may be helpful for family members suffering the shock of unexpected nursing home entry for a previously 'fit and healthy' relative.

CULTURAL CONSIDERATIONS: I WANT TO GO HOME

What consideration should be given to the resident from another culture when death is imminent? This account of Georgiou's death illustrates the unfortunate and unhappy consequences of ignoring a resident's primary cultural need. Reflection on practice shows that, in this instance, the cultural needs of the resident and his wife may have been more adequately met by careful listening, lateral thinking and continuous re-evaluation of the plan of care. As well as offering Georgiou some choice about where he wanted to die, the outcome may have turned a widow's guilt, frustration and resentment into long-lasting satisfaction and fulfilment. While there will never be another Georgiou, what we learn from his story may broaden our vision by alerting us to consider cultural factors more carefully.

Georgiou's name was on the waiting list intermittently for nine months, while his wife struggled to care for him at home with minimal assistance, putting off the inevitable. Then, the inevitable happened. He fell, broke his leg and was admitted to hospital. 'This is it,' Anna decided. 'I won't be able to take him home this time. He'll have to go to the nursing home.'

Revised forms were completed, the assessment team's decision was clear. Taking into account Anna's failing health and in the absence of extended family support, admission to a nursing home appeared to be the only course of action. The local doctor was relieved to have the situation resolved.

Georgiou however, perceived to be too confused to be asked for his opinion regarding moving to a nursing home, had firm ideas of his own. He didn't like the hospital food, he missed his wife who could only travel the long distance from home to hospital once a day and had to leave early to catch her bus to get home before dark. He became restless and agitated and Anna could see he was fretting. 'Well,' she reasoned with the social worker, 'he won't be able to wander off now, so he'll be easier to manage at home. Will you please tell the nursing home I've changed my mind. I'm taking Georgiou home instead.'

Knowing Anna well, from our many phone calls and her frequent visits to the nursing home, we kept his name on the waiting list. The doctor, social worker and community nurses were quite sure the situation would soon break down and Anna would be forced to admit Georgiou for long-term care.

About six months later Anna visited to confirm her husband's place on the waiting list 'just in case'. It was clear she was at breaking point. Georgiou's fracture had healed and he was as active as ever. Only the night before, he had mistaken the drying cabinet for the toilet and then managed to get himself wedged behind the bathroom door. Anna could cope with his incontinence while he was in bed, but his unpredictable wandering was causing increasing frustration and strain. Georgiou would allow Anna to wash and feed him but would have nothing to do with the visiting nurse. Attempts at respite care had failed miserably; Anna spent her time worrying while Georgiou occupied himself trying to get out of bed so he could go home. Also there was a new problem: Georgiou had been diagnosed with lung cancer. He was losing weight and seemed to be in pain. The doctor knew it would be difficult to proceed any further with tests and tried gently to persuade Anna that Georgiou needed specialised nursing care to keep him comfortable and pain free.

Anna understood all about comfort. She knew how Georgiou relaxed when she lay beside him at night, gently stroking his forehead or massaging his back. In spite of all the complexities of incontinence, she had somehow managed to nurse him in the bed they had shared for over 40 years. She also knew that he would be less likely to attempt to get out of bed at night while she was beside him. Yes, Anna knew all about that kind of comfort, but as for symptom control for cancer, of that she had no knowledge at all, so it was best to ignore those harsh realities. So she continued to do her best. As Georgiou became progressively weaker Anna became increasingly tired, her arthritis worsening because of the constant strain of lifting and turning him. Finally, when she allowed her blood pressure to be checked, the doctor had to be quite firm, 'Who will look after him if you have a stroke?'

As often happens, coincidental factors came together at the right time. A bed became vacant in our nursing home and Anna's decision had to be made quickly.

Georgiou, by now quiet and withdrawn, did not seem to object to the move and Anna set about labelling clothes, cooking special delicacies and visiting at every meal time. We were quick to make assumptions — Anna would now enjoy the rest she deserved. No longer having the worry of caring for her husband day and night, at last she would be able to look after herself. We would persuade her to visit only once per day, although she lived close by. 'Anna, you must take care of yourself; we'll take care of Georgiou.'

There was, however, another side to the story which, despite all our caring, was never fully appreciated. Steeped in her own cultural expectations, Anna felt she had deserted her husband; handed him over to strangers. Although she had no other family in Australia, her close-knit Greek community kept a watchful eye over events. While she received some sympathy and understanding from her friends, she believed she was shunned by others, blamed for giving in too easily. Her guilt increased when she saw Georgiou's condition deteriorate. Unfortunately, no-one ever took the time to explain that the tumour was growing rapidly, so Anna was left to draw her own conclusion — he was fretting. Georgiou became restless and agitated whenever she visited; withdrawn and morose when she left. When well-meaning staff could see Anna's health declining they offered plenty of suggestions: 'Why don't you stay home and rest. We'll look after him. We'll ring if we think he needs you.' Anna knew perfectly well that her husband wouldn't eat the nursing home food and would probably not eat anything unless she was there to feed him. While it was nice of the nurses to offer, how would they know when he needed her? In spite of frequent reminders about the nursing home laundry, Anna continued to take all his soiled washing home, returning it spotless and perfectly pressed. As far as Anna was concerned there were no other options, this was her labour of love for her husband. It was also a source of pride that her friends could see she was a dutiful wife.

However, it was not easy for the staff. They were puzzled when the normally cooperative Anna became critical and suspicious of all nursing care offered to her husband. She disliked the hard, hospital linen and longed to check her husband's skin but the nurses seemed defensive about it. He certainly had no pressure marks when she cared for him at home, protecting his skin with the softest of linen which was carefully removed and meticulously washed immediately it was soiled. These disposable pads must certainly cause chafing and what was this medicine they were giving him? 'It's to help the pain,' was the repeated explanation. When the injections started, Anna became absolutely convinced her husband was being drugged in order to keep him quiet. When she had time to discuss the situation with her friends they agreed that it must be the morphine and 'once they start with that, it's the end!'

Georgiou's condition changed. As the result of pain relief, he became clearer in his thoughts and his faltering English easier to understand. Whilst accepting all care offered, he continually appealed to each nurse to 'please let me go home'. Although he had lost the physical energy required to climb over the bedrails that Anna had insisted upon, no-one had thought to suggest to Anna that she could let the bedrails down when she was sitting with him. Now there was an intolerable steel barrier between Anna and her husband. At each visit, hands clasped through the rails, Georgiou pleaded with her to take him home.

Again the problems escalated. Staff became impatient with Georgiou's repeated requests to go home and defensive of Anna's intense preoccupation with every aspect of his care. Why was he still in the same shirt that he wore yesterday, with its unsightly stain from spilled food? Why haven't his teeth been cleaned? Where is his own small blanket, the one that gave him so much comfort when tucked up round his shoulders? Checking whether he was in a wet bed became an obsession for Anna. Furthermore, she had become quite friendly with two other women from the 'old country' who regularly visited their husbands in the nursing home. They could frequently be seen in a cluster, talking rapidly, leaving staff with the impression that more criticism was being levelled at them. From all angles, this was becoming a very difficult situation. Everyone was frustrated and no-one had an answer.

When Georgiou's death was imminent Anna's visits increased in length and frequency. Having stayed all through the night on several occasions she was counselled on this night to go home and get some sleep. Although expecting the inevitable, when Georgiou died at 11 p.m., Anna was totally unprepared for the phone call and become hysterical. Her doctor responded by prescribing a sedative.

ON REFLECTION...

What may be learned from this unhappy ending?

The point at which the situation seemed most difficult was an opportune time for assessing and re-evaluating the plan of care. With a fresh look at the goal and direction of care, viewing Georgiou in the context of his culture, his family and his community, the following outcome may have been achieved.

Alternative (hypothetical) scenario for Georgiou's death

One week before Georgiou's death it became apparent to the charge nurse that the situation was becoming intolerable for all concerned. Staff were frustrated in their desire to give good nursing care. It seemed nothing they did was good enough for Anna. Georgiou would not communicate with them, except to constantly repeat his desire to go home. Everyone could see Anna becoming more and more stressed while the staff themselves were becoming more and more resentful of her. Clare (the charge nurse) arranged for a case conference, inviting the doctor, Anna, a Greek community welfare officer and one of the nurses who had developed a rapport with Anna. In summarising Georgiou's physical deterioration it became apparent that his care needs had changed. No longer resisting the necessary regular position change and pressure care, no longer attempting to climb out of bed, Georgiou was compliant and patient, even accepting small amounts of food and fluids. It was evident that much of his distress and restlessness had been caused by pain and now he slept peacefully for long intervals. However, the previous agitation and aggression had been replaced by a wistful longing and yearning, evident by his plaintive, repetitive pleading, 'I want to go home. Please take me home.'

Ensuring Anna understood the purpose of the review meeting, Clare asked Anna what options she saw for the immediate future. Clare then presented her revised draft plan of care for the group to discuss. Anna was pleased to be given an outline of all Georgiou's care, and for the first time the side effects of morphine were explained to her. The doctor carefully outlined Georgiou's diagnosis and prognosis, clarifying the goal of care. Anna was asked, 'It seems as though Georgiou may only have a few more days to live. What do you think he would want and what would be most important to both of you in these last few days?' Anna was unequivocal in her reply, 'He wants to come home and I always promised him since the first time he got sick that I would never leave him. I promised him I'd look after him till he died. He wants to die in his own home.'

All present were deeply moved by Anna's clear reply and further challenged by the charge nurse's suggestion: 'Let's see if it is possible for Georgiou to go home. I think he'd accept assistance from the district nurse now. What do you think, Anna?' Anna agreed that if she could be offered 24-hour on-call nursing support she could manage him. 'He's so thin now. I could turn him easily by myself.' The doctor agreed that his urinary output was now so low that renal failure was a possible factor. Incontinent episodes were far less frequent, he was no longer accepting anything by mouth other than small sips of fluid, his pressure care was under control and a special mattress over-lay could be loaned to Anna. Anna agreed that she could manage but her main anxiety was the morphine. An immediate phone call to the community nursing service confirmed their willingness to resume the care. Regular administration of morphine would not be a problem, they had the necessary equipment to provide a continuous morphine infusion. They would visit twice daily and more often if required. They also offered respite care to allow Anna to rest or attend to shopping while a staff member sat with Georgiou.

The next step in the process involved a meeting at the nursing home between the community nurse, the charge nurse and Anna. Thorough transfer notes were prepared and the doctor confirmed he would continue to care for Georgiou at home. Discharge planning was an infrequent occurrence for the nursing home and there were mixed feelings as the staff said goodbye to Georgiou and Anna. It was made clear to Anna that Georgiou's nursing home bed would remain open should things not work out at home.

It was 11 p.m. and Anna lay beside her husband, counting every breath. He had become agitated and restless but was quickly soothed by her comforting touch. She decided to phone for the nurse, just in case. Although they had given her their night number she had never used it in the six days and nights since Georgiou had been home. She held his hand, gently repeating in her own language, 'It's all right my dear, you're at home with me. I won't let you go. You're safe here in your own bed.' By the time the nurses arrived he had died. Although calmly reconciled to the fact of his death, Anna was grateful to have someone to talk to. Unsure of formal procedures, she gratefully accepted their offer to call the doctor and arrange for the funeral director to be notified. She was determined to make coffee for them all. What pleased her most was to hear them say, 'Well done, Anna. You've cared for him beautifully and you've kept your promise.'

Pre-admission communication

Assessment of Georgiou's cultural needs should have been part of pre-admission planning, so it is important that the person responsible for admissions to the nursing home has some understanding of such complexities. Rather than a mere administrative formality the waiting list became the focus of support for Anna, enabling a smoother transition for the big step from home. However, it is worth noting that this important aspect of pre-admission care does not attract the government funding it deserves. Neither does it come under scrutiny for the purposes of accreditation or formal monitoring of continuous quality improvement.

Options made clear

On admission, while giving reassurance regarding security of accommodation, it may be important to reassure families that other options may need to be explored if the desired outcome is not achieved. Perhaps if this had been explained to Anna, some of the difficulties may have been minimised. While the nursing home is usually the final site of care, the dying resident and family may, in certain circumstances, benefit from having other options presented.

Carers' perspectives

Viewed holistically, Georgiou's care in the nursing home needed to be seen in continuity with the care he had received at home. Both Georgiou and Anna may have benefited from a continuity of care which acknowledged Anna's desire to assist in his personal care and which also recognised her own skills and expertise. Well-meaning nurses constantly reminding Anna to 'have a rest and let us do the work' may, in fact, have caused resentment and frustration rather than relief. It is therefore important to ensure the carer's participation in the plan of care, so their voice may be heard concerning their priorities and their desire to be actively involved in the care.

Community liaison

Continued liaison with the visiting nursing service may have brought a speedier resolution to the problem. A trial period of admission to the nursing home with a specific review date may have been one solution. Advantages of such continued liaison include the opening up of the nursing home to provide a welcoming atmosphere for health professionals from the community. Such breaking down of barriers can be mutually beneficial, particularly when sharing of cultural resources is involved. A further important feature of continued liaison is improved communication — such as when Georgiou's death occurred. A phone call in these circumstances enhances inter-agency relationships and communication, particularly regarding the common query, 'I wonder what happened to…?'

Allaying fears and anxieties

When communicating with residents and carers from another culture it is important to understand their fears and anxieties. This may best be achieved by inviting a sensitive professional interpreter or counsellor to the case conference. Anna's fears may have related to her perception that her husband was a 'problem' that the staff were anxious to dispose of as quickly as possible. Knowing she could refer to a senior staff member at any time may have fostered a relationship of trust.

Myths about morphine

Anna's fear of morphine administration may have been alleviated had full explanation been given when the drug was commenced. Always meticulous in her oversight of Georgiou's medications, Anna was confused and anxious over the introduction of this powerful drug. Appropriate education is a good antidote to anxiety. However, assumptions are easy to make and not always correct. It is therefore important to check first the particular issues that require extra attention. For example, the moral issue of giving a drug commonly understood in some cultures to hasten death may be more important than explanations about dosage and medical effects. Issues such as euthanasia may remain silent fears in the minds of relatives, leading in turn to lack of trust and insecurity about the care being given. The *Oxford Dictionary* defines euthanasia as a word of Greek origin meaning the bringing about of a gentle and easy death, especially in the case of incurable and painless disease. Anna may have been reassured by a full explanation of the derivation of the word from her own language.

Reviewing the care

Exploring options for care involves risk-taking. It is therefore important to fully explain the plan of care and discuss options should the current plan of care be unsuccessful. Possibilities in this situation (as described in the hypothetical alternative) may have included a trial period at home, while the nursing home bed remained secure as a back-up. Respite care and shared care arrangements, while not without their difficulties, provide an important alternative to permanent residential care in specific situations. At the conclusion of any review it is important to ask the family whether they desire a further review, leaving the way open for further questions and discussion. Such reviews are, of course, time consuming. However, extra time spent gaining trust and clarifying queries in the beginning often leads to reduced problems later.

Culture-specific nursing homes or culturally sensitive care?

There was a definite, albeit small, Greek community within the nursing home. Rather than being seen as a threat, how may this richness be acknowledged? Examples include: arranging a special relatives' meeting for those of similar cultural background; providing culture-specific literature for staff, including translations of often-repeated phrases; arranging appropriate guest speakers; or facilitating discussion in staff meetings. Even so, much time may be wasted in arranging such meetings if they do not provide the support relevant to the carers' needs. Relatives' trust may be gained more readily if their opinion is sought first as to whom they would like to meet with and under what conditions.

The particular and not the general

It is also important to avoid generalisations when addressing cultural differences. For example, staff should guard against making one prescription of care fit all residents of a particular culture, 'Greeks always prefer it this way'. The plan of care that suited Georgiou and Anna may not necessarily be appropriate for the next resident of the same cultural background.

Resources for staff

While the standards for nursing home care require cultural diversity and ethnicity to be acknowledged in every area of the resident's life, there is no prescriptive list of strategies or ways to achieve this. Despite the requirement for culturally sensitive care, it is not always easy to discern the implications for each particular resident. However, there are publications available to guide staff of nursing homes and such educational material should be readily available for all staff. The important question remains, 'What is the culturally specific care appropriate to this particular resident and his or her family at this time in these circumstances?' Staff involvement is critical. There may be, in some circumstances, a tendency to withdraw from a resident's care because of misunderstanding or frustration with the family's involvement. This may be interpreted by the family as neglect. When an attitude of active partnership between staff, resident and family is fostered, culturally sensitive care is enhanced.

Where is my wife?

Georgiou and Anna had been married for over 40 years and, having no children, had lived exclusively for each other. Sensitive assessment of their relationship may have led to increased understanding about their need to be together in the closing days of Georgiou's life. The importance of close tactile contact in this situation should not be underestimated. For this couple, the marital bed provided the most important factor in the dying process.

Intimacy

When intimacy is understood as a powerful ingredient in the care of one person for another, then the implications of the cold barrier of steel represented by bedrails will become evident. Cultural factors may prevent family members from asking questions of staff with the result that nursing home routines may be perceived as inflexible rules. Staff who are sensitive to these cultural factors will not wait until a problem emerges; they will initiate discussion with relatives, checking perceptions rather than making judgments. If Anna could not be persuaded about the negative implications and risks attached to the use of bedrails, she may have benefited from encouragement to lower the bedrails while she was visiting, thus enjoying closer contact with her husband. Providing other options such as drawing screens round the bed or closing the door to facilitate privacy, may also be appreciated by resident and spouse in some circumstances. These options are best determined by sensitive questioning rather than thoughtless assumptions.

QUALITY ISSUES FOR ENHANCED PRACTICE

The gerontic nurse

- Cultural issues impact on every aspect of a resident's care; these issues are not merely an appendage to a generic care plan. Thus, careful assessment, involving resident and family, highlights specific cultural considerations at each point of the resident's care.
- Careful pre-admission assessment often provides important clues for ongoing relationships with resident and family. Family processes then become a very important component of the care plan.
- Gerontic nurses have an important role in educating family members about the administration of morphine and any other drugs likely to cause side effects. Discussion prior to commencement of the drug may also allay fears and anxieties.
- Careful assessment at the time of admission should identify to what extent a family member wishes to be involved in the resident's daily care.

Management

- Nursing home admission procedures need to clearly state the options for alternative sites of care and the procedures to be followed when such options are being negotiated.
- Palliative care policies, including administration of narcotics, should be available to family members in writing (with the possibility of interpretation and translation if this is needed).
- An assessment form that provides some of the resident's pre-admission history is a valuable asset for staff and should be required reading in circumstances of such cultural complexity.
- Policies regarding ethnic mix in each nursing home are a helpful guide to ensuring, wherever possible, that relatives from a non-English-speaking background have access to others in a similar position.

- Involving a culturally appropriate counsellor in care planning and review meetings may be an effective way of communicating with families. Interpreters should also be called when required.
- Equipment such as special mattresses may be an appropriate alternative to bed rails.

Indirect carers

- A volunteer may have the sensitivity and skills to create group support for families with similar ethnic background. Introductions may be all that is required for the group to continue in an informal way, appropriate to the specific needs at the time.

DEMENTIA: WHY BOTHER?

Carers may sometimes overlook the unique life histories of those residents whose lives are complicated by dementia, disordered brain function, fragmented memory and/or erratic behaviour. When such a resident is acknowledged holistically in their particular family and community context, when the meaning of that life is not reduced to the mere physiological process of dementia, the potential exists for providing better care. Caring for such a person is not easy, the way forward is not always clear and no person has all the answers. The challenge lies in reversing the negative 'What's the use?' attitude of some carers which often reflects the stereotype of broader community attitudes. This story begins with the frustrated sigh of those who utter a despairing 'Why bother?' and ends with an attempt to probe more deeply into the experience of the person whose dementia runs its final complex course.

'For heaven's sake shoot me if I ever get like this!' Mary and Brian are providing practical, nursing care for Dot who lies in bed, leaking urine, legs crossed and clamped together, resisting every intervention. Her hospital gown is always folded up around her chest in order to save on linen; the family have long since ceased spending money on clothes for her. Now that she's dying it seems cruel to struggle with her and there seems to be little point in spending time on passive limb exercises. Her rigidity and weight make it hard for staff to turn her. Lying mute and immobile she is like a log; nevertheless she still has the strength to resist. Her skin hangs loose, there's nothing left of that firm ballroom dancing figure. Sometimes she mutters unintelligibly; mostly she seems to be in a trance. Mary and Brian are just two of the nurses who painstakingly reposition Dot every two hours day and night, resenting the time and effort expended on her care. When they are rushed, Dot's head may be grazed as it flops against the bedside cupboard. She often has skin tears on her forearms from hasty, grasping hands.

'Here, have some nice pureed pears, Dot.' Pressure care and hygiene needs having been attended to, Brian now attempts to feed Dot. Her toothless mouth opens to the touch. Her dentures were broken ages ago; there didn't seem any point in getting them fixed. She usually eats everything put in her mouth anyway. But lately, she is not so cooperative. Despite Brian's efforts the nice pureed pears stay in Dot's mouth with no intention of going anywhere. Brian thinks to himself, 'What's the use! I'd be better off spending my time with residents who appreciate their meal.'

Dot has occasional episodes of fitting, and she is on anti-hypertensive medication although her blood pressure is never checked. She's also on psychotropic drugs but no-one knows why. Now the doctor wants antibiotics given. Some of the nurses refuse to give the medication but sign the drug chart anyway. They have given up forcing the tablets which she invariably spits out. 'Why bother? What difference does it make?', they say with a shrug. Perceiving her life to be meaningless they hope Dot will die soon. During the day Dot's bedroom is quiet and lonely as the other residents are in the lounge and Dot has few visitors. Her son seems awkward and embarrassed by the whole situation. Because she needs attention so often at night, her bedside light is always on low, casting an eerie monotonous glow.

Dot does not always lie quietly and just when the nurses think death is near, her activity level intensifies. Her fingers are bent and contracted but still she manages to scratch her groin raw. ('Why won't they let us tie her hands? Her skin would then have a chance to heal.') On this particular day it seems as though the very devil incarnate is let loose in that frail body and mind. 'Get the b… h… out of here!', is the typical response to a gentle: 'Good morning, Dot.' 'Why don't you f… off and leave me alone? Ouch! You're trying to kill me.' The gentlest of touch brings a tirade of abuse; language her family had never heard her use before. Staff react with embarrassment or amusement; some are offended, others frustrated; some simply stay away from her bed, while others devise elaborate defences to help them cope.

There are one or two nurses who know the other side of Dot — the gentlest of ladies, always considerate of others, much loved for her sweet singing voice and proud of her trim, dancing figure. They grieve as they watch Dot deteriorate, the Alzheimer's disease taking its predictable course. They mourn the loss of dignity afforded her by those who fail to understand her old-fashioned sense of modesty. They long for a way into her mind's mysterious maze.

Taking a different approach to 'why bother', the regular night nurse, who had known Dot for many years, began to probe more deeply. Was there any diagnostic cause for Dot's screaming when touched? Would it be worth an X-ray? Yes, it does always seem to be the right shoulder that hurts more. And hasn't she been on cortico-steroids for many years? Would she have osteoporosis? What about secondary bone cancer from her mastectomy in 1975? So…maybe she really does have pain. After discussion amongst some of the staff and the doctor a carefully formulated plan emerged. However, as with 'the best-laid plans', it somehow went astray.

Nurse A at handover: 'We've decided to start Dot on a small dose of oral morphine, strictly four hourly.'
Nurse B at the next handover: 'Debbie has got a morphine order but I don't think Dot's in pain. What she needs is a good sedative to quieten her down. Anyway, suit yourself about the analgesics. I haven't given her any.'

While the nurses took some considerable time to be convinced of the need for consistency, Dot continued her seesaw pattern of withdrawal into her own inner world or of lashing out with fists and tongue. Gradually, a routine was sustained. Dot's response to morphine indicated that she had most probably been in pain. Even though she became more manageable, most of the staff continued to treat her with careless indifference, as though it was too late to establish a new relationship with her. Incapable of answering questions or directing her own care, her quality of life remained in the hands of those few staff who knew her best. At least she seemed comfortable, pain free and at peace during her last few days.

ON REFLECTION…

Dementia: a mysterious malady

While dementia may be caused by a specific pathological condition like Alzheimer's disease or multi-infarct damage, the dementia itself may also be shaped by the individual's cultural and personal life history and by their immediate social and physical environment. We may never fully understand the reality of another person's experience, especially in the advanced stages of dementia; however we are able to structure their environment in order to allow for the possibility of a meaningful encounter.

The story is told of a volunteer who was asked to sit for some time each day with a resident in advanced stages of dementia who had stopped communicating with anybody many months ago. The volunteer made a point of using perfume whenever she visited and of talking quietly in the most natural way she could, as if they were having a conversation. After six weeks the resident reached out and took the volunteer's hand; more importantly, she now reaches out for her hands each day as soon as the volunteer enters the room. This connection is probably cued by the volunteer's perfume, as the resident is blind.

Another story comes from a night nurse who claims a special relationship with a resident who has not spoken for many years. The resident seldom shows any sign of meaningful communication, yet this night nurse is sure the resident knows her by her voice. 'I sing to her each night and her eyes light up.'

Why bother?

Recognising the challenge is the first step in addressing the problem. Caring for residents who exhibit little response and seem not to notice whether they are cared for well or poorly is viewed by many as a thankless task. With imagination and ingenuity, together with a focus on the professional rewards for maintaining high standards of care in every situation, the 'bother' may be turned into a unique opportunity for excellent care. Mutual support, praise and humour are important ingredients in this recipe that takes a fair bit of 'bother' but is worth it in the end. Why bother? We must bother in order to correct erroneous concepts that describe the person with dementia as 'the living dead' or 'just a vegetable'. We must bother to turn around the community's perception that in dying with dementia one loses all traces of dignity. We must bother to ensure staff and relatives are well informed about the processes of dementia. Increasing incidence of dementia, together with population trends in ageing, strongly suggest that we or someone close to us may be totally dependent on someone who bothers to care. And every person with advanced-stage dementia needs an advocate. While none of the listed interventions brings with it a guarantee of success, it is worth asking the question 'Why bother?' because we may find the key which opens the door for this particular resident to die with dignity in spite of the devastating implications of this mysterious malady.

Advocacy

Nowhere in aged care is the issue of advocacy more important than in caring for the dying person with advanced Alzheimer's disease or other dementia-related disorders. At a time when families and friends may have ceased to look for anything positive in their relationship with the resident, staff are challenged to use their experience, their knowledge and their sensitivity to provide the subtleties of care. Who could be relied upon to speak for Dot? Who would presume to speak of Dot's pain and fear, of her expectations and satisfaction? Who would complain if the care were below standard?

Evaluation and research

In the absence of concerned relatives, valuable feedback may be given when staff reflect together on their practice. A brief evaluation session may centre on the following questions: How well did we care for Dot? Were there any mistakes made? What may we learn from this experience in order to care better in the future? Moreover, when such evaluation is carefully documented it may prove to be a significant contribution to areas of research.

Nutrition and hydration

When well-meaning doctors, concerned family members and opinionated staff contribute advice on this area of care, the potential exists for everybody's viewpoint to be heard except that of the resident. Residents who are dying may make their wishes felt concerning this very basic need for food and fluids. Pursing of lips, pulling out of tubes, refusing to swallow may be in fact very clear indicators: 'Please do not force me to eat or drink. I am no longer hungry or thirsty.' Medical and nursing staff need to be clear about the difference between dehydration and malnutrition, between small amounts of plain water given for comfort and constant coaxing to ingest 'a well-balanced diet' at the point of death. Maybe Brian and other nurses like him would have benefited from expressing their feelings about having to feed a dying resident whose dementia made it such a thankless task.

Accurate assessment

Knowing Dot thoroughly meant the integrating of current symptoms with her past history. It meant investigating physical causes for her antisocial and offensive behaviour, it meant challenging apathetic attitudes. Ultimately it meant according Dot the dignity she would have enjoyed had she been able to speak for herself.

Variety of experience

Who made the decision that Dot should remain in her room, no longer to hear the music she had previously enjoyed? Who decided that it was no longer appropriate for her to be wheeled out into the sunshine? Was she being punished for her behaviour? While many residents with dementia respond negatively to increased stimulation, Dot may have responded well to soft music and gentle touch. She may have relaxed in response to a warm bath with aromatic oils or to tender therapeutic massage of her contracted limbs. If boredom and touch starvation can lead to worsening of psychiatric symptoms, who knows what effect such factors may have on the progress of dementia? The sensation of sun on an elderly person's skin, the sound of birdsong or familiar traffic sounds may be sufficient to stimulate memories, relieve monotony and calm the fear of being overlooked. Or should we concentrate primarily on physical symptoms such as Dot's itchy groin? The sunlight may do wonders for that too! It is easy to offer a variety of experience to those who make a meaningful response. It is often only by trial and error that we find the appropriate strategy for the person with dementia.

Pain management and symptom control

A well-thought-out policy on drug administration includes reference to appropriate use of narcotics as a form of pain control. Decisions are authenticated by drawing to the attention of staff, visiting doctors and families, the nursing home's philosophy and policies with respect to this important area. This book is not a manual for specific pain management and symptom control, however diligent updating of skills in this area is necessary for high-quality care of the dying resident. For example, when Dot was ordered morphine in regular doses she should not have been denied the therapeutic benefits of this drug merely on the whim of one particular nurse.

Abuse

There is unspoken frustration in the 'Dot' situations, especially when death will not hurry. The incidence of abuse in the community towards elderly persons with dementia, attests to this. Often such abuse, even from members of a loving family, is the result of carer stress due to inadequate support. The same kind of abuse may occur in nursing homes. The rough, hurried treatment of a vulnerable, dependent resident by a tired, over-stretched nurse may also constitute abuse. This issue has been barely recognised in the past and is now becoming a subject for research. Frank discussion on the matter should assist towards strategies for solving the problem in specific situations.

Medications

What factors contribute to the prescribing of medications in such circumstances? And what happens when the drug chart is not an accurate reflection of reality? What fosters the attitude, 'Don't worry too much about the drugs, half the time she won't take them'? It is not the intention of this discussion to focus on medication administration in nursing homes, except to emphasise the importance of consistency of care based on sound clinical knowledge, in order to avoid the scenario pictured above.

Understanding the incomprehensible

The 'why bother?' attitude of staff may reflect a lack of understanding of the disease process and associated manifestations. Recent research in this area has much to offer in the way of deepening staff understanding and suggesting practical, compassionate care interventions. Education in the form of guided reading and attendance at in-service sessions or external seminars, may open the way for staff to interact with Dot on a more empathetic level. Although communication may still be difficult, staff may find that a knowledge-based, confident response to an agitated, distressed or confused resident may communicate genuine understanding. The power of close human touch may also communicate more than any words.

Relentless and unrewarding care

Some of the hardest and most unrewarding care is provided to the Dots of our nursing world. What may be done to overcome the resentment which says, in effect: 'Why should I bother giving my time and energy when she doesn't even know I'm here?' Responses may well come from colleagues who share the frustration but who also applaud good care. For example, the nurse in charge may comment: 'Dot looks so comfortable and well cared for today. Well done!' or 'That hand massage must be very soothing for Dot. Look how her face has relaxed too.' or 'Someone has taken extra time with Dot's hair and nails, and I observed David massaging her hands. Thank you!'

'Shoot me if I ever get like this!'

What prompts this kind of response? Why would a nurse (metaphorically) choose violent death at the hands of a colleague's shotgun rather than dying of dementia in a nursing home? What if the resident is also silently pleading, 'Please let there be an end to this — for all of us.' or 'If I had a gun I'd shoot you for being so hardhearted and cruel. How would you like to be treated like this?' Guns are not amongst our tools of trade. We may need to dig more deeply into our 'tool bag' to find the most appropriate way of caring for the Dots of the nursing home world. What would it signify for nurses and personal care staff to be proud of the care they give and to hope that one day, if they themselves were in need of such care, these standards would be upheld?

QUALITY ISSUES FOR ENHANCED PRACTICE

The gerontic nurse

- When planning a case discussion, invite all interested staff. Allow time for staff to express resentment and frustration, as well as offer positive suggestions.
- Support and encourage other staff by acknowledging the difficulties in caring for residents like Dot.
- Revise the care plan to include suggestions of what works well, removing any previous plans which have proved unrealistic; acknowledge goals which have been met; and set a date for next review.
- The charge nurse may provide positive feedback to staff, highlighting specific aspects of care.
- A staff member may show interest in writing Dot's life story. There may be elements of her past which provoke certain behaviours; telling her story may assist staff to see Dot in her total life context.
- Arrange a medication review that realistically assesses Dot's compliance and ensures she is only given medication which is congruent with the goal of care.
- The intuitive gerontic nurse may have the ability to reverse Dot's negative self-image, encouraging all staff to focus on her increased self-esteem.

Management

- Promote staff education by providing well-researched publications, including the latest research on dementia.
- Reward staff for good care, while acknowledging the difficulties when the task seems 'unrewarding'.

Indirect carers

- Involve allied health staff and volunteers in caring for residents like Dot where possible, so the care is shared and the resident receives a variety of care that is not all task centred.

THE SHORT-TERM RESIDENT: RON'S CHOICE

Although Ron's admission to the nursing home suited 'the system', and his wife's subsequent admission seemed in the couple's best interests, the outcome was not so clear. Each time Ron was moved, he seemed to agree it was in his best interests. Was he merely acquiescing to a system that rendered him powerless? Some months later Ron moved again, this time to another room, his fourth new environment in a little over a year. Although this final move was felt to be the ultimate in good decision making, Ron's subsequent death prompted many questions. Ron's story is one examination of relocation and its impact on the morbidity and mortality of frail aged residents.

Ron's admission to the nursing home solved two 'system' problems. As a long stayer in the state geriatric centre, he was finally 'placed' — and we filled our vacant bed promptly without loss of revenue. In hindsight, it seems this move, so satisfactory for the system, created an insoluble problem for this 82-year old.

Before his stroke, Ron lived at home with his frail wife Mary and her 85-year-old sister. Together the three formed a fragile system of mutual support, with Ron the only one physically able to maintain the tasks of shopping and housework. Ron's stroke and admission to hospital changed these three lives dramatically.

Mary's sister was admitted to a nursing home close to her other family members. After two months in a public hospital Ron was transferred to a geriatric centre as a short-term admission, awaiting placement. Mary, assessed as needing hostel accommodation, dug her heels in and refused to move without Ron. Community support was arranged for her while the search commenced for vacancies in a facility where Mary and Ron could be accommodated together.

Almost a year passed, as suitable accommodation was hard to find. The longer they waited, the more reluctant Mary became to move at all, especially without Ron. With no prospect of suitable accommodation for the couple, a decision was made to 'place' Ron. Ron's tenure in the geriatric centre was becoming less firm, so when the centre was contacted about an appropriate resident to fill our vacancy you can guess what happened. Ron was *sold* to us rather like a used car, and we to him. We needed urgently to fill a vacant male bed and in the opinion of both parties Ron seemed a most suitable candidate. No doubt the social worker did the same job of selling us to Ron, for before we could blink she was back on the phone wanting to arrange transfer.

We found Ron to be all that was promised, a lovely, gentle, unassuming man to whom the staff responded warmly. Sadly, this dignified man had the submissive air of those who perceive themselves to have no power, but what could you expect after he had been wrapped up and sent like a parcel? He settled into a four-bed room very quickly, finding he already knew one of the other residents from years back.

The gentle atmosphere of the room seemed to suit Ron, who was so disabled that physical self-care was impossible, but he responded to company. Ron and his friend often listened to the cricket together in silence after lunch. We felt sorry for Ron; he'd had a difficult year and was still separated from his wife. We wanted to help him settle in and feel at home. Despite his dysphasia he gave every indication that he was pleased his future was settled.

Reviewing our room allocation we discovered that Mary and Ron could, perhaps, be accommodated together after all. After reassessment it was discovered Mary's deteriorating health meant she now qualified for nursing home admission, albeit at a very low level of care. After complex negotiations Mary moved in. She and Ron had been apart for 15 months.

They were offered our only double room. Ron was so eager to please, it was hard to tell what he thought about the prospect of a fourth move. The charge nurse was getting to know Ron well and, as his advocate, tried to delay the move until Ron could make a clear decision. As usual, timing was difficult — the bed suddenly had to be filled and, to avoid disadvantaging other residents, a decision had to be made quickly. So Ron moved again. Was there a hint of regret as he said goodbye to his old roommates? If so, he quickly concealed it, determined to do what we was expected of him, resolutely turning to face change again.

Eager to cooperate, Ron once more seemed to settle very quickly into his changed environment. He seemed so resilient. Yes, it was nice being with his wife, but it was also evident they had grown apart. For reasons best known to herself, Mary had found it impossible to visit him during those 15 months; other family members were either absent or uninvolved. However, we were very pleased, it seemed so neat and satisfactory to get them back together. But togetherness is more than mere proximity, and Ron's disabilities meant their levels of function were quite different. After the space of her own home, Mary found the small double room claustrophobic and she roamed the nursing home on her walking frame. Unable to follow her, Ron spent the days alone, just sitting. There wasn't much they could do together. Perhaps we overlooked his needs, he never asked for much. Once he and Mary were together again we assumed she would meet his social needs.

We were all shocked when Ron died suddenly, six weeks after his last move. Perhaps he'd had the final say. He had taken control of his life in a way that no system, social worker, nurse or wife could. Ultimately, perhaps, it was his choice.

ON REFLECTION…

Relocation

In recent times there has been recognition of the stressful effects of relocating a frail aged person, whether from home or hospital to a nursing home, or transfer between nursing homes. This is called relocation or translocation stress. This syndrome may be simply understood in terms of the trauma and stress everyone feels when moving house, even if the move is seen as positive.

For the frail, dependent resident, a move means a whole new social environment: new staff, new roommates and new support systems. If the resident's self-care and communication is compromised, such a move may be enormously disruptive. Deficits may impair a resident's ability to adapt to the new environment. If the move further diminishes their sense of control, if they feel they have no choice or personal power in the situation, significant stress will result. Significant stress, at any age, is acknowledged as a precursor to serious illness.

Factors likely to diminish or increase relocation stress include the ability of staff to receive and support the new resident, the resident's innate ability to cope with loss and stress and the amount of power and control the resident is perceived to have in decisions related to the move.

How does this apply to Ron? It is difficult to measure the first two factors anecdotally. However, Ron's compliant behaviour may indicate a diminished sense of personal power. Thoroughly institutionalised, he was willing to cooperate with any suggestion without attempting to express his own opinion. We will never know how he really felt about his final move. Did this move affect his survival? All we can say with a degree of certainty is that, for some older people, relocation seems to be a factor working against survival.

The value of a pre-admission visit

In the majority of situations the pre-admission visit to the nursing home is attended by family members, the prospective resident being too frail to manage multiple visits in order to make an informed choice. This may leave the resident with fears of the unknown, magnifying the anxiety related to change. On the other hand, seeing a new environment before moving enables residents to begin the process of adaptation. They may imagine themselves there, fantasise about the people they have met and what their relationships will be, picture their possessions in the new environment, rehearsing the new in preparation for change. This lessens the stress of the actual move. While it is not always possible to arrange a pre-admission visit, it is likely that Ron would have benefited from being involved in the choice.

Security of accommodation: the individual versus the many

Should we have waited for Ron to indicate clearly his decision about moving again? This was our dilemma. In residential aged care, the empty bed factor forces decisions that may later be regretted. Had we delayed, other residents would have been found quickly to fill the double room. Enshrined in residents' rights is the need for security of accommodation. Though we can never guarantee every resident the same bed position for life we encourage residents to regard their bed position as their own space.

In circumstances such as these, there may be times when an individual resident is disadvantaged by being in a collective situation, but if the needs of all parties involved are given due consideration, no more can be asked.

Power, choices and the older person

Research has shown those who believe they have options feel more powerful and less stressed. In aged care, reduced stress may enhance survival. It seems Ron had neither choice nor the illusion of choice in any of his moves. When staff accept society's stereotypical view that old people have no power, then residents' wishes will be easily disregarded.

Because of such unbalanced power relations, the extent to which elderly residents' needs are met depends on the goodwill of carers. Compliant residents do not complain about lack of consultation. They have made an adaptation to their environment that ensures their survival. Staff enjoy dealing with compliant residents and so are motivated to respond to their needs, if not always promptly. The noisy, complaining resident may get immediate attention, but not necessarily good or thorough care. Unfortunately, the 'compliant' residents please everyone except themselves.

Fill the bed today!

Urgent requests may compromise good resident outcomes and, in some situations, influence a resident's survival. Time taken to prepare a new resident for a move is time spent in promoting that resident's health and harmony within the home, but this is not always possible under the current funding system which makes filling the bed a more urgent priority than resident satisfaction. While current legislation allows some increased flexibility by way of pre-entry leave it is often difficult to achieve the necessary negotiations in complex situations.

To facilitate smooth, though urgent, admissions, nursing homes keep comprehensive waiting lists. Maintaining a stable waiting list is difficult. No matter how much care and time is taken, the possibility always exists that there will be no suitable prospective resident at the time required. This may lead to inappropriate or rushed admissions with negative consequences for that resident and the rest of the home.

Placed 'like a parcel'

The description of Ron being 'wrapped up like a parcel and sent' is an analogy for the way nursing home 'placements' are often arranged. The term 'placement' connotes an object being picked up and put down, rather than the careful and sensitive care surrounding such a major move in a person's life history. When priority is given to the person rather than the process, then the person may feel less like a pawn who is manipulated to fit the system.

Power and powerlessness

The importance of a perception of personal power in everyday life is evident at every level of society and every stage of life. In aged care, when so much else is against the survival of the individual, promotion of feelings of personal power and control over one's destiny is an important factor to consider and include in all stages of care, starting before the resident is admitted.

QUALITY ISSUES FOR ENHANCED PRACTICE

The gerontic nurse

- When a resident seems overly compliant in response to significant life changes, staff should sensitively probe the resident's situation and reflect on the dynamics of the resident's care situation for factors inhibiting the resident's full participation in decision making.
- Access to objective, factual data regarding a married couple's past coping mechanisms and future hopes and fears may assist understanding the couple, rather than making decisions based on assumptions and generalisations.
- Difficult decisions are sometimes made easier through the collective wisdom of a group of staff. Particularly where relocation decisions affect a resident with no family, staff may be encouraged to advocate on the resident's behalf.

Management

- Careful pre-admission assessment where a married couple are both prospective residents should entail a thorough understanding of the couple's expectations. This may include the level of intimacy they would expect and enjoy, based on their previous history together.
- Awareness should be promoted of the positive examples of providing accommodation for a married couple. This concept should also be applied to any two persons, regardless of marital status or sexual preference, who choose to live together in order to maintain an accustomed, intimate relationship.
- Community health professionals have much to contribute to the resident's pre-admission history. In complex circumstances it may be beneficial to arrange a meeting with those who have intimate knowledge of the resident's former situation.

Indirect carers

- Carers who have previously had a professional relationship with the resident in the community may continue visiting as a friend, thus removing another barrier between the nursing home community and the wider community.

THE LONG-TERM RESIDENT: THIS IS MY HOME

Although the average length of stay in Australian nursing homes is less than one year, a significant number of residents remain more than five years, forming a core of long-term residents. Where there is also a stable staff, the death of a long-term resident may mark the end of many significant relationships. Should all deaths in the nursing home be treated with equal significance? Are there some residents whose deaths have a greater impact than others? As in the wider community do some residents command respect commensurate with their standing in the nursing home community? Each nursing home will have unique stories about the impact of the deaths of long-term residents. We dedicate this chapter to one of our loved and respected long-termers, a woman of 99 years, our oldest resident at that time, whose influence was of great significance to staff. Her real name is used with permission of her next of kin.

Ita was a proud spinster ('*Miss* Ita English, if you please. I have never married nor have I regretted it'), cultured, whimsical, forthright, perceptive and astute. Clipped and precise in her enunciation, Ita was increasingly outraged by the decline in the English vocabulary. A wonderful storyteller, intensely devoted to the memory of her family, Ita would enchant us with tales of her schooldays and youth in a small rural community. It had not been easy for Ita to take the very big step from independent living to the nursing home. However, always philosophical as well as practical, when she had outlived all her relatives and close friends, when her physical disabilities increased, Ita decided there was nothing to be done but to 'put myself in a home' Reluctant to give up her independence, she was admitted initially for a trial period.

Recalling the lives and deaths of many residents in her care, the charge nurse wrote at the time of Ita's death:

> Grey hair swept up into a carefully secured crown Ita reigned as the 'Grand Old Lady' of the nursing home for over 11 years. Her mind alert and her memory recall remarkable, she was acutely observant and her tongue could be razor sharp if she considered criticism necessary. Although she did not leave her room for the last four years of her life, she always knew before 9 a.m. who was doing the cooking for the day. There would always be someone talking to Ita as she was so prepared to share the experiences of her long life and her interest in the outside world. Conversations with me would always begin, 'My dear, did you know…?' In a discussion about her age Ita said, 'My dear, I have lived through the reigns of six monarchs' and then proceeded to list them all, noting the list included 'Edward, the uncrowned King'. When Ita celebrated her 99th birthday she was proud to sit up in bed and have residents and staff sing 'Happy Birthday' and share her cake with them. After this day Ita was able to tell people she was in her 100th year but she considered that she had lived long enough. When asked to what she attributed her long life she replied: 'Good, clean, simple living and a belief in God.' Ita said her prayers every night and would often tell me who she had prayed for. Her nightly prayer went something like this; 'Thank you God for today, and may I walk with you tomorrow.' Ita was in full control of her life right up until the hour she died, six weeks after her 99th birthday.

Being in control meant knowing every staff member by name. Many, many members of staff found their way into Ita's corner in the very end room to share news of a birthday, an engagement, a broken romance or to confide work pressures. As with any true confidante, Ita would never disclose those secrets, except to advise the director of nursing that various staff members were on her mind and in her prayers. Another measure of control was to ensure that not one item of her personal possessions was ever moved without permission. Hence, the walking frame, not used for four years, remained by the bed, finally being removed only after thorough consultation. A further example of Ita's autonomy (and perhaps a contributing factor towards her longevity!) was her hair care. No member of staff could ever remember Ita's hair being washed. 'It's not dirty so why wash it!' Thorough, daily brushing ensured Ita's hair retained its shine, length and thickness until the day of her death.

In her many philosophical conversations about life and death, Ita was quite clear that she had lived long enough. Much to the chagrin of the staff Ita had decided she would not be around for her 100th birthday; she had no desire to fulfil other people's desire for publicity, drama and celebration. Sensing our disappointment she was, nevertheless, quite determined. Perhaps she also knew that the gastric ulcer she had 'grown to accept as one of life's constant companions' would end her life.

On the day the ulcer finally eroded, Ita refused to regard it as a cause for panic or undue disturbance. Word spread quickly through the nursing home and one by one staff came to say their goodbyes in many and various ways. For one special nurse, in clear and firm voice, Ita recited part of her favourite poem: 'Oft, in the stilly night,/ Ere slumber's chain hath bound me'.

Staff offered Ita the calm reassurance they knew she would appreciate: 'Ita, it's Ruth. I'll be on till nine o'clock.' Flowers arrived — not the impersonal arrangements delivered by outsiders but jonquils from the laundry staff's home garden, a posy picked from the nursing home garden and daphne from another staff member. One nurse who had known Ita for nearly 11 years — 'I started four days after Ita came here so I've known her all that time' — came for a final visit. Staff who had known Ita for a much shorter time or not at all personally, also came to pay tribute and express solidarity: the new occupational therapist, the ground-floor charge nurse and those who were going off duty. Others stayed away only because their sadness was too much to bear, or they didn't know what to say.

While many days in the life of a nursing home are predictably routine, there are others where chaos reigns supreme. This was one of those days: staff shortages, another resident requiring immediate hospitalisation, doctors coming at inconvenient times, no volunteer available to sit with Ita and no staff member to spare. Amid the flurry someone checked with Ita about her desire to see the priest. When Father Coster arrived from the other side of town with apologies for the delay, Ita's reply was typical of her thoughtfulness for others, 'Fancy your coming all that way'. The director of nursing, hesitant about demonstrating any favouritism amongst residents yet also mindful of a close relationship developed through daily conversations on the morning round, chose to sit with Ita for a while. No words were adequate, no words were necessary.

As Ita grew weaker her physical distress was evident. Hasty discussions were held amongst staff and with Ita's next of kin. Should we send her to hospital? If she is haemorrhaging internally shouldn't we arrange for a blood transfusion? Questioned about how she was feeling, and whether there was anything she needed, Ita responded with gentle and patient stoicism, 'It's the pain'. Ita was told her doctor was on his way. Content with that reassurance, Ita expressed a desire for no other intervention. Staff ambivalence was evident. No-one wanted to watch Ita suffering, yet no-one wanted to see her moved. The doctor was now in regular contact by phone, for he too was distressed. She was his oldest patient and his favourite. Caught in the dilemma of suspecting a perforated ulcer but knowing there may not be time to get her to hospital, the doctor agreed with staff that Ita would not wish to be moved. Her previous expressed wish to avoid active treatment was honoured.

Amid the flurry of activity in other areas of the nursing home, Ita's corner retained an air of calm, a centre of peace amid anticipated climax. Ita's charge nurse, on duty since 7 a.m., was still there at 5 p.m. trying to arrange a substitute for the regular evening nurse, who was sick, in order to ensure Ita would be surrounded by familiar faces. The ground-floor charge nurse, already busy with crises in her own area, remained long past her official going home time to show care and support for her colleagues. Offers of voluntary assistance came from night staff: 'I could come on earlier just to sit with her'. No-one wanted a stranger to be in charge of Ita's final nursing care. Ita, the all-knowing, counselled her charge nurse, whom she knew had been there all day. 'You go, my dear. You've already done more than enough.' After a quick consultation with Ita, her two close friends, staff and doctor it was decided sufficient morphine should be given to maintain her comfort, including increased amounts in the event of haemorrhage. In the end, the disease process took its course; a philosophy espoused by Ita. She did not want to live to be 100.

As Ita lived, so she died — in full control of her surroundings, able to make decisions and, as always, thoughtful and considerate of others. Nursing home life must always go on. However, it was a very subdued atmosphere that pervaded this community the following day as staff, residents and their relatives heard the news. One nurse spoke for us all, 'It will take someone very special to fill that bed.'

ON REFLECTION...

Hospital or home

Death as a crisis in a strange place or death faced with equanimity in her own bed? Ita's life was one of calm reflection, showing a distinct disdain for undue attention or hasty, ill-considered action. It was important, therefore, to see this crisis in the context of Ita's whole life. While we suspected an internal haemorrhage there was a degree of ambivalence as to the appropriate response. However, for those who knew her well, her close friends, doctor and staff, the decision was reached by consensus. The conservative approach adopted matched Ita's attitude to life and death.

One resident's place in a 50-bed nursing home

Ita's place in the nursing home was frequently acknowledged when she reminded people, 'I used to be on the ground floor, you know.' Ita exercised her right to know

every detail about the daily life of the whole nursing home. This state of affairs, in the case of a different resident, may be perceived as unhealthy interference or inappropriate intrusion. However, for Ita, being acquainted with ordinary daily affairs was the normal response of a mentally alert resident to her rightful place in her home of 11 years.

Friend and confidante of staff — she was our teacher

While many elements in this and other such stories about long-term residents readily emerge, other factors remain unacknowledged. Ita's wisdom and life experience had a profound influence on her carers. While it is not generally thought to be appropriate practice for a resident's advice to be sought regarding a staff member's personal problems, for an 18-year-old student nurse the wisdom of someone more than 80 years her senior is a gift to be cherished. Mutual exchange of this nature benefits the resident by acknowledging their worth and usefulness to society and benefits the carers who may receive new insights from one so wise.

Nursing home history

Each nursing home develops its own way of acknowledging significant events. In this case, it was important for the charge nurse to record, in a book she was writing, her feelings of joy and sadness at the death of this greatly loved resident. Other ways of acknowledging the death of a long-term resident may be through the nursing home newsletter, participation in the funeral oration or by encouraging staff to write a response in poetry or prose or song in memory of the resident.

The cleaner's silent tears

Reactions of a number of staff have been described in the story of Ita's life and death. However, it is not so easy to record the unspoken feelings of the cleaner who had mopped around that bed five days a week for eight years. A higher profile is often given to nursing staff's reactions to death, but it is the reaction of staff in the kitchen, maintenance, cleaning and domestic areas that is often left unacknowledged. Some staff may require encouragement to express their feelings or to feel they have 'permission' to say goodbye to a dying resident.

Favouritism and fuss

For those who dislike more attention being paid to one resident than the others, reactions and responses described above may be perceived as unfair. While there may never be consensus, misunderstanding and clarification of concerns may be approached through staff discussion where all staff are invited to express their opinion. Some staff find security in their former hospital practices where undue emphasis on one particular patient was frowned upon and feelings surrounding a patient's death were not freely expressed. However, the long-term environment of the nursing home offers greater opportunity for normal reactions and responses to death, as in the general community. Thus, it is not inappropriate for significant respect to be paid to a significant person.

Filling the bed

While funding requirements generally mean the bed must be filled quickly, it is important to note the staff member's comment, 'It will take someone very special to fill that bed'. Some would regard leaving the bed empty for two or three days as a healthy mark of respect for such a long-term resident. For others, however, it would make no difference who filled the bed and when — it would always be Ita's bed. Acknowledging such a variety of opinions opens the way to prepare the nursing home for the next resident. Other ways may need to be found to ensure the memory of a long-term resident is appropriately maintained, while living also with the reality of another older person's need of care. One can imagine Ita saying, 'My time's up. It's time to make room for the next person.'

QUALITY ISSUES FOR ENHANCED PRACTICE

The gerontic nurse

- Each resident should have the opportunity of stating whether or not they wish to be hospitalised in the event of a medical/surgical crisis. Provided this preference is clearly documented and regularly reviewed, it should form the basis of informed decision making.
- When staff's opinions differ as to whether the resident requires hospitalisation, the clear 'terminal wishes' statement or other appropriate assessment documentation should be the guide.
- In the event of a crisis such as imminent haemorrhage, arranging a quick meeting of all available family and health professionals removes the burden from one person as the decision-maker.
- When a clear diagnosis is made, medical and professional nursing judgement come to the fore in anticipating likely consequences. For example, in the case of haemorrhage, readily accessible linen, adequate medication orders and ready access to the prescribed drug of choice, are practical means of preparation which contribute to a more comfortable death.
- Immediate communication assists other staff, particularly unqualified staff who may be dismayed at the prospect or event of haemorrhage; these staff may require reassurance and factual information.

Management

- Each nursing home has its own way of incorporating significant lives into its history. Encouraging staff to write 'in memory of' is one way of including a variety of voices in the history.
- Appropriate debriefing may be required following such a significant death, particularly if the circumstances are sudden and critical, as in haemorrhage.

- While acknowledging the particular significance of a long-term resident, staff should be encouraged to value each resident's life and death as unique and significant.

Indirect carers

- In the absence of family, involving close friends in decision making at the point of death empowers those friends and acknowledges their significance in the resident's life.

RELATIONSHIPS: TOGETHER OR NOT?

Vera and Bruce were not a conventional couple, neither did they have the insight to understand their increasing need for outside help. According to the strict criteria of aged-care assessments, their differing physical needs meant they were to be separated. One assessment visit failed to uncover all the complexities of this relationship. Perseverance and sensitive probing resulted in other possibilities being explored with the result that Bruce and Vera achieved, in their new environment of care, a fulfilment and closure of their lives together, which would have been impossible in their own home. Thus, the nursing home provided the context for a fitting end to their former fragile, fragmented lives.

For many years Vera and Bruce had struggled to care for each other at home, refusing community support, apart from meals-on-wheels. All that came to an end when the assessment team was finally called in by a concerned relative. The geriatrician was shocked to see this couple's squalid living arrangements. Apart from concerns about Vera's hygiene and nutritional status, it was quite clear to the doctor that Vera's cardiac failure made hospitalisation imperative. She also had leg ulcers which had not been treated, except for Bruce's clumsy attempts at bandaging with rags.

Without Vera, Bruce would also need supported care, for they had been truly interdependent, sharing the necessary daily tasks — what one could not manage the other could, well... almost. Since Bruce's stroke some years ago, Vera had assisted him with tasks he couldn't manage with one hand. Now she was too ill to help him, Bruce reluctantly agreed to consider nursing home admission 'some time in the future'.

When Vera came to our nursing home there was very little information available about her former life. The letter of transfer mentioned Bruce as her 'friend' but the relationship was not clear and, in deference to her privacy, staff did not pursue it. The hospital nominated Vera's son as next of kin, but we were never able to contact him. No-one ever visited. Although Vera was quite lucid at times, she seemed unable to give a coherent account of her life before entering the nursing home.

It was not until Vera had settled in, that the community social worker phoned about Bruce, and the story of their life together was told. Bruce was still struggling to manage independently at home, fretting for Vera and refusing all community assistance. His health had deteriorated markedly. Unable to get to the nursing home to visit, he could only worry, but once he knew Vera was well settled he seemed reassured. Declining our offer of transport, he seemed content for messages to be passed via the social worker to Vera on his behalf.

In response to messages from Bruce, Vera also began to fret, calling for him constantly in the evenings and at night. We were keen for Bruce's place on our waiting list to be confirmed, so a case conference was arranged with all relevant health professionals invited. Bruce declined to attend, determined to stay in the security of the home he and Vera had shared for many years. He feared leaving home, in case, like Vera, he was not allowed to return. He feared hospital admission. Bruce had now been reassessed for urgent nursing home admission, mainly due to self-neglect. Now, given the option of living in the nursing home with Vera, he agreed to leave home.

It was not possible to obtain a coherent opinion about Bruce's admission from Vera. Staff were divided over whether Vera and Bruce should share a room, evident by the various comments, 'She wouldn't even know if he was there or not, so why move the other resident?' 'It would be a different matter if they were married.' 'They've lived together for so many years, why shouldn't they spend their last years together?' In the end we decided to give them a shared room.

Within days of his admission Bruce's condition improved dramatically. Reunited with Vera, he resumed his accustomed role of carer and sat beside her all day, holding her hand and talking to her as if she understood every word. It would be nice to report a corresponding improvement in Vera, but we were never sure what she understood as her condition continued to deteriorate. When the charge nurse took Bruce aside to prepare him for Vera's death he said immediately, 'I know she's slipping away. All I want is to be with her.'

While most staff were generally accepting of Bruce's participation in Vera's care (for example, he still wanted to bandage her leg ulcers), some felt it was unfair that Bruce was taking up a nursing home bed when his condition had improved. However, his contribution to Vera's comfort was apparent. Always a light sleeper he would call the staff if Vera needed attention. One night, only a few weeks after his admission, Bruce appeared at the desk, tall and dignified in dressing gown and slippers, 'I think she's gone.'

In the days that followed Vera's death, shy Bruce was overwhelmed by staff support — 'I've never been kissed by so many girls!' After the funeral in the chapel it seemed only natural for the small party of mourners to share afternoon tea in Bruce and Vera's room.

Although grieving for Vera, Bruce subsequently settled into the nursing home, making friends and living a self-contained life. His general condition continued to improve due to his improved nutrition, until clearly he was too independent to remain in the nursing home. And yet we were loathe to begin the process of uprooting him again. It seemed our hesitation was justified, for in a long conversation with a nurse, he spoke of his past. 'I'm afraid I'll go on the bottle again if I leave. And anyway, I feel so close to Vera here, every night I look out this window where I can see our star.' With a sideways glance at the nurse he added hesitantly, 'I told her it wouldn't be long before I joined her.'

Our dilemma about the appropriate site of care was solved exactly one month after Vera's death. Suffering a further fatal stroke Bruce did indeed join her.

ON REFLECTION...

Assessment details to include care of spouse or partner

Given the strict criteria for approved entry into aged-care facilities, people in circumstances like those of Vera and Bruce do not neatly fit the system. It was only after careful and persistent inquiries that their individual and shared needs became apparent. It would have helped us considerably if the assessment details had included a brief account of their partnership and the effect it would have on Bruce when Vera was transferred to the nursing home.

Ambivalence in decision making

Opinion will remain divided as to the most appropriate course of action in circumstances such as those outlined above. The question remains, what is the best course of action for this person in this particular context at this particular time? Setting a review date may guard against the long-term consequences of a wrong decision. Having a clear admission and discharge policy which allows flexibility is another way of leaving options to be negotiated.

Flexible arrangements to provide for shared accommodation

Vera's and Bruce's health did not decline at the same rate; therefore their accommodation needs were not the same. Their story highlights the difficulties in addressing short-term needs in a long-term residential setting. Apart from the question of nursing home design allowing for shared accommodation, the need exists for more flexible funding arrangements which allow, in certain circumstances, for a partner's accommodation needs when one partner needs long-term care.

Bruce's shame

Careful psycho-emotional assessment may have revealed Bruce's feelings of shame at not marrying Vera. He may have felt a lack of acceptance without the legitimacy of his partnership that made him reluctant to come to the nursing home. Such factors require careful documentation so staff have *facts* to guide them, rather than innuendo and gossip.

When a resident's condition improves

Bruce's story is not uncommon; there are many stories of nursing home residents who have shown dramatic improvement following care in an environment of physical and emotional security. Provided sufficient time is allowed for thorough planning, including continued inter-agency liaison, transfer of a resident to another level of care may be appropriate and beneficial. Again, the door needs to be left open for regular review; another resident's condition may deteriorate following such a transfer. While caregivers strive to make the best judgement at the time, based on thorough assessment, there will always be the possibility of error. Providing opportunity for continuous assessment and re-evaluation is the best means of minimising negative outcomes.

QUALITY ISSUES FOR ENHANCED PRACTICE

The gerontic nurse

- A comprehensive social history is necessary to identify a couple's past coping mechanisms, alerting staff to factors such as Bruce's fear of 'going on the bottle again'.
- Careful assessment of previous health and lifestyle habits may lead to a partner retaining some role in the daily care of the resident. When this is clearly identified in the care plan inconsistencies are minimised.
- Goals and plans of care may not always be clearly evident and in such cases, a clearly defined period of review may offer a way forward.

Management

- Aged-care facilities may have an intentional mission statement or admission policy which allows some flexibility for providing accommodation on the basis of social justice. The concept of 'ageing in place' is intended to allow greater flexibility. However, a humane approach to budgeting may allow for a 'low-care resident' to be accommodated on grounds other than economic.
- Admission policies and procedures for room allocation should be made clear to prospective nursing home residents and assessment teams, to assist all parties in making a choice based on comprehensive information.
- Staff will be reassured if decisions about 'unusual' nursing home admissions are made on the basis of clear policy direction, rather than on an ad hoc basis.
- Time taken for a meeting with community health professionals may uncover important information that influences the resident's ongoing care. Time taken at this point often saves time later.

Indirect carers

- The use of volunteers may add quality to a relationship such as Vera and Bruce's. To be taken for a drive to their familiar neighbourhood may have helped them to re-live old memories and assist in drawing to a close the former chapter of their lives.

CHAPTER THREE

This chapter explores the complexity of communal life, highlighting the opportunities and challenges for residents, their families and carers who find themselves in a community not necessarily of their own choosing.

INTERCONNECTIONS: WILL YOU BE MY FAMILY TOO?

In a shared bedroom strangers are brought as close to each other as family. This communal space draws each occupant into the mundane elements of the other's life. Residents are also observers and, at times, participants in the personal triumphs and tragedies of their roommates. We may never be sure what impressions are gained by other residents when care is focused on a roommate who is dying. This story describes quite different reactions from two women who had shared a room with Emily for several years. Representing a microcosm of the nursing home these reflections illustrate the contrast between an assertive, alert, articulate resident and one who is confused and solitary, living in the impenetrable inner world of dementia. Emily, centre of attention in her death, demonstrated in a profound way, her unique influence on the other occupants in this room.

Emily had remained inert, immobile, impassive and inarticulate in her corner bed for 10 years, prompting the charge nurse at the time to write her impressions:

> A gracious, patient lady, unable to utter a single word of joy or complaint but her beautiful blue eyes seemed to say everything. Although she had no family to mourn her passing, for those of us that knew and cared for her she left us with a lasting impression of endurance and dignity.

What did Emily's passing convey to the other two residents who shared her room? First, there was jealous Jessamine. Resenting any movement towards Emily, particularly by two nurses at a time, Jessamine would react in one of her many attention-seeking ways in order to divert staff towards her own needs. Jessamine frequently tested staff's patience with her repetitive calling out, 'Help me, help me, help me! Will somebody please help me!' Never able to explain exactly what kind of help she needed (and therefore never able to express satisfaction with help received), Jessamine's behaviour provided a stark contrast to Emily's silent endurance. Jessamine's world however, was not entirely self-centred; as she saw Emily's life fading away she paid her more and more attention. Daily, venturing closer to the bed, she would make her way right around as if to check on every angle, perhaps making sure Emily was well covered and comfortable. Towards the end, she would sit beside Emily, holding her hand and rocking her own body to and fro. On these occasions she would stop calling out for help, engrossed in a world of mysterious communication with her roommate.

When Emily died, staff were concerned that Jessamine might not understand. She appeared reluctant to leave Emily's bedside that night. Next morning she sat in her chair gazing silently at the empty bed opposite. Gently staff tried to explain to Jessamine that Emily had died and a different person would soon be occupying that bed, but Jessamine reverted to her self-preoccupation, resuming cries of 'Help, help, won't somebody please help me!'

Elizabeth's reaction to Emily's death was different. Physically disabled but mentally alert, she watched from her more distant corner, very little escaping her attention. Finding it hard to imagine life without any family visitors, Elizabeth watched the different nurses' interactions with Emily. Some would touch her gently, spending that extra few minutes ensuring Emily appeared relaxed and comfortable, double checking the position of her limbs, attending to her hair, ensuring her bedclothes looked neat and tidy. Others would come in two by two paying scant regard to Emily as, across the bed, they discussed their previous night's social life. Elizabeth made her own judgements as to which nurses she would prefer at her deathbed. On the long night of Emily's death, Elizabeth struggled to stay awake but must have dozed between 2 a.m. and 3 a.m. She woke to find more activity in the room but there was no undue noise or panic. Skilled staff attended to Emily's body for the last time. The night nurse assisted Elizabeth to her wheelchair after confirming that, yes, Elizabeth would like to say her last goodbyes. Elizabeth's tears were explained to the director of nursing the following morning. 'You should have seen the way they cared for Emily. She looked so beautiful. I won't worry any more about dying in a nursing home.'

While Elizabeth's family visited regularly, her older sister was frail and the nieces and nephews all had their own lives to lead. She could see herself soon to be in Emily's situation with only the nurses to care for her. Only after more tears could she explain the reason for her grief. It was a mixture of joy and sorrow, satisfaction and expectation. In Emily's death, Elizabeth could see her own. She confided that the one fear which had dominated her older adult life was that she would be left to die alone in a nursing home bed. 'And do you know something else?' she whispered, 'You'll probably think I'm stupid but I don't want to look ugly and for my family to have to see me that way.' 'That way', for Elizabeth, meant without make-up and without her hair carefully coiffed. Elizabeth could now see that death need not be filled with the horror she imagined. Overwhelmed by the care and attention she had witnessed towards the lifeless body of this frail woman who could never articulate her feelings, Elizabeth had renewed confidence that staff would understand her own particular needs. She had come to place her trust in those who would be her family too, when the time came.

It seemed quite natural for Elizabeth and Jessamine to attend the funeral together. There was very little known about Emily's past and the chaplain deferred to the charge nurse for the reading of a short eulogy. Tribute was paid to the silent influence of this resident who provided an opportunity for the staff to care for her as though she were one of their own family. Jessamine listened intently to these words and later, ignoring her meal, she made her way carefully and deliberately down the passage to the nurses' station. 'They said at Emily's funeral that you were all her family. If there's no-one at my funeral will you be my family too?'

ON REFLECTION…

Shared rooms

Accommodating several older persons in one room is not necessarily the best way of providing care, especially when the hallmark of today's nursing homes is a homelike atmosphere. However, when a room is occupied by the same residents over a number of years, a sense of community often develops through shared experiences. Here, these three residents, all differing widely in their background and needs, were united in a close bond by Emily's death. As Elizabeth and Jessamine watched over her, observing the many different aspects of her care, it appeared they were putting themselves in her place. What will it be like when I die? Will they care for me as well?

Lack of family

It mattered little that there were only half a dozen people at Emily's funeral for this was her family — her roommates and the staff. What thoughts crowd the minds of those residents who have few family members or none at all? 'Who will be at my funeral? Will anyone miss me when I'm gone? What has my life been worth?' When staff show their affection through paying due respect to a deceased resident, when staff show their own sadness at the loss of a friend, then others are reassured that when their turn comes, their life and death may have some meaning.

Written tribute

Elizabeth was alert enough to ask for a copy of the tribute to Emily printed in the staff meeting minutes. Our practice is also to record the deaths of residents in the regular newsletter forwarded to residents and relatives. This had new meaning for Elizabeth, whose self-perception was very much dependent upon what others thought of her. In her need for affirmation she could see that even after death she would not be forgotten.

The public face of care

It needs only a small gap in the screen around the bed, or voices loud enough to be heard elsewhere in the room, for other residents to receive a very clear picture of the care provided to a roommate. Indifference, roughness, carelessness are reflected not only in staff's physical demeanour but in voice and attitude. Gentle, sensitive care, together with thoughtful conversation directed to the resident, may also be noted by others. As clearly indicated by Elizabeth's response, these actions serve as significant signposts for other residents who may watch and listen and reflect. Carers may also reflect on the impact their words and actions have in the perception of other residents.

QUALITY ISSUES FOR ENHANCED PRACTICE

The gerontic nurse

- Sensitivity to the needs of a resident who has no family may uncover a specific role for the nursing staff. For example, one or two nurses may like to be designated as 'primary nurses'; given extra responsibility for getting to know the resident's needs as death approaches.
- Questions and discussion at handover may uncover other staff members' feelings and suggestions for a resident who is unable to verbalise their own needs.
- Open communication about a resident who is dying may provide reassurance to those who are onlookers, but who may be fearing their own imminent death.

Management

- Within available resources it may be possible to include particular recognition for a nurse designated as 'primary nurse'.
- Such a role requires careful role description, review and evaluation.
- Given legitimacy by management, the role of primary nurse becomes recognised by other staff and may encourage others to take on a similar role.
- The role of indirect carers as resident advocate may also receive acknowledgement by management, provided a system is developed to utilise their skills.

Indirect carers

- In the absence of family members, others who know the resident may contribute their thoughts and feelings about the resident's imminent death.
- There may also be one particular carer who would act as resident advocate, contributing to the plan of care developed by the team.

FEARS AND ANXIETIES: DON'T YOU EVER PUT ME IN THAT BED!

It sometimes happens over time that several deaths occur in one particular room or even one particular bed. Superstition may mark that bed as 'unlucky' and, hence, the least popular bed in the nursing home. For Ben, the case was quite clear. He had witnessed enough changes in his room to be left with a feeling of anxiety about his own future. While there were many positive outcomes of the resident changes in Ben's room, his lasting impression was real and his fears could be allayed only by extracting a promise from his trusted charge nurse in response to his plea, 'Don't you ever put me in *that* bed!'

Ben had had enough. Several residents had died in his room in recent months and, as he reported, 'Always on a Friday and in that bed'. To begin with, two long-term residents, declining at an almost equal pace, had died within 36 hours of each other. They had, of course, occupied two different beds but in Ben's mind it was that particular bed that attracted more than its fair share of death.

Alfred and Jose were the two heaviest residents in the nursing home (heavy in terms of their build as well as the nursing care they required). Each required lifting, feeding, toileting, changing, unable to cooperate in any way. Alfred was as noisy as Jose was quiet and together they were regarded as a challenge best suited to the charge nurse's wisdom and skills. Ben knew every movement they made; he often called or rang his buzzer for attention when he felt either resident needed a nurse. Death came slowly to both Alfred and Jose as Ben watched intently, noting every change. Alfred, no longer noisy and restless, relied on the nurses to change his position frequently while Jose simply gave up eating. Both in their 90s, they had long outlived their families and rarely received visitors. Their routine of care being similar, Alfred and Jose were mostly spoken of together. 'I'll wash Alfred and Jose,' was the repeated offer during allocation of duties. Showing no impatience or resentment, the nursing staff accepted the presence of these two old men as though they would always be there.

Ben often joked about placing bets as to who would live longer, Alfred or Jose. However, when the time arrived, Ben was quite concerned. He woke one morning to see Alfred's bed screened and during the evening he heard Jose's breathing change and then stop. 'I knew he'd had it!'

Ben waited with interest to see who would replace his long-term roommates, 'Please try and get someone who can at least talk to me.' Nothing in his known world of nursing home life could have prepared him for Albert's arrival. Cheerful in spite of severe physical disabilities, this friendly newcomer tried to engage Ben in some form of communication. Ben, an Australian digger, never lost the look of surprise to be sharing a room with Albert. Never known for tact he would inform staff, 'Have you met the new bloke? He's as black as the ace of spades!' When Albert died three weeks after admission Ben was not prepared for the shock. Seeing the bed empty he enquired of the night staff, 'Where's he gone?' 'Upstairs,' came the enigmatic reply. Full of the importance of this new information, Ben relayed it to the next nurse who came in. 'Did you know they'd taken the new fella upstairs? I didn't know there was another floor up there.' Ben had taken literally the night staff's euphemism for death.

Always eager to get on with the next meal, the next conversation, the next piece of gossip, Ben set about wondering afresh who would be his next roommate. Calling his trusted charge nurse the next morning he issued his command for the day, 'Clare! Don't you ever put me in that bed!'

ON REFLECTION...

Communication between residents

What had been communicated between Alfred and Jose, who shared the same nurses, suffered similar physical ailments, required the same level of care and yet never spoke a word to each other? It seemed inevitable and yet uncanny that these two residents died within 36 hours of each other. We may never know what passes between two such residents seemingly isolated in their own beds, yet in close proximity in a shared room. There are many moments during a day when no staff are present to detect a knowing look from one resident to another. Nursing home staff are apt to underestimate perceptions and feelings of such residents, making inappropriate statements which may be overheard by another roommate.

Setting the record straight

Why is a euphemism for death preferred by so many health professionals? Most nursing home residents are more familiar with death than their carers or their younger relatives. Death is a fact of life, the inevitable conclusion, the final stage in their life's journey. To tell Ben that his roommate had gone 'upstairs' implies the ascent of a person to a higher realm, a phrase arising out of a particular religious belief or superstition but not necessarily appropriate as far as Ben was concerned.

To say that a person has died is to communicate in a clear and unambiguous way that the person will not be returning. When such an event is not clearly acknowledged many complications may arise. For example, Ben may wonder how his own death will be communicated to his roommates; will someone suggest that he had merely been transferred elsewhere? Informing residents of another resident's death requires sensitivity and an informed assessment of their ability to receive such a statement. Even for those residents who are inarticulate and seemingly unconscious of their surroundings, it is not necessarily appropriate for a nurse to conclude that a resident need not be told. 'Telling it straight' is not intended to signify a statement devoid of emotion. Caregivers may also feel extremely sad when a resident dies. When such emotion is conveyed to other residents, the feeling behind the statement may also bring reassurance that they too will be missed when their time comes.

Humour and grief shared

There may well be occasions for humorous exchange between staff and residents. A lighthearted comment such as, 'Are you scared you'll be next?', may have been sufficient for Ben to know his fears and anxieties were acknowledged. He may not have welcomed a deep and meaningful discussion about his own impending death; merely the recognition that he was not untouched by the deaths of his roommates. Ben may have been expressing the grief which finds its way to the surface through humour. Or, he may have welcomed nurses sharing their own grief with him. 'Ben, I can't believe that Jose has died. I've looked after him for five years and I've grown very fond of him. I'll really miss him.'

Other exchanges between staff and Ben may have included, 'Ben, how are we going to survive without Jose's constant groaning and grunting — this room will be so *quiet*.'

The issue of humour between staff and residents relies on staff sensitivity and knowledge of the residents' likely responses. In order to avoid offence or hurt, staff need to know where to 'draw the line' between humour and derision, lighthearted fun and hurtful criticism. Excessive or prolonged laughter and joking may mask a denial of death, either on the part of residents or staff. These issues may need to be worked through with an experienced facilitator.

The issue of shared grief also depends on the relationships developed with staff and residents in a particular situation. Tearful and sad responses would be considered normal in most instances, a sign of healthy grieving. However, sensitive and intuitive staff would be alert for signs of deep-seated grief which may hide unresolved fear.

The dreaded bed

Ben, for all his straightforward humour and lack of tact, had no desire to be moved to a bed which he had dubbed 'the deathbed'. This reaction points to the very important issue of each resident's location in the nursing home. Taking into account the issue of security of tenure, each resident's bed location should be kept under continuous review. Some well-meaning staff decided that Ben would be better off out of that room altogether. On careful questioning by the charge nurse, it was clear Ben did not wish to be moved. He did, however, request a clear promise that he would never be moved into 'that bed'.

Preparing for his own death?

Ben, in his commentary on the death of his roommates, may have been giving voice to thoughts of his own impending death. 'I see a lot of death around me, but my time's not up yet.' 'I can afford to joke about it because I know it's not really affecting me — I'm well and truly alive.' 'I know my time will come some day, but I don't want to think about that yet. I have still quite a lot of living to do.'

From the particular to the general

Staff who know the residents well may have the opportunity to engage in general conversation about death, using the particular example of a resident who has just died. There are many prompts for a dialogue, such as: 'What do you think about all this dying, Ben?', 'When you see your roommates dying, does it make you think about your own death?', or 'Do you ever wonder what is the meaning of death, or what happens to us after we die?' As the topic of death will one day closely affect every resident and every carer, it is helpful to take up these opportunities for discussion. Informal discussion may sometimes lead to deeper issues which may be more helpfully discussed with a chaplain or bereavement counsellor.

QUALITY ISSUES FOR ENHANCED PRACTICE

The gerontic nurse

- Ben's situation suggests active listening is needed to uncover his underlying fears. Documentation of Ben's fears is important, as is a review which may not necessarily be a formal case conference; rather, it may take the form of another 'casual' conversation.
- Nurses share a privilege and a responsibility when caring for residents in a shared room. As other residents watch and listen to activities and conversations in another part of the room, they may be making their own judgements as to quality of care. Nurses have a remarkable opportunity of exemplifying quality, even when unconsciously performing their caring role.
- Gerontic nurses, by their professional education, have a holistic approach to life and death which allows grief to surface and be discussed naturally, and to ensure that humour also finds its legitimate place.

Management

- It may not always be possible to keep a promise that a resident will never be moved into a particular location. However, if such a preference is articulated it should be documented in such a way that future circumstances will take the resident's preferences into account.
- Communicating the death of one resident to other residents will depend on the circumstances of the death, the residents involved and the particular philosophy and policies of the nursing home. It may be helpful to have a documented procedure so all staff are aware of the 'local custom'; for example, the nurse in charge of the shift may be the person responsible for conveying news of a death to other residents as appropriate.
- Superstition is not the sole province of residents; where it is perceived that staff or visitors may also have fears and anxieties about a particular bed, the above point may well include them.

Indirect carers

- Where fear, superstitions or anxiety is perceived about a particular bed, it may be considered necessary for some appropriate ritual to be enacted. For example, the chaplain may acknowledge the residents who have died in that 'dreaded bed'. A brief, informal ceremony may ensure memories are preserved, while assisting the affected resident to grieve and overcome fears.

PUBLIC AND PRIVATE: COMMUNITY OF DIFFERENCE

We were reviewing the care of Connie's husband Petro. An intensely private man, he had resisted moving into a nursing home, believing such a move would be the ultimate insult to his frail body, and the unthinkable betrayal of their recent marriage. Connie carefully chose the nursing home closest to their own home so she could visit twice daily. Their preference had been for a single room. After three months Connie commented, 'I'm glad Petro is sharing his room with other men. He would be so lonely on his own. Although he has no wish to socialise he watches the others, takes an interest in them, rings the bell when one of them needs a nurse — all this keeps him occupied and less self-centred. And, more importantly, I know that when a nurse enters the room to care for the others, they will also check on my husband.'

Connie related the anxieties of her friend whose husband was in another nursing home. 'She constantly worries about his being in a single room. Twice he has fallen and was unable to call a nurse.' Connie's friend feared her husband would die of loneliness and boredom or, on the other hand, that his complex medical condition would not receive the constant supervision it needed.

Connie had also befriended Luc, the Vietnamese roommate who, through dementia, had lost language and speech and through circumstances not clear to us had lost contact with his family. By trial and error Connie managed to identify Luc's taste in food and brought him some Greek home-cooking. William, another roommate, was the cause of many disturbances in the room. His alcoholic dementia manifested itself in verbal and physical aggression and he sometimes threatened Petro. However, his aggression was often short lived and there were many periods each day when William rested quietly on his bed, sometimes singing to himself. When, as a result of a major seizure, he was confined to bed for many days in a semi-comatose state, Petro showed a compassionate interest. When William died, Petro confessed to a great affection for him, in spite of the trouble he had caused.

Sharing the visiting

Connie's initial expressed wish for a single room for Petro changed as she saw the benefits of a shared room. Petro was not easy to please; they had married late in life and Connie was often frustrated by Petro's constant demands for meticulous detail in every aspect of his life. She had found herself cut off socially by many of her friends and yet she wished to remain loyal to Petro, wanting to fulfil his wishes to the best of her ability.

Connie found that visiting Petro was becoming a source of irritation rather than an occasion for pleasure. So, she began to introduce herself to the others in the room. Finding she quickly gained their trust, friendships developed. When Petro became tiresome with his complaints and demands, she found she could 'switch off' and go and talk to William and Luc. When her home-cooking failed to satisfy Petro ('You know I can't eat that! I'm not hungry anyway'), she found in Luc an avid fan who always made known by his gestures that he expected her to offer him food.

Connie had a sense of humour which contrasted starkly with Petro's rather dour demeanour. She found she could usually evoke a response from William, whose wry sense of humour lifted her spirits. Petro's solemn scepticism also frustrated her. 'Come on Petro, you'll soon be walking again if you do the physio each day,' was met with 'No, no, no, I'll never be able to walk properly again.' Her cajoling got her nowhere, so she would turn her attention to William or to Luc. While there was no question of Connie's faithful commitment to Petro, her visits were made more enjoyable by the company of others. She, too, was profoundly affected by William's death.

ON REFLECTION…

Cultural mix

There may be benefits in having ethno-specific nursing homes or special accommodation for those with dementia but there are also benefits in having a broader and multicultural community. If, at the age of 50 and at the height of his business career, Petro had been asked his preference for shared or single accommodation in a nursing home he may not necessarily have chosen to share with three distinctively different companions from widely differing socioeconomic and cultural backgrounds. Yet here a community developed, where those perceived as the stronger helped those perceived as weaker, where families established friendships, where the residents themselves complemented the complex medical and nursing care each required. Given the increasing number of non-English-speaking older residents residing in Australia this issue requires careful consideration and architectural planning.

To share or not to share

This story is not intended to idealise accommodation in shared bedrooms, nor to suggest that merely by placing residents of different backgrounds in a room together they will develop lasting friendships. There is much evidence to the contrary. However, the point is made about decision making from unquestioned assumptions, particularly assumptions from an individualistic framework. Many older persons would prefer single room accommodation; while there are others for whom sharing is an antidote to feelings of isolation.

Solidarity is not always evident

When death is 'in the air' in a shared room not all responses are quietly sensitive and empathetic. William had been dying for some days, although it seemed to Matthew (the fourth resident in the room) like weeks. Nurses would sympathetically give Matthew a daily report, assuming he would feel concern for his roommate. On one particular morning Matthew, always one for catching the nurse out, said with a voice of alarm, 'I think he's stopped breathing…oh, no he hasn't, he must have decided to keep going!' On another occasion Matthew expressed his impatience, saying to the nurse, 'Lord almighty, hasn't he gone yet!'

While other roommates and their visitors may have shown compassion towards William as his death approached, Matthew saw him only as a nuisance factor. No-one was going to make him feel any different. Whether or not he had an intense hatred of William, one thing was certain, he showed no sympathy or sorrow at his death.

Equality of care

It is not easy to discern whether or not a resident has a legitimate concern over the amount of care received in comparison with others. One resident may have the impression that the dying resident is receiving more than his fair share of care, leaving the other to feel insecure, jealous, angry or frustrated. This issue is particularly sharpened in the context of a shared room where it is easy to see how much attention the other residents are receiving. Sometimes explanations are helpful, 'Matthew, I know we're coming in and out a lot to check on William, but you understand he's very ill?' Other situations demand a different kind of reassurance, 'Now Matthew, before I attend to William, is there anything *you* need?'

QUALITY ISSUES FOR ENHANCED PRACTICE

The gerontic nurse

- Paying attention to residents' reactions to others in the room is part of caring for the resident in a specific context. This involves checking frequently the needs and reactions of other residents and/or their families to make sure their responses have not been overlooked when a resident in the shared room is dying.
- Where possible, specific requests, such as closing the curtains surrounding the dying resident, are documented and regularly reviewed.
- When it is not possible to plan strategies, the staff remain sensitive to the feelings and reactions of all who share the room. This means remaining alert for unforeseen events; ensuring the plans remain flexible and subject to revision when the situation requires change.

Management

- Architectural decisions need to be based on flexibility and choice, as there is no one ideal model of room size which suits every nursing home resident.
- Careful public relations allows prospective residents and their families to make choices based on reliable information.
- Given the complexity of human nature, it is difficult to tell in advance whether a particular mix of family members and residents will form a friendly community, even though their country of origin may be the same. Residents and families may be helped to settle in by being introduced to others beyond their own shared room. Comprehensive policies and procedures may ensure this happens.
- Where single rooms are predominant, the provision of carefully designed furniture or spaces for visitors to meet communally may help to dispel any loneliness and isolation experienced.

Indirect carers

- Some facilities designate a person or small group to provide special hospitality to new residents and their families. This is a significant role for volunteers or other indirect carers to adopt, and may make a considerable difference to the resident and family entering a new environment.

DISHARMONY AND CONFLICT: THIS IS MY SPACE

This story continues the theme of shared rooms, showing that harmony is difficult to achieve when residents of diverse backgrounds live in close proximity. Unless the nursing home has specific admission criteria which focuses on one group only, the mix of socioeconomic backgrounds as well as cultural backgrounds is likely to manifest itself in negative as well as positive outcomes. Alec found he had to share his new home with a variety of roommates, with the added intrusion of their visitors. Never having had a place to call home, he resisted sharing his space. Nevertheless, he was not immune from the effects of death as he watched Bert and then Eric take their place and then take their leave.

Alec's chosen isolation and total lack of visitors stood in sharp contrast to Bert's family who visited on a roster system for several hours every day of the week. What a remarkable cameo: the dying Bert surrounded by his wife and various combinations of their six children ('we fostered a few'), their grandchildren and the family dog. Whenever Alec, from the bed opposite, could make himself heard he would send a resounding, 'Shut up yer noise can't yer! A man wants a bit of peace and quiet.' As the tension increased over Alec's preference for uninterrupted rest on his bed 24 hours a day, and Bert's family's constant chatter, Bert's wife complained about Alec's intolerance. When offered the choice of a bed in another room: 'Oh no,' she said, 'I'd rather put up with it. I promised Bert I'd never put him in an old men's home and he can see that this is different. If I move him again he'll think I'm breaking my promise. No thank you. We like it here, we look out the window and feel that this is Bert's corner.'

Alec was equally adamant. 'You told me this is my home till I die' and, pointing to his pillow, 'This is my home. I wouldn't feel at home anywhere else. This is my corner.' So much for promising tenure on admission. The homelike qualities had also been conveyed as an article of faith; now there was no retreat. There had to be another way through this seeming impasse. It was agreed by staff that Alec's situation should take precedence because he had occupied his bed for five years before Bert's admission. A family meeting was held with Bert and his wife who were shown an alternative bed with access to the garden, where the family would have more space. Bert's wife was fully involved in the move, maintaining a perception of her own power over the situation. As for Alec, he suffered unanticipated feelings of guilt for many days afterwards. 'It's my fault he had to move downstairs.' When Bert died Alec wanted to make his peace with the family but not in person; his words of regret and condolence were conveyed by the charge nurse. Even then, Alec had not finished with death.

Eric came to live and to die in the bed opposite Alec. We thought Alec had a rather special relationship with Eric; he would often press the buzzer if he thought Eric needed nursing assistance. Most important, Eric was very quiet and his only visitor was his equally quiet son. Eager to assist Alec to express his feelings, our aim was to convey to him honestly and clearly that Eric was dying. 'Alec, you know Eric is not at all well.' 'Neither am I,' said Alec, 'I've told them I don't want any breakfast.'

At this busy part of the day there was no time for a deep and meaningful discussion as to why Alec might be rejecting his breakfast. Was he feeling rejected, seeing Eric receive all the attention? Or, was he merely unconcerned, preferring to concentrate on his own private world? It seemed appropriate to take the cue from Alec, that he had not been particularly attached to Eric and he was not suffering great emotional trauma at Eric's impending death.

The next morning revealed a surprising reaction from Alec when a nurse approached him. 'Good morning Alec, did the night staff tell you that Eric died in the early hours of the morning?' With seeming indifference, Alec shrugged his shoulders and responded, 'I always remember the one before him. He had a beautiful death. They called all his family and all his enemies around him. He said goodbye to them all. There were dozens of them, people everywhere. He sat up as though he didn't have a care in the world, then lay down, closed his eyes and never opened them again. It was beautiful.'

Alec's story seemed to bear no resemblance to any facts whatsoever; was this saying more about Alec's own impending death?

'How would you like to go, Alec?'

'Ah, it's no use predicting, you never get what you want. If I die in my sleep in the morning I won't know how I died, will I? I used to be a grave digger and you get used to death. It didn't mean much as all the graves were the same except that if it was for someone you knew, you'd put a bit of extra trimming on the side.'

All Alec had to say about his recently departed roommate was to recount the time when Eric had told him off for swearing. A refined gentleman with a distinguished professional career, Eric could have lived on another planet as far as Alec's life experience was concerned. Having arrived in the nursing home from his single boarding-house room, with a small battered suitcase half-filled with a few possessions, Alec had pleaded not to be sent back there. 'I'll drink meself to death if I go back there.' Alec lived an isolated but contented existence in his corner, curtains pulled around him most of the time, but showing a deep philosophical wisdom about his place in the world. He had made little overt connection with any of his roommates. The end of Alec's story indicates life's strange mixture of truth and fiction, of dreams and reality. Alec called for the night staff at 3 a.m., sat up, gave them a rare, beautiful smile, laid his head down on his own pillow and died.

ON REFLECTION…

Private living in a public space

Alec had been a loner all his life, his poor health being discovered by the caring landlord of his cheap rooming-house accommodation. It was not easy for him to move from his poorly lit, solitary, barely furnished room to a large, airy, bright, shared room. Once established in his new home, Alec was fearful his health would improve to the extent he would be asked to leave. His twin fear was of having too much company. He shunned visitors and refused all coaxing to come out of his room. His own bed and the small amount of space around it was sacred and when others 'crossed the line' he was greatly irritated.

Who's intruding on whom?

Bert's large family were an obvious intrusion into Alec's space, especially when he could hardly hear the races on his radio. Alec was also an intrusion into their space, calling out for them to stop their noise and so causing them offence. Each party claimed their rights. It seemed neither party was willing to modify their activities, so the only solution seemed to be separation. One compromise was suggested by staff; Alec could sit in the lounge for one to two hours per day, while Bert's family were to confine the large number of visitors to that period. Reluctantly, Alec tried this new arrangement, but after two days pleaded to be allowed to stay in the security of his own bed in his own room. There may have been other solutions we did not think of, but the only way out seemed to be for one of them to move.

QUALITY ISSUES FOR ENHANCED PRACTICE

The gerontic nurse

- When difficulties arise between roommates, options for resolving the conflict should be presented; and time allowed for the residents and their families to negotiate these options.
- It may be possible to have some idea of the likely family involvement when a resident enters the nursing home. This information is useful to share when introducing the new resident to others in the room.

Management

- The pre-admission visit is one of the most appropriate occasions for establishing the resident's feelings about, and family responses to, a shared bedroom.
- It is also helpful to have any responses to such a discussion recorded on an assessment form.
- When room changes are considered necessary, it is important to involve families and relevant staff. Time spent in a meeting to discuss the issue may save time in correcting misunderstandings later.

Indirect carers

- Other carers, such as volunteers, activity workers, therapists, may observe or hear about difficulties experienced by residents in a shared room. These carers should be encouraged to communicate this information to the nurse in charge, and wherever possible, decisions should be made in a team context.

CHAPTER FOUR

This chapter provides insights into the disruptive nature of death within a close community. It also highlights the nature of partnership when indirect carers take their place among other carers.

GRIEF: IT WON'T BE THE SAME WITHOUT HIM

When our much-loved Jon died suddenly, shock waves went through the nursing home. There had been nothing to warn us that his death was imminent. What a different place the nursing home would be without his singing and his mischief. How could we ever bear a new resident being admitted to Jon's bed? This story, a memorial to all our residents, shows how appropriate mourning within the community can preserve the memory of those residents who have died; while leaving us free to greet, appreciate and form new and enriching relationships with those residents who take their place.

'Jon hasn't been down for supper; he must be dead!' The nurse laughed, making a joke of our beloved Jon's invariable routine. As it turned out the joke was unfortunate, because Jon was, in fact, dead. When the nurse took Jon's usual strong black coffee to his room, there he was on his bed, looking peaceful after a lovely day, looking as though he would burst into song given the slightest encouragement — but dead. The sense of shock that accompanied Jon's death was profound, both for the staff on duty when he died and for the staff who heard the news over the next few days. It was hard to accept the loss of a resident who was cherished for his unique characteristics. One staff member summed it up when she said, with a heavy sigh, 'It won't be the same without him.'

And it couldn't be. How could anyone but the mischievous Jon drive us from despair to laughter many times in the space of a day? With his roller coaster emotions he would be full of complaints and blackness in the morning but by lunch time would sing us teasing little folk songs from his childhood in another country. A survivor of tragedy and relocation, he also survived the institutional demands for conformity, being perfectly himself up to the hour of his death.

In the early days, when nursing homes were still places of custodial care, Jon enraged the cautious and rule-bound among the staff by his tottering trips to the pub on the corner. He would come back triumphantly with one small bottle of beer. It hardly seemed worth the effort, but his prize was the achievement, not the beer. His determination challenged the stereotypical view of a nursing home resident. Staff with a more enlightened outlook saw Jon's behaviour as a model of risk-taking and self-determination. Jon had been exercising his rights long before the 'Charter of Residents' Rights' was enshrined in print. Trust him!

Not that alcohol wasn't an important part of his self-medication. Having been a brewery worker for many years he never let an opportunity for a drink go by, especially a free one! The brandy in the Christmas raffle basket did not go unnoticed and was of special interest to Jon. Back and forth he shuffled in the evenings, through the front foyer and past the raffle basket. Finally he was intercepted scuttling back to his room with the brandy clumsily concealed in his cardigan. He had managed to drink the better part of the contents on the way, walking stick and unsteady gait notwithstanding.

There came a time when Jon's risk-taking became even more challenging. His increasing unsteadiness brought him down in the car park with a crash. There was no-one around, but staff were quickly summoned from the adjacent building by Jon's roars — not roars of pain, although he had bloodied his nose and grazed his hands — but roars of rage at his powerlessness against the infirmity of old age. We found him unable to move, face down on the cement, pride hurt but fearful his independence may be curtailed.

Why did we feel so deeply the shock and grief of his sudden death some months later? Because he was real, he was a character; because he socially engaged us in fun and mischief; because of his freely expressed feelings and his ability to enrage and charm us; because he challenged us out of a routine approach to care by his defiance in the face of age; and for his songs.

As Jon's will instructed, his funeral was to be at a distant church on the other side of town, making it impossible for most of us to attend. Death had snatched him away so suddenly; we had hoped to say goodbye to him in the nursing home chapel. Cheated of this opportunity, a group of staff and residents gathered less formally to share their memories of Jon. We laughed and we cried, felt sad and flat after the death of someone we cared about, but somehow also clear and freed. In the end, we were ready to greet the new resident who would not take Jon's place but would join the community on his own terms, bringing his own special qualities to be admired or despaired, unfettered by the ghost of Jon.

ON REFLECTION...

The emotional impact of sudden death

When a resident dies suddenly, staff may experience shock; often recognisable in such comments as: 'I can't believe he's gone' or 'I was just talking to him last night'. Transient shock is normally experienced following news of a death. If the death has been unexpected, the feeling of shock may be profound or persistent. In the case of Jon's sudden death, many staff members expressed feelings of disbelief and shock manifested in physical expressions of dismay and spontaneous crying.

Funeral attendance

Funeral attendance may assist some staff in adjusting to the reality of the resident's death and letting go, an important precursor to staff establishing relationships with new residents and continuing high-quality care. For some, funerals may represent unwelcome personal memories; for others, the funeral represents the stark reality and finality of death that they may wish to avoid.

Remaining professional, yet remaining close

Long-term residents need to engage emotionally with their carers, particularly if family and social networks are diminished. In the past, health professionals were taught to 'maintain emotional distance' and avoid 'getting involved'. In residential aged care, becoming involved is not only right, but an important part of holistic care. Being 'family' to a resident facilitates the close and special bonds that can promote a high level of job satisfaction for committed staff. Sometimes the richest care results from the carer going that 'extra mile'. However, staff relationships with residents are different from personal relationships outside the workplace. Emotional interaction with residents is appropriate when staff work within the role boundaries of professional and ethical standards of conduct, which protect the resident from emotional or material exploitation. By remaining in their defined roles, staff can provide emotionally nourishing care for residents without being burned out or expecting residents to meet their needs.

It is difficult to define acceptable professional involvement in aged care; what is acceptable differs from the acute-care setting, largely because of the long-term relationships in the aged-care context. Many staff members develop their own standards within the framework of professional training, modified by experience and the context of their work. Others are guided by the standards of their colleagues and the norms of their workplace.

In aged care, where resident deaths are becoming more frequent, maintaining an awareness of role protects staff from the emotional exhaustion of repeated bereavement. In addition, making use of opportunities to grieve appropriately assists carers to remain emotionally available to other residents, even though staff may experience loss when a resident dies. Because Jon was a long-term, well-loved resident, any crisis in his life had the potential to affect staff deeply. The informal memorial gathering assisted staff to deal with his death in an appropriate manner, acknowledging their personal sense of loss.

It is every carer's responsibility to reflect on the emotional support they offer residents. If an unsound pattern of relating is recognised, counselling may uncover areas in the staff member's personal life which could compromise their ability to provide high-standard care for residents.

Playing favourites

Many carers have favourite residents; those whose appeal gets under the carers' veneer of impartiality. This may be because of a particular behavioural adaptation, or because they remind us of a loved grandparent, or even of ourselves! However, by remaining self-aware, the same standard of care can be given to those residents we feel positively about and those who arouse our negative feelings. The ideal of unconditional positive regard, or of the carers' putting aside personal beliefs and prejudices in order to empathise with and accept each resident, is an important element in securing the same high standard of care for all residents.

Guilt can affect our care

For carers there are limitless opportunities for guilt, and some staff will be more prone to guilt than others. Guilt results from a violation of our own standards, as part of our internal moral system. Some staff may have experienced guilt for liking Jon more than other residents — or because they didn't like him at all! Had Jon died after a fall on one of his increasingly tottery walks to the pub, there is no doubt the staff on duty would have felt guilty, whether this was justified or not.

Unresolved guilt is a most painful and destructive emotion. It makes us wary of similar situations being repeated. Healthy ways to manage feelings of guilt include, examining our reactions for irrational beliefs ('Was I negligent in allowing Jon to go alone to the pub, or was I upholding the standards of independence and acceptable risk?'), learning from mistakes and self-acceptance ('I did the best I could at the time, but on reflection I will manage that situation differently in future.'). Talking to a sympathetic, trusted colleague can often assist acceptance of our own human failings. Dealing with guilt that arises from our real or imagined failings frees us to view each new situation of care on its own merits, rather than through the restricting lens of the past.

The need to grieve

Close bonds between residents and staff result in feelings of loss when a resident dies. For the sake of the ongoing life of the nursing home, it is necessary to acknowledge and deal with that loss. This is especially important for the sake of each new resident who must be admitted promptly to maintain the bed occupancy rate, and who has a right to the highest standard of care and emotional commitment from staff. Staff members who have not come to terms with their emotional response or mourned the resident who has died, may unconsciously resent the new resident.

Funeral attendance is one of the most natural ways to complete the relationship. If this is not possible there may be occasions when it is appropriate or advisable to hold a memorial service. A chapel or hall is not necessary. We held our own informal gathering for Jon in the dining room.

In most cases staff continue debriefing naturally, without need for intervention. Often this happens at the morning-tea table, or when a group of past and present staff get together socially and reminisce: 'Remember Ivon and how he used to yell in the shower?' or 'I still miss Lily, she was a real lady.'

Learning of a death well after the rest of the community is informed may obstruct the grieving process and manifest itself, for some staff, in feelings of isolation. This is attested to by the experience of staff who have returned from extended leave, or days off, seeming to be the only person who has not heard the news. By then the other staff have moved to a different place in their grieving process and are understandably unwilling to go back over painful ground.

QUALITY ISSUES FOR ENHANCED PRACTICE

The gerontic nurse

- Residents may be given the opportunity to respond when told personally of a sudden death. An informal discussion may be prompted among several residents by the invitation, 'Is there anything you will particularly remember about Jon?'
- Rather than removing all traces of the deceased resident, other residents may like a photo, or other reminder, to remain on display until such time as it is naturally replaced by a current resident's photo.
- Residents may also like to mark with respect the deceased resident's accustomed place at the dining table, by leaving the chair vacant for a short period.
- The charge nurse may need to give particular attention to personally notifying specific staff who may be affected by the unexpected death of a favourite resident.

Management

- Open communication is essential, particularly in the circumstances of sudden death. A clear, factual statement disseminated as soon as is practicable, minimises the opportunity for speculation and misinformation.
- Communication may consist of a notice prominently displayed, provided the practice is consistent so that every death is communicated in a similar fashion.
- When death occurs suddenly it is important to ensure indirect carers receive appropriate notification. This is especially important for volunteers or others whose contact with the resident may have been irregular, but nevertheless significant. Such notification acknowledges the importance of indirect carers as part of the team.

Indirect carers

- Volunteers and others not involved in direct resident care can contribute to informal de-briefing by sharing anecdotes about their relationship with the resident; thus helping the whole team to acknowledge the resident's life and death.
- The music therapist's response may be to write a song about the resident, setting it to music and encouraging other residents to join in.

MIXED EMOTIONS: IF ONLY WE'D KNOWN

If ever there was such a thing as a 'bad' resident it was Philip. At times every interaction seemed to become a power struggle. Even so, there were moments of cooperation so that Philip's likeable qualities attracted a thread of commitment from his carers, although it was often stretched thin. Some staff were able to be more patient than others, able to look beyond his difficult personality to the person who struggled as much with life as he did with his carers. At times Philip tested us all to our limits. When he challenged our intention to care day after day we couldn't help but imagine how much easier our work would be if he was not there fighting us. So it was with mixed feelings we received the news that Philip had died during his admission to hospital. Our feelings of guilt, relief, sadness and anger illustrate the uncomfortable mixture of emotions staff often experience after the death of a difficult resident.

We learned of Philip's death indirectly. The public hospital rang Philip's next of kin promptly but did not notify the nursing home. Although we were annoyed to be informed second hand, there was a sort of justice in it. For although Philip's sister had visited infrequently, she came when Philip needed her. On these occasions she showed warmth and understanding, born of a bond that superseded the many years of hurt and rejection involved in dealing with this difficult man. Compared with Philip's sister, we were novices in the art of negotiating Philip's alienating mood swings.

Although his sister was next of kin, we were Philip's primary carers. We had struggled with him over his routine, his demands, his loud, rude calling out, his physically aggressive gestures, his careless splattering of food, his obesity, his verbal abuse and his total egocentricity which seemed incompatible with community living. At times staff felt they had either taken too much from him, not been firm enough, or 'let him get away with murder'.

And yet there was something about Philip that ensured he had his share of supporters willing to overlook his antisocial behaviour and advocate for his independence. Like Philip's sister, some staff were able to see beyond the forbidding Philip to the person who was lovable, to remember his smile and humour, to take a longitudinal view of what we knew of his life and concede he wasn't all bad.

Even so, no-one from the nursing home had visited him in hospital. When his bed was empty day after day, the relief of being without him made telephone enquiries perfunctory and few; in case it seemed we were eager to have him back. Perhaps it would have been different if we'd known he was dying.

The week before his hospital admission, Philip's behaviour became even more challenging, although he had been noticeably ill. While he was forlorn and pale, it was easy for us to feel sorry and forgiving. When he rallied with a fierce salvo of rudeness and complaint we felt betrayed. Surely he could remember our kindness? But that was not Philip's way. Staff at a review meeting considered his motives and discussed possible strategies for dealing with this escalating disruptive behaviour. The charge nurse advocated for him, suggesting that fear of death and guilt for past wrongdoing could be motivating his unacceptable behaviour. It seemed she had a point.

Since Philip refused to listen to any reason it was agreed he should receive a formal letter from management. The letter acknowledged his recent illness and reiterated our commitment to caring for him, while suggesting he had an obligation to cooperate and refrain from some of the more violent aspects of his current behaviour. 'While we recognise it is difficult at times to live so close to other people, it is not acceptable for you to throw objects at other residents, or to physically threaten staff.'

After a short lull the battle was on again. Philip's doctor repeated pathology tests in a vain hope there may be some easily correctable physiological cause for his violent temper. It had all been done before. However, on this occasion the tests showed that Philip was acutely ill. Imagine our relief when he was bundled out the door to hospital. Imagine our mixed feelings as he waved us goodbye, old eyes moist. Perhaps he knew he wouldn't be back.

Word came from the hospital that he was a model patient. We will never know if he was on his best behaviour due to strange surroundings or if he was just relieved to have the medical attention he needed.

ON REFLECTION...

Confession

Philip, we'll never joke with you or share complaints about you over morning tea, or see your cheeky grin again. We are sad now we didn't visit you in hospital, but if we'd known you were never coming back we would have. We would have afforded you the care given to every member of our community who is dying — if only we'd known. Even so, it will be a relief to fill your bed with someone who doesn't test our patience to the limit at every interaction. It will be easier not to have our caring intentions challenged. Some of us will always feel that, ultimately, we failed you. Just as you made sure you were never overlooked when you were alive, you will never be forgotten — but we will remember you with mixed feelings.

Facing regrets

Life isn't neat and tidy and neither is death. It can be unsettling to juggle a mixture of emotions, such as relief, sadness, anger and guilt after the death of a resident. Fortunately, most adults have the ability to manage such a complex emotional task. Acknowledging each emotion without judgement makes it easier to learn from the experience while reflecting on the resident's care.

Learning from conflict

It is not possible to like everyone. No matter how determined we are to offer residents an equal standard of care, some residents will always seem easier to like. It is, however, a challenge to achieve excellent care for a resident we dislike.
We are not responsible for the personality of others. We cannot fix every difficult situation. We have not failed if a resident prefers to take the role of 'bad patient'. What we can do is learn from these situations, so that the next difficult resident may benefit. Reflection may teach us something about ourselves and the motivations of others. Instead of thinking, 'Here we go again, just like Philip, this is going to be a nightmare!', we may discover an opportunity for some really satisfying and innovative care.

Conflict and the caring personality

Many staff who work in aged care do so because of their need to care. The motivation to look after people arises from our personalities, just as an athlete may gain satisfaction from competition or an actor from performing. When motivated by the desire to care, we feel fulfilled and gain satisfaction from performing the carer's role.

A component of this positive feeling is the gratitude of those who receive our care. When we meet someone who is in need of our care but refuses it, the relationship may seem unbalanced and we may feel confused and personally rejected. For the resident who needs to be independent the imposition of care may seem like oppression. Any close involvement with a resident tests our objectivity but it is possible to put our feelings aside and meet the challenge by attempting to understand what motivates difficult behaviour. While we were temporarily blinded by our long involvement with difficult Philip, the review meeting and problem solving by the doctor was a step towards regaining objectivity. Constant conflict between carers and residents indicates a need for further investigation — of both the carers' methods and the resident's total health.

Our obligation to 'difficult' residents

Close involvement with a resident who resists care tests everyone's patience. It is important for us to examine our own motivation in any situation of conflict with a resident to avoid negative feelings about that resident resulting in less than optimum care. It is essential that carers ensure that even residents labelled by staff as 'difficult' are offered ample opportunities for conflict resolution and a return to positive regard by staff. Luckily, as in Philip's case, there are usually some staff who are able to be tolerant with the most difficult residents. Likewise, there are always some residents who can tolerate the most difficult staff!

The carer's side of the emotional equation

Understanding our own contribution to conflict with a resident involves some degree of self-examination; without self-awareness, effective communication is not possible. Because our work is people oriented it is likely that some situations at work may remind us of events and relationships in our personal life; some understanding of the dynamics of human behaviour (motivations, attitudes, values and belief systems) is indispensable for the conscientious carer.

Recent loss in staff members' personal lives may predispose them to some emotional discomfort when dealing with loss at work. For instance, following the recent death of a grandparent a nurse may feel particularly upset about the next death of a same-gender resident. A personal reaction of this type is normal and often unavoidable in the initial bereavement period. When this reaction continues after subsequent resident deaths there may be a need for counselling.

Sometimes staff may identify positively or negatively with residents' personal qualities. If this is not acknowledged, the feeling of aversion or attraction will affect the quality of care for that resident. This process may also be responsible for a resident taking an apparently irrational dislike or liking to a particular staff member.

One of the tasks of old age is to reflect on life, recalling pleasant memories of earlier years and revisiting old traumas and unresolved conflicts. Some residents may replay old, unresolved conflicts in an attempt at resolution, assigning roles to unsuspecting staff. Who knows what conflicts Philip may have been reliving through the staff. One thing's for sure, we certainly responded!

QUALITY ISSUES FOR ENHANCED PRACTICE

The gerontic nurse

- Philip's story is a reminder to staff to check continually and repeatedly for physiological causes of a resident's behaviour changes. Accurate documentation and communication of the outcome offers reassurance to staff that all possibilities are being considered.
- The charge nurse may consider debriefing staff at the end of each shift, following difficult interactions with a resident who is perceived as 'difficult'.
- A team meeting with regular review may assist in establishing whether it is best for Philip and for the staff to have consistency of staff allocation or frequent changes.
- Focusing on the positive elements of Philip's personality may assist staff to see him as not totally objectionable.

Management

- Consistency of practice when a resident is transferred to hospital may be enhanced by written guidelines. Such guidelines would prompt the charge nurse to contact the hospital regularly, and to record the outcome. In this way, staff retain their link of care to the resident.
- Protocols based on local factors may also guide staff about visiting a resident in hospital.
- When incorporated into the overall plan of care, the volunteer's role is acknowledged and supported.

Indirect carers

- Volunteers may play a pivotal role in the care of a resident who is perceived as difficult to manage. Volunteers have no need to focus on tasks or nursing interventions, freeing them for more creative care. Extra attention from a volunteer may defuse other responses perceived as demanding or attention-seeking.

SUPPORT STAFF: I'LL MISS HIM TOO

Nursing and allied health are the largest staff group and have pivotal roles in resident care; they tend to dominate any discussion of care of the dying. Elizabeth Kübler-Ross was one of the first writers in this field to acknowledge the place of non-nurses in providing hospice care. In residential aged care, indirect-care staff and others not on the payroll often interact with residents in a way quite different from nurses. By normalising an otherwise institutionalised existence, these staff take a unique place in the resident's life. When the resident is dying, those staff who are not nurses must not be overlooked, but acknowledged as partners in care with nurses and the rest of the nursing home community.

At 9 a.m. on Tuesday morning, Jane the administrative assistant arrives at her desk. The first knowledge she has of Bill's death is when she reads the urgent memo requesting arrangements for the new resident. As she opens the waiting list file her thoughts are on Bill, recalling a relationship that stretches back many years to the time Bill's name was first put on the waiting list. She recalls their first meeting and the day she showed him around the nursing home, introducing him to staff and helping him begin the difficult transition from home to nursing home. She sighs as she reaches for the phone, wondering what sort of death Bill had and if she will have time to attend the funeral.

Mareeka the part-time receptionist wipes away a tear, for she has always personally delivered Bill's mail ever since he came into the nursing home. She had developed a special bond with him; she doesn't really know why. She watched with concern as he was dying, feeling inadequate at the bedside. In the end she just left his mail at the nurses' station, feeling too distressed to see him any more.

In the kitchen, Sally the chef wipes Bill's name off the white board. After all the residents she's seen come and go she doesn't feel too sad any more. Still, she used to enjoy delivering Bill's scrambled eggs on Fridays. It was a sort of ritual and she can still hear Bill saying, 'You cook the best eggs this side of the black stump!'

Other staff were affected by this resident's death in different ways. The accounts clerk worried about Bill's wife as she finalised the account, wondering how she'd manage to deal with the paper work on her own and how she would cope with widowhood. The cleaner had to stop himself asking for a tip for the races on

Wednesday as he mopped around the empty bed. And the laundry attendant thought of Bill as she changed the name on his shelf; they used to talk about old friends and familiar places as she put his clean clothes away, both having lived in the same neighbourhood.

Domestic staff may also have a special relationship with residents, often attending to personal tasks that go beyond their role description. 'I used to put Maisie's glasses on for her every morning,' said Belinda, the regular domestic, 'and she used to tell me what beautiful eyes I have. On the morning she died she told me she loved me. I told her I loved her too.'

Maintenance staff in nursing homes require a special sort of tact and sensitivity, often being the accidental observers of intimate resident care as they go about their work. A special bond developed between the maintenance person and Annie, whose dementia led her to regularly tidy up, hoarding many treasures in her large hand bag. No longer frustrated when his maintenance book disappeared, Jack commented, 'I know where to find it now. I always ask Annie. I don't want to offend her by looking in her bag so I ask if she would read me my jobs for the day. I tell her I'll get in trouble if I don't do them, so she's always eager to bring out the book to give me my orders.'

The local news agent proprietor has a special relationship with those residents on his list for daily delivery of the newspaper. Although pressed for time, he always includes a friendly word; a racing tip or two; comments on the football; and sharing the headline news with those residents who may be more articulate and responsive to the news of the day. 'What's the weather like outside?' is an important point of contact between residents and the external community.

The hairdresser

Susan the hairdresser had always attended Bill first. At his request, Bill had a regular weekly appointment whether he needed it or not. 'I haven't got much hair but what I have got I like to keep well trimmed.' Susan had her own explanation, 'I always give him a nice shave too, and when I'm not too busy he enjoys a facial massage as well.'

On the morning after Bill died, Susan wondered why he hadn't come for his appointment. Since no-one had bothered to tell her he'd died, she went looking for him, finding to her astonishment a stranger in Bill's bed.

ON REFLECTION...

Different yet equally important

Indirect carers may provide residents with the greatest sense of dignity and life satisfaction during their time in the nursing home. Having no knowledge of residents' intimate medical and physical details, the support staff relate to the residents according to their personal characteristics, rather than their disabilities. Interaction is not constrained by the residents' biomedical problems.

Obligations in the caring relationship

All carers, nurses and non-nurses, have similar obligations in relation to their care of the residents. Although non-nursing staff have limited access to a resident's formal records they face the same requirements as personal care staff in the need to keep their care of the resident professional, maintain confidentiality and observe the best standards of care. They are also just as likely to experience loss when the resident dies.

The importance of communication

The grapevine may keep this group of support staff informed about a resident's deterioration and impending death, but it is important that there is a formal mechanism in place to inform them when a resident has died. An effective mechanism for achieving this communication is to circulate to all relevant personnel a list of resident admissions and discharges immediately any changes occur. Apart from being an organisational necessity; prompt, formal notification acknowledges the place of indirect-care staff in the resident's life and death, as well as allowing an opportunity to deal with their sadness appropriately before going on with their daily work.

When the caring relationship is not so clearly defined as it is for nursing and personal care staff, and where tasks are not the main priority, a bond may develop which is quite intense. There are many support staff we have not named in this chapter; for every nursing home is different in terms of their staff mix. In reflecting on the circumstances surrounding Bill's death we needed to remind ourselves that the hairdresser and the podiatrist should be notified for they too had a unique relationship with him. If only a limited number of staff are able to attend the funeral, support staff should not be overlooked; they too have a legitimate need to make use of this opportunity to say goodbye.

QUALITY ISSUES FOR ENHANCED PRACTICE

The gerontic nurse

- The charge nurse has a particular responsibility to communicate with non-nursing staff and indirect carers, thoughtfully providing relevant information without breaching confidentiality.
- When a resident's death is imminent it may be appropriate to list one or more indirect carers who have a specific place in the team, and a defined role in the care plan.

Management

- It is important to establish procedures for advising all relevant staff immediately after a resident's death. Staff who attend the nursing home infrequently may require a separate form of communication.
- Debriefing sessions arranged for nursing and allied health staff following a resident's death may also be appropriate for indirect carers.
- Some means of acknowledging the contribution made by indirect carers may be developed by a general communication thanking all staff and other carers for their contribution to a resident's care.
- Where a particularly close relationship has developed, senior staff may need to be alerted to offer support to an indirect carer.

Indirect carers

- Non-nursing staff may consider sharing observations or conversations they perceive to be significant, particularly when a resident is close to death.
- Indirect carers may also offer comfort and support to nursing staff by sharing their own feelings at the time of a resident's death.

ROBERT'S WISH: I WANT TO DIE

This is the story of Robert's wish — and ours. He wished to die and we wished to care. For a while it seemed the two could not be done together. The rocky road to an agreed plan of care for Robert has helped us focus on important issues earlier in the course of each resident's journey. The story has a happy ending, because when Robert's wish was finally acknowledged, both resident and staff achieved the outcome they desired.

In the end, death crept up on Robert. His file was finally closed after two years of struggling with his symptoms, with the staff, with life. Who was this 'difficult' 80-year old? There is little in his clinical record beyond the details of his daily care requirements and his complex medical problems. Despite the many entries headed 'behaviour' there is no social profile, nor a psychosocial assessment. Although the reason for Robert's admission is not recorded either, we knew it was due to his wife's failing health and inability to continue caring for him at home. Was that why he was perceived as so difficult?

The death of Robert's wife, a year after his admission, coincides with a recorded increase in medical problems and very difficult behaviour. After his wife's funeral the previously grumpy old man who was always outspoken in his demands and maintained some relative physical independence suddenly became withdrawn and increasingly dependent. Several months later, bedridden and incontinent, he had lost 17 kg in weight. Although there was some speculation about his reaction to his wife's death, the question of Robert grieving was never formally addressed.

What Robert had to say about all this is not recorded; perhaps he was never asked. If we had asked Robert what was troubling him, could he have told us? Soon urinary retention was recorded as a major problem. Was this a metaphor for held-in feelings? Whatever the cause, Robert was sent to hospital where a permanent urinary catheter was inserted. So that problem was settled — or was it?

On his return to the nursing home, all attention focused on the catheter. Robert played his part by pulling at the catheter enough to induce bleeding, pulling the catheter out, and refusing to drink enough to keep the 'damn tube' patent and free of debris. Now his behaviour was recorded as: 'withdrawn', and again, no mention of emotional factors.

The next focus of attention was nourishment. Robert's oesophageal stricture had been managed by providing a soft or vitamised diet, but now he was unable to retain even this carefully prepared nourishment. Here was one of the last things we could do for him and he was rejecting it! Or was it really our attitude he couldn't swallow? By focusing on the physical we missed the larger picture. For as well as rejecting our excellent physical care Robert became far more 'demanding'. What was it that he demanded? Something that we were unable to give.

However, Robert's demands finally won him the attention he needed. At a special review of care, which Robert declined to attend, he 'spoke' very clearly through the staff's frustration, and the director of nursing agreed to speak with him to try to elicit his feelings. He responded to her impartial approach by tentatively expressing the frustrations of life in the nursing home when he would 'rather be at home'. He acknowledged that his wish to be at home made him 'hard to get on with' at times. At least someone was listening.

Robert's physical and emotional state continued to deteriorate. In the following months he was twice admitted to hospital for investigation of his medical problems. Despite thorough investigation, no diagnosis was ever made. Is there a diagnosis for 'tiredness of life'? Once back in the nursing home he began to call out in a high-pitched whine that could not be ignored. As before, this secured the physical attention he needed although he was never able to articulate his emotional needs.

By now, debilitation and inactivity made it almost inevitable 'the old man's friend' would intervene. After numerous episodes of choking on the nourishment we offered, he developed pneumonia. The subsequent public hospital re-admission proved to be a turning point in Robert's struggle. He returned with a letter stating simply that further hospital admission was inappropriate because Robert wished to die. As palliative care was now the appropriate management, he could return to the nursing home.

The letter brought a mixed reaction. Some staff read it as abandonment by the hospital, but others understood that finally we could really care for Robert in the best and most appropriate way. Finally his wish had been acknowledged. What Robert understood of all this is hard to know; perhaps he felt the staff's ambivalence and lack of cohesion in his care. We all needed time to get used to the new information.

For a while his clinical notes continued to focus on catheter, nutrition and hydration, but it was about this time that Robert's wish to die was first recorded. Whether the issue was raised by Robert or by staff, he was certainly at the case conference arranged to plan this new direction in his care. Clear guidelines were established about nutrition, hydration and medications. It was determined that these things were Robert's choice. The case conference summary included the following:

> Robert's wish: Robert stated clearly his wish to die. He was given the reassurance that we did not wish to cause him further distress by urging him to eat, drink, or sit out of bed against his will. All nursing measures for comfort will be given. Robert's wishes are our priority.

Despite the clear message, it took a while for all staff to catch on. Some were angry with him, others understood, seeing how frail he had become. Each dealt as they could with his now frequent assertions that he wanted to die.

That was not the end of it for Robert. It was a long time since he first expressed his wish for death, yet he was still alive. The catheter still blocked, he still had to fight with some staff over nourishment. Sometimes his nights were uncomfortable and disturbed. He resented any activity, such as hygiene or repositioning. Once invited, it seemed death didn't come quickly enough, but at least he was no longer perceived as demanding. He was dying.

In his last days, when all unnecessary medications were ceased and morphine syrup commenced, Robert was finally able to relax, and so were we. It was surprising the amount of tension his struggle to let go of life had created. Almost immediately, changes were observed in his circulation and respiratory pattern. He did not call out any more.

Death crept up on him, and us. The night his death was imminent, Robert seemed to hang on to life as if waiting for someone. In the morning, his friend the charge nurse, his provider of milk and ice cream, care and exasperation, was on duty again. Returning to his bedside after handover she found Robert's wish had been granted.

ON REFLECTION…

Listening for meaning beyond the words

A resident who states, 'I want to die!' needs careful assessment to discover any underlying meaning. Sometimes the statement may arise from the distress of a correctable physical symptom that, once resolved, returns some life satisfaction to the resident. However, at Robert's review meeting, his stated wish to die seemed to be an acknowledgment that his life was drawing to a close and a request for his preferred type of care. He was not requesting euthanasia but telling us he no longer had the energy or will to continue living as we were insisting he should.

It took a long time for Robert to communicate this to us; while we concentrated on the physical, Robert's emotional needs were being overlooked. As advocates, it is up to staff to tailor their care to meet the resident's current and changing needs, listening carefully to whatever voice the resident can use. At times this may mean interpreting physical symptoms, as well as treating them. Signs that needs have changed may be perceived in a resistance to a previous routine, change in physical appearance such as marked weight loss, loss of appetite, or unexplained 'difficult' behaviour. When the unexpected occurs, this should alert staff to the need for a thorough formal or informal review of that resident's care.

Empathy involves the carer entering the resident's world by attentive listening, observing and open communication. When this occurs at a significant level, when carers achieve a deep level of understanding of residents' experience, the way is open for life-changing experiences, even at the point of death. Even when communication is difficult, trying to understand the residents' perspective increases the likelihood of appropriate responses. As another writer has put it, we need to listen to the music, not only the words.

Clouding the issue — we knew him so well

Why did it take so long for staff to understand Robert's wish? Familiarity with the resident means we are in a position to be sensitive even to small changes, but sometimes that same familiarity blinds staff to the larger picture. Perhaps, in this episode of care, we experienced a role conflict common to nurses working in aged care. Although we are professionals, personal care staff also become family to their long-term residents. Perhaps the caring staff experienced some denial; what family can be totally detached? Part of the carer's role must be to maintain a certain objectivity, for where the roles of carer and family overlap, issues of care can be clouded.

While the health of a resident slowly declines, our aim is to enhance quality of life by providing appropriate and responsive care. The rewards for carers, trained in the curative model of medicine, are subtle. We will not often cure. Sometimes, in the desire to provide optimum care, we overlook a dignified death as the preferred outcome for the resident, and for us.

Residents are more than a list of symptoms

Psychosocial care demands that carers are neither dismissive nor neglectful of the emotional, behavioural and social dimensions of the resident as a person. In recent times we have also become aware of the holistic philosophy of care, which promotes the social, emotional, spiritual and physical components of the resident's life as equally important. If we adopt this perspective from the first day of a resident's admission, not just when the resident is dying, the care will have a depth that provides satisfaction for all, and a smoother transition to appropriate terminal care when appropriate.

QUALITY ISSUES FOR ENHANCED PRACTICE

The gerontic nurse

- Care plan documentation requires an appropriate balance of psycho-emotional factors along with the physical. As a communication tool, the care plan then becomes the guide for all carers.
- When the goal of care is changed, for example to palliative care, it is essential to ensure appropriate communication to all carers.
- It is particularly important with regard to food and fluids, that there is a consistency of approach which includes giving adequate instruction to kitchen staff.

Management

- Staff education on issues of euthanasia may help to differentiate between the statements, 'I want to die' and 'Please kill me'.
- Staff education on listening to what is behind a statement like 'I want to die' may open up opportunities for more creative practice.
- Clear procedures are needed for alternative meals for a dying resident when loss of appetite occurs.

Indirect carers

- Kitchen staff have a role in the care of a dying resident. For instance, the attractive serving of a very small meal may change the resident's perception and may help staff to achieve a realistic goal of care. However, their role is enhanced when they receive clear and consistent communications about the resident's changing requirements.

STAFF STRESS: TOO MANY DEATHS

In this 50-bed nursing home, the number of resident deaths per year has increased from 12 to 28 each year during the past four years, representing a 32 per cent increase. There is no standard or predictable number of deaths per week or per month; however, when the statistics show an average of one or two deaths per month, six deaths in one week seems extraordinary. In the interests of care for the living, as well as care for the dying, it is important to reflect on the impact of so many deaths in so short a time and to inquire as to who is most affected. Practice and quality issues inevitably arise. This section, through a series of vignettes, explores the tragic, the humorous and the urbane as life goes on in the midst of so much death.

Responding to the incredible

'That's two, one to go!'

After the sixth death in a week, 'That's two lots of three. We might as well make it three lots of three now.'

'What will we do today for a change? Lay out another body?'

'The linen bill will rocket to the sky — we can't afford any more complete bed changes.'

'What a shame Percy died, just when I'd finished the most perfect care plan.'

'What's the new lady's name?', 'Which new lady? We've got four!'

'I can't bring myself to get to know the new man in Ben's bed. That will always be Ben's bed as far as I'm concerned.'

'We should put a sign up, "Beware, all ye who enter here, you may be gone within a week." '

'Make sure the bed has a chance to get cold before you put the next resident in it.'

'Perhaps we could start getting a commission from the funeral director.'

'Who's taking bets on which resident will be the next to go?'

'It's not a bad idea to have a good clean out, then start again with some new residents.'

'I came to work in a nursing home. This is more like a funeral parlour!'

When the fifth death in six days occurred, a newly appointed nurse commented, 'Will they (the Department) come and investigate why we've had so many deaths?' Others said, 'We use too much morphine. It's bordering on euthanasia.' Some looked on the unusual phenomenon as a failure: 'It's because we've had so many agency staff; no-one's provided any continuity'; 'We need more staff when there are so many new admissions'; 'If we had more time between one resident's death and the new resident's admission, at least we'd be able to adjust better'; 'We don't even get to pay our proper respects to the dead!'

Questions of documentation also arose. How could we have time for keeping thorough records when so many residents were dying? Most of the documentation could withstand any investigation of inadequate care. Where it was relevant, the resident's planned palliative care involved intense family consultation and careful assessment by a medical palliative care specialist before introducing narcotics. However, there remains a gap between the professionally documented care and staff perceptions. When the sixth death occurred, the sharpness of its impact was denied by reactions of nonchalance, humour or resigned incredulity, 'I can't believe this is happening!'

The following vignettes capture the unique story surrounding each death and also some of the staff's varied reactions.

Death on a public holiday

Two deaths on a public holiday were a bit much for everyone. The director of nursing could do little other than to show some solidarity by her personal presence. Foremost on her mind, of course, was the waiting list — how to fill two beds without losing too many days' funding? The 'big picture' is a term often used these days. The big picture encountered at 2.45 p.m. on Melbourne Cup Day was of a nursing home engaged in much living and much dying; an atmosphere of exhilaration mixed with grief and incredulity. There was even talk of winners and losers in the nursing home, as staff speculated about who would be next to die, and how long this last lap of life would take for those who were not yet in the race.

The lounge was decorated for Cup Day; there was a lively, festive air. Champagne glasses tinkled amid prize-winning hats: one nurse had made her own hat by entwining her long hair with ribbons. Annie was aglow with pride for winning the best decorated hat (by a resident), George smiled demurely with his prize for the smallest hat and Fred, one of several new residents, beamed with amazement at being permitted to drink champagne and place a bet on his first day in the nursing home, 'I didn't know it would be as good as this!'

Staff had momentarily left their sad scene where Ben had just died, to join in the Cup Day celebration; and also to spread the word of another death and to receive some comfort. It was now several hours since the first death of the day at 4 a.m. and some staff had moved on a bit further in the race of the day.

While the horses were running their fastest, Ben's wife had left his bedside to sit proud and tearless in the relatively private space of the dining room, surrounded by their four sons. Within this atmosphere of profound grief and sadness, humour also found its place. 'Trust Dad to interrupt our lives and call us to attention right in the middle of the Melbourne Cup!' It also seemed fitting to celebrate this uniquely personal 'race' which Ben and his family had fought so hard to win. They had wanted him kept alive at all costs, suggesting more tests, more treatment, still hoping for a cure. Now that the doctor had explained that the rare neurological disease was progressing rapidly, they all decided on a new 'winning post'. They had no wish to see Ben suffer further. This well-loved patriarch, youthful looking and distinguished even in his dying moments, seemed to be satisfied that he would pass through this last barrier with every member of his family around him. No more laying of bets as to the finishing time for this race. Ben did not keep them waiting long; in a matter of two to three hours he reached his goal.

This little picture, unique in its personal detail, was not incongruous with the 'big picture'. The race went on, its aftermath taking several more days.

Ben's wife and Ronald's wife had developed a close relationship while visiting their respective husbands who were roommates. They would sometimes fill in for each other, when one chose to have a day off from visiting, confident that the other would say hello to her husband too. Taking a day off from visiting brought relief but it was also fraught with anxiety and guilt. When Ben died, Ronald's wife knew this would be an experience she would share some time in the future. Each knew this new status of widowhood would one day unite them further. Ronald's wife was helped by observing the rituals surrounding Ben's death, storing up her private thoughts, formulating her own plans about how she would manage when Ronald died. Little did she know that this would be her own experience in three days' time. When Ronald died unexpectedly she was reminded of these recent events. 'It's still a shock, but somehow Ben's death helped to prepare me.'

ON REFLECTION...

Humour, the strong defence mechanism

It is not easy to maintain balanced professionalism in the face of such rapid change, particularly when it represents a new phase for long-term residential care. Defences such as anger, incredulity or humour are healthy responses to unexpected events. What is not so easy, is channelling those energies into good practice, particularly when it involves careful attention to so many new residents in a short space of time.

Confining the comments

While it is acceptable for professional staff to respond with humour to crises such as death, it is important to confine the comments to an area where they are not overheard and misinterpreted. Some families also enjoy responding with humour, while for others a solemn response is more acceptable. Sensitivity is needed when using humour with residents, who may be offended by staff treating death in such a lighthearted way. Other residents may respond positively to humour, legitimating their own reactions. Some visiting health professionals may receive the wrong impression if death is described in a glib manner; others will be able to empathise with a humorous response.

The context of the next vignette is anger, resentment and frustration; a far cry from the humour referred to previously.

Death on a Saturday

As Director of Nursing, my reaction to the phone call was less than sympathetic: 'Ho, hum, another death! I could go into automatic gear and complete the administrative tasks in record time as I have rehearsed them so often in the last few days. Do I really need to interrupt my Saturday? Couldn't someone else phone the next person on the waiting list, notifying them of the vacancy? No. Nobody else could possibly find their way through the disorganised paper trail of the waiting list file. It will have to wait until Monday.' Pragmatism was at work; however, my hunches had become rather well honed over the years, so I obeyed that 'inner voice' in response to the sense of distress detected in the nurse's phone call.

Eva, the weekend relieving charge nurse, rang to notify me of Doreen's death at 8.45 a.m. Eva had taken the usual handover from the night staff in which Doreen's condition was described as 'deteriorating' but no specific indicators were given to suggest that death was imminent. It was 8.30 a.m. before Eva got to Doreen's bed in the last room at the end of the corridor. Immediately, her professional judgement prompted her to ring the family to advise them to come immediately because Doreen was dying. Ten minutes later, Eva phoned to tell them Doreen had died.

Eva had been on annual leave for three weeks and was not well-acquainted with all the recent resident changes. She translated her anger, embarrassment and frustration into a very apologetic explanation to the family for not giving them more warning. Her private reaction was to blame her colleagues, 'Why didn't they warn me? I hardly know this resident. Why didn't they tell the family their mother was dying? Why hadn't the family been given some opportunity to say their goodbyes? Why have I been left to pick up all the pieces?'

Eva was relieved to see me and to accept my offer of speaking with the relatives, with whom I had established (or so I thought) a trusting relationship. Doreen's son-in-law came right into my office.

'There's no-one at Reception,' he said in an accusing tone.

I held back from asking, 'Do you expect the Commonwealth to subsidise a receptionist in a nursing home 24 hours a day including weekends?' I had not met this particular family member before, but discovered he had come to support his wife who was already keeping a vigil at her mother's bedside. My condolences were quickly interrupted. 'Why weren't we told she was dying?'

Defensively, I thought, 'What sort of a son-in-law are *you*? You don't even know where your mother-in-law's bed is. How dare you demand some sort of special treatment at the time of death when you've never been involved in family meetings? What complaints can you make at the time of death when you never visited while she was alive!' Mutual hostility erected a barrier. 'How can we possibly be all-powerful and all-knowledgeable, able to predict who is going to die — and when! Doesn't he understand we've already had four deaths this week. Doesn't he understand this is my precious day off?'

Deflecting my own frustration, I turned to Doreen's clinical record; it didn't help. While I read a very comprehensive report from four days previously, describing the charge nurse's discussion with Doreen's son and daughter, there was no mention of her condition since. 'Why did I have to be away for the last two days at a waste-of-time conference, when I could have served a more useful purpose here? Surely, if I had been here, I would have seen the signs of impending death. Why can't I rely on professionally qualified staff to pick up these subtle nuances — that's what they're paid for!' My anger was tinged with regret that this family, who had always been so complimentary about their mother's care, were now greatly disappointed. 'I had so much wanted to be with her,' said her daughter.

Aware that mouthing platitudes or being verbally defensive would be counterproductive, I remained professionally objective. From the family members' perspective it seemed this was not a 'good death'. Whether we failed Doreen, we would never know. We had certainly not met this family's expectations. That we *did* know.

ON REFLECTION…

Subjective blaming or objective analysis

Reflecting on this episode, it is important to learn from omissions without unnecessarily blaming other staff. The director of nursing responsible for resident care needs also to find a way of dealing with personal and professional disappointment when, in his or her opinion, care does not reach the optimal level.

Dealing with unrealistic expectations is also a matter for professional staff to grapple with. As imperfect human beings, it is not possible to offer perfect care. It requires some wisdom to accept imperfections without reacting defensively and without apportioning blame.

Communicating without predicting

The essence of professional long-term care is to be alert for subtle changes in a resident's condition and to communicate these changes clearly to staff coming on duty, even if what has been detected is more in the realm of 'hunch' than objective assessment. As family members become increasingly involved in planning and evaluating care, it is also important to maintain communication with them, and to document the details, so that other staff are informed. In residential aged care, the part-time nature of the workforce places an obligation on professional nurses to make a comprehensive report, written or verbal, when handing on the care of residents. This is particularly important when caring for a resident whose medical condition is chronic and where changes do not appear in dramatic or acute form. In handing over a hunch, care is provided for colleagues, as well as for residents and families.

As the following vignette shows, some deaths are so unpredictable there is no time even for the slightest hunch.

Death on Day One

Joy's name was placed on the waiting list only a few days prior to her admission. Such was the rapid change in resident population that her admission occurred sooner than expected. Joy's two daughters were delighted; Betty had flown home from the United States to help her sister Joan choose a nursing home for their mother. Their goal and dream was to have their mother in the home of their choice before Betty returned to the USA for the Easter holidays. Notified of the vacancy on Saturday — and with Betty's return flight booked for Sunday night — Betty and Joan pleaded 'special circumstances' in order for their mother to be admitted on Sunday.

So, on Saturday, Joy's daughters made hasty plans to bring their mother's belongings in, complete with a welcoming bowl of flowers. The admission went smoothly, with Joy settling in immediately. 'I like it here,' she told her daughters. Having spent most of the day with their mother, Betty and Joan left, content with their decision. Their next appointment was at the airport overseas departure lounge.

After tea in the nursing home, Joy was found wandering in the corridor. 'I'll help you find your room,' offered the kitchen hand. This intuitive staff member gently redirected Joy and waited, intending to call for a nurse once Joy had settled herself on her bed. To her utter amazement, Joy uttered a sigh and died.

An urgent message was relayed and Betty's plans to fly home were cancelled. 'We're not sad,' Joan told the staff. 'Of course we're shocked, but we believe mum was greatly relieved to find her final place, so close to her own home and familiar surroundings. And Betty was thrilled to see mum settled after all the uncertainty of recent weeks.'

ON REFLECTION…

Was it worth all the paper work?

This very short episode of care involved a seemingly disproportionate amount of resources. The daughters had required a lengthy interview as part of the waiting list procedure because they wanted to confirm every detail before Betty's return to the USA. They had carefully prepared for their mother's transfer, taking several hours to acquaint themselves with all aspects of nursing home life. Betty wanted to have a clear picture of the nursing home in her mind; she planned to phone her mother regularly from the USA. Following Joy's unexpected death, a great deal of informal counselling was required. Betty and Joan wanted to speak with the kitchen hand to gather fragments of the last few minutes of their mother's life; they also needed longer conversations with senior staff. While the amount of resources for such a short stay may not be considered 'worth it' these two devoted daughters have a lasting memory of acting well in decision making on their mother's behalf. 'This was the next best thing to mum dying at home,' they concluded. And, we concluded, of course it was worth it.

Preparing families

Statistics have shown that the many deaths within the first three months of admission to a nursing home are a significant factor in aged care. How well do we prepare families for this not uncommon phenomenon? Without unnecessarily raising the family's fears and concerns it is possible to use the waiting list interview to mention these factors. It may be reassuring to give families a general statistical overview of average length of stay. It may also be appropriate, when discussing expectations, to mention the number of residents whose lives flourish after entering long-term care, the number who live for several years and also the number who die soon after admission. These matters are best discussed in a conversational tone which does not presume to predict or forecast, but creates an awareness of some realistic parameters to guide families.

The final vignette in this chapter shows some inevitable complacency surrounding a resident who takes a long time to die.

Death at the wrong time

Ellen had been close to death for so long that staff believed, 'She'll last for months yet'. Ellen was pale and terribly thin, suffering the slow but relentless end stage of Alzheimer's disease; however, Ellen's family were content to watch and wait. A clearly documented palliative care plan included the family's wish for no intrusive interventions, their one exception being the continuous subcutaneous infusion of a low dose of morphine. It was now several weeks since Ellen had been able to swallow oral medication. Because she was unable to communicate her pain verbally, nursing staff feared that Ellen was suffering from her advanced osteoarthritis each time her position was changed. A palliative care consultant advised that a morphine infusion would provide the best pain management now. Once the morphine infusion was commenced, Ellen was so comfortable and free from pain and anxiety that it seemed she would live on and on. No-one predicted she would be our sixth death that week.

ON REFLECTION...

Myths about morphine

Some ill-informed staff complained that residents, including Ellen, were receiving morphine when it was not warranted. When Ellen died, comments were made similar to those alluded to at the beginning of this chapter, 'We shouldn't be giving so much morphine. It's just like euthanasia.'

Such statements indicate that not all staff are fully informed about the aims of palliative care. When staff are persuaded by the myths of morphine usage and allow their personal prejudices to colour professional judgement, education is needed. Sadly, such reactions are not confined to unqualified staff. This vignette reinforces the message distilled from other stories: while allowing staff an opportunity to vocalise concerns, a continuous focus on education in order to update the knowledge base is a high priority, whether the context of care is acute or long term.

No time for debriefing

The weary charge nurse sighed, 'I haven't had time to lift my head from all this paper work. Why did Ellen have to choose this time to die!'

Senior staff were aware of the emotional and physical implications for staff, of an inordinate number of deaths in a short time. Palliative care literature emphasises the need for adequate debriefing after death has occurred. In this book, we also emphasise the value of reflection on practice following each death. We also emphasise the funding constraints which allow little room for such debriefing and reflection. Given the circumstances of many deaths in a short time, what opportunity existed for such thoughtful reflection?

In an attempt to salvage the situation before 'all these deaths' were forgotten in the busy period following the admission of six new residents, it was decided to provide an opportunity for staff to gather informally to remember the six former residents, to express their feelings and to acknowledge the residents' place in the nursing home history. The small meeting room was prepared, with subtle lighting and music and...not one person turned up! Perhaps this was an artificial attempt to structure the debriefing, or perhaps it was too soon after such a busy, stressful period. Perhaps debriefing happens less formally, for example in the tea room or at the nurses' desk. If this is the case, is there any need for a structured session? This had not been our past experience. There could have been a number of reasons why no-one turned up on this occasion. Staff may have been too exhausted or they may have simply had enough of death. Ironically, the 'real' reasons could not be discerned because there was no time or energy to pursue them!

QUALITY ISSUES FOR ENHANCED PRACTICE

The gerontic nurse

- When closing the file after the resident has died, satisfaction is gained by writing 'outcome achieved', particularly when palliative care goals of comfort have been met.
- Each new resident deserves a fresh approach, so that the settling-in process is not compromised. It is not the concern of a newly admitted resident or their family that their admission has come at a very busy time for the nursing home.
- When several residents in a short space of time require multiple assessments and detailed documentation, the opportunity exists for the whole care team to share the workload. Staff at all levels may acquire new skills through practice.
- Efficient documentation and filing processes result in deceased residents' files being closed as soon as possible. This makes room for new residents' files to be readily accessible, ready to be used as working documents.
- When multiple admissions occur close together, it is essential that correct name labels are used. Double checking minimises the risk of error when several new admissions are processed, particularly when some have similar names.
- Recording essential details immediately, rather than waiting until the end of the shift, is of vital importance to avoid confusion or serious error of documenting in the wrong file.

Management

- Written and verbal acknowledgement from senior staff which recognises the stresses, sadnesses and the extraordinary efforts of staff, may offer welcome encouragement for busy clinical-care staff, particularly following so many deaths.
- It is important to have clearly documented procedures, so admissions and discharges can proceed smoothly and quickly, and error is minimised.

- As each life and death is unique, so it is important not to neglect the public acknowledgement of each person's death, together with appropriate announcement of each new resident's arrival.
- When non-nursing staff encounter death at a close personal level, as did the kitchen hand who escorted Joy to her bed, careful attention to debriefing may be beneficial. This episode also called for praise and commendation for the staff member's actions.
- Praise and acknowledgement is also welcome for clerical staff who, at these times, work under increased pressure.

Indirect carers

- Clerical/administration staff are also under significant pressure when so many deaths occur in a short space of time. It has been estimated that the administrative processing of a new resident's admission requires several hours. Such procedures are 'office work' and do not include any documentation related to the resident's clinical care. However, this clerical work is of vital importance to efficient record keeping.

CHAPTER FIVE

This chapter provides examples of significant relationships formed when the doctor, the chaplain, the volunteer, the student and the activities staff are included in the team.

THE DOCTOR: THAT'S HOW DEATH SHOULD BE

Holistic care, as a means of achieving a dignified death, occurs when nursing home residents are attended by a doctor who understands their needs and when staff are committed to enabling residents to die with dignity. A partnership of trust established among resident, family and doctor increases the resident's potential for a peaceful death, free from distressing symptoms.

However, when a clear goal of care is lacking or when conflict exists it is the resident who suffers. This chapter describes the important features of a team relationship which resulted in one resident's dignified and pain-free death and contrasts it with a fragmented form of care which led to frustration for staff, anxiety and bewilderment for the family and less than optimum care for the resident. The vignettes highlight the need for developing cooperative strategies for use by funding bodies, doctors, community palliative care services and nursing home managers. The challenge is for each nursing home to develop, in a consultative manner, its own philosophy statements and policies for achieving a dignified death for residents.

Mapping medical objectives in response to Beverley's changing needs wasn't easy. Dr Thomas was not entirely free of emotional involvement, having cared for Beverley for 39 years and now caring for Beverley's children and grandchildren. Beverley was not a stereotypical 88-year old. A twinkle in her eye, a wink and a nudge revealed her quick reaction to any conversation with the remotest double meaning; she lived up to her reputation of being 'a real bright spark'. Her ribald sense of humour provoked a variety of comments and opinions. Beverley was forthright about her past relationships and maintained a discerning regard for the male nurses who cared for her. As for her 'Dr Tom' she would boldly assert, 'He and I have been sweethearts since the day we met.'

Dr Thomas had seen Beverley through her various episodes of depression and her successful surgery for bowel cancer 20 years earlier; however, she was reluctant to admit that her current 'funny pains' may be due to cancer. Following Dr Thomas's frank discussion with Beverley's daughter and granddaughter the question of extensive tests was put aside in favour of conservative treatment. Beverley pre-empted any further decisions by confiding to Clare, the charge nurse, 'I think it's the cancer back again. Please don't tell Dr Tom that I know. He'd worry too much.'

From that day, Beverley was resigned to the cancer taking over. Seldom without humour, never without stoic patience, she succeeded in making light of every encounter with her Dr Tom. It was also Clare in whom Dr Tom confided, 'Have I done everything I should have? Should I call a surgeon? Maybe I've missed something.'

It was agreed that time should be set aside to review all aspects of Beverley's care with family members present. In due deference to Beverley's stated wish, the case conference was held without her involvement. Beverley had discussed at length with the charge nurse and the chaplain her readiness to die. 'I just hope it will be quick and without too much pain,' she said. And to the chaplain she confessed, 'I've not lived what you would call a perfect life but I hope I haven't done anyone harm.'

Dr Thomas told the review meeting that pathology tests indicated Beverley was dehydrated. He discussed the options and mentioned his own ambivalence about sending her to hospital for intravenous fluids. He wanted to do all in his power to ease her suffering and to care for her to the best of his ability. He also knew that in hospital she would be beyond his direct supervision and that she may feel he had abandoned her. Nursing staff outlined their views. It was clear to them that Beverley would rather die in her own bed in her own room in the nursing home than in a strange hospital bed. Recalling a recent painful and regrettable experience when a resident had been sent to hospital in the middle of the night on the well-meaning advice of a relieving night nurse and locum doctor, the charge nurse suggested a way forward. 'It would help us, Dr Thomas, if you would consider writing in her notes that, as it is the wish of Beverley and her family, no further treatment for dehydration is appropriate and that she should not be hospitalised. That will give clear direction to the whole team.' The family members nodded.

'I'm sure that's the best decision,' replied Dr Thomas. 'I've already thought about it. I'm very happy with that decision if we are sure that we are all agreed.' Later, in discussion with the charge nurse, he confided, 'Do you know, this is one of the rare occasions when this sort of thing is spoken about openly. I often think, in similar circumstances, that this is the way forward but I'm also unsure about how others will react. There's always the fear that nursing staff or family will think I should have been more decisive about vigorous interventions.'

Now the goal of care was clearly recorded in the doctor's notes and the formal care plan: 'Comfort measures, including pain relief. Not to be hospitalised.' Beverley had not admitted to Dr Thomas the amount of pain she was suffering. He needed no convincing, however, when shown the pain management chart comprehensively recorded by the nurses. It was also clear that once she could no longer tolerate oral pain medication the time had come for small but regular doses of morphine to be administered via a needle permanently in place under the skin to save Beverley the intrusion of frequent injections. When the family became concerned at Beverley's apparently increasing drowsiness the charge nurse asked Dr Thomas to reinforce her explanations to them about the positive effects of morphine. It was apparent to Dr Thomas that the charge nurse, Clare, had the benefit of several years' palliative care nursing. While reluctant to prescribe morphine at first, or to increase the dose, the doctor's fears were allayed when Clare offered him a copy of the relevant chapter from her clinical textbook on palliative care. 'I don't have much occasion to use morphine in the community,' Dr Thomas explained, 'and you know all the fears that used to surround the side effects of such a powerful drug.' Unused to symptom management according to palliative care principles, he directed the nurses to '…just write down all your suggestions and when I come in I'll write the necessary prescriptions.' Clare reminded him that her own responsibility as a professional nurse was to ensure she had a comprehensive knowledge of drug administration, but that prescribing was quite clearly his role.

After several phone calls to Dr Thomas, Clare was able to clarify all the issues surrounding the morphine administration; Beverley's physical symptoms were at last controlled. It was clear that the doctor's focus on this rather special patient had shifted. Phone calls were no longer sufficient. In the last few days of Beverley's life he called in at least twice a day, 'just popping in' before or after surgery. On some occasions he would bypass the clinical notes and go straight to Beverley's bedside to sit with her. Once, Clare saw him tenderly stroking Beverley's shrivelled arm, unashamedly allowing his tears to fall on the pastel bedspread. 'I'm ready to let her go now,' he said at the nurses' desk, 'I wasn't last week, but now I'm ready. Please continue to keep her comfortable.'

It seemed as though he had only been gone a few minutes when Clare phoned to inform him of Beverley's death. Returning to the bedside he wept. These tears were not only for Beverley, his long-term and greatly admired patient, but also for his brother who had died recently and for his mother who was critically ill in the intensive care unit of a major hospital. 'This is how it should be!' he stated with great conviction and heavy sadness.

Dr Thomas was overwhelmed to receive a letter of condolence from the nursing home that acknowledged his own grief and his difficulties in separating from this very special patient. Thanks were also expressed for his cooperation in carefully documenting the redirected goal of care. Shared grief at Beverley's death was acknowledged while staff and doctor recognised an immense feeling of satisfaction at the outcome of her dignified, peaceful and pain-free death. Some time later, Dr Thomas mentioned his mother's death. 'Sorry I got a bit emotional when Bev died but I couldn't help contrasting her death with my mother's situation. I'm sure my mother wouldn't have wanted all that intrusive treatment but there seemed to be no option at the time.' He repeated with a sigh of resignation, 'This is how it should have been.'

The story of Beverley and her Dr Tom stands in significant contrast to another experience of death in the nursing home, characterised by a frustrating lack of consultation and openness on the doctor's part.

Lola's quality of life was already compromised by Alzheimer's disease and a major stroke. Seldom registering any meaningful response, Lola was dependent on nursing staff for her every need. She did, however, appear to eagerly eat all the food offered to her. Staff were pleased to feed her as she opened her mouth for every spoonful, always enjoying her cup of tea and showing no signs of the swallowing difficulties evident in many other residents. Lola's doctor was called when a significant droop was noticed on one side of her face and her limbs showed evidence of increased weakness. Lola looked imploringly at each nurse who approached and she seemed anxious when her family appeared mid-morning, followed by the doctor who was grave and officious. 'It looks like she's had another stroke. She'll have to go to hospital,' the doctor decided within earshot of Lola and to the consternation of the staff. Lola's family, accustomed to always deferring to the doctor, stood in silent acquiescence. 'May I have a word with you to clarify some concerns, please?' asked charge nurse Clare. Impatient and brusque, the doctor was in no mood for further delays. However, Clare's request to wait and see for 24 hours did not seem unreasonable and he was reassured that staff would call his surgery immediately if there were any signs of deterioration in Lola's condition.

Lola's family could speak little English, so Clare arranged for an interpreter to come to a case conference the following day. Unfortunately, the doctor was unable to be present, declining the offer of alternative times. While there was no further deterioration in Lola's condition, there was one dramatic and specific change. Lola refused all meals. Against the frequent offers of her customary sweetened, milky tea Lola's protest was clear. She held her tongue over the spout of the feeding mug; she pursed her lips and clenched her teeth against every teaspoon of food offered. With the interpreter's help, Clare explained to the family that Lola appeared to be giving clear direction concerning her own future. The family were not discouraged from bringing small amounts of home-cooked food to try but it soon became evident that Lola's decision was final. She had suffered enough. With great sensitivity, Clare also explained to the family that Lola was refusing medications and she promised to discuss this with the doctor when he called. A proposed change to the plan of care was drawn up, in accordance with the nursing home's palliative care philosophy and drug policy. The plan was accepted by the family at a meeting the doctor declined to attend.

The doctor, however, had a different view. He was astonished that there could be an alternative plan. 'If she's not eating she will, quite clearly, soon become dehydrated and I have a responsibility to treat her symptoms.' When asked about the goal of continuing Lola's blood pressure medications, tranquillisers and sedatives, he became defensive. 'I wouldn't order them if she didn't need them. If she's not taking them, you'll just have to do the best you can,' Reiterating his clearly perceived goal to 'treat', he began arranging hospitalisation. Persisting in her role as resident advocate, Clare tried to indicate the result of the case conference in which the family seemed reassured that all Lola's needs for a comfortable and dignified death could be met in the nursing home. With apparent disregard for the family's wishes the doctor replied, 'It's easy for you. You're not the one who will suffer the consequences of litigation.'

The sequel to this story is complex, signifying a period of turbulence for family and staff, complicated by the hospital's response in treating Lola with intravenous therapy and performing numerous tests. Resolution of the preferred site of care was finally brought about by the return of a family member from overseas, who immediately took steps to have Lola returned to the nursing home and arranged a change of doctor. Lola's journey towards death did not occur swiftly or without further complications. Having been hydrated and given a wide variety of medications while in hospital, Lola seemed to be marking time. She lingered on for some weeks, causing further anxiety among the family and increased ambivalence among staff regarding her refusal to eat and drink. Somehow, the provisional plan of care had become lost in a maze of indecision and differing opinion, complicated by the perceived need of a relieving doctor to treat Lola's recurrent infections with antibiotics. One doctor's clear and decisive (although unpopular) directives had now been replaced with a variety of doctors' different responses, the result of rapid turnover of staff from the clinic in question. Seen in the context of holistic or palliative care, the outcome of Lola's death several weeks later was neither dignified nor peaceful. Recalling the contrasting experience of Beverley's death and Dr Thomas's cooperation, the staff reminded each other, 'That is how it should have been.'

ON REFLECTION...

Doctors' feelings

Many doctors develop long and close relationships with their older patients that may or may not continue when the patients enter a nursing home. One of the disadvantages of being a lone practitioner is the isolation and lack of opportunity to discuss or reflect upon emotional complexities of the doctor–patient relationship. In offering a partnership of care the nursing home environment has the potential to provide doctors with professional support. While the intensity of feelings depicted in Beverley's story may not necessarily be common, there is a distinct possibility that this episode is not an isolated instance of a doctor needing to speak freely about matters other than the strictly clinical. The genuine warmth of appreciation and affection demonstrated by the nurse's letter of thanks demonstrates that the doctor–nurse relationship is enhanced by such a gesture.

Palliative care experience

The principles of palliative care include appropriate medical intervention, with a clear indication that, for optimum care, it is believed that the doctor should lead the multi-disciplinary team. Many general practitioners willingly care for dying patients and their confidence increases with experience in terminal care. However, many have had little or no undergraduate preparation and training in the principles of palliative medicine, caring for only small numbers of terminally ill patients each year. Now that community hospice and palliative care services are becoming well accepted by health-care personnel, appropriate resources are available for general practitioners and nursing home staff to call on. While the partnership between Dr Thomas and the charge nurse led to appropriate palliative care for the resident, the following extract from the nurse's personal journal signifies a more comprehensive approach. A doctor from another suburb, normally engaged in caring for hospice patients, had come to treat an old friend whose stay in our nursing home was complex but brief. The appreciative nurse wrote:

> Thank you, doctor, for making it easy to apply palliative care principles. For once, you, the doctor, gave the lead and made it less hard for us. Always one step ahead, you initiated the morphine, you suggested ceasing all other medications, you came without waiting to be called.

Although textbooks may suggest the doctor is the leader of the palliative care team, as Beverley's story demonstrates, real leadership comes from the shared decision making and pooled resources of a team where every member is valued for their special knowledge and abilities.

Shared responsibility

In the story of Beverley and Dr Thomas it was quite clear that the pooling of opinions and a frank discussion about the changed goal of care resulted in the burden of responsibility being shared. While recognising the unique duty of care pertaining to both doctor and nurse, there is potential for enhanced care when individual responsibilities are managed by a team approach.

Clearly defined plan of care

A plan of care, constantly reviewed as the result of careful and continuous assessment and agreed upon by resident, family, staff and doctor provides a clear point of direction and communication for all involved in the dying resident's care. In Beverley's situation, the potential for ill-advised staff to change the direction of care was minimised. Beverley's care, particularly regarding the treatment of dehydration, was no longer subject to differing opinions of staff resulting in inconsistency of care; the concisely worded medical direction was unambiguous and became the pivotal point of reassurance for staff and family. These factors contributed to the achievement of our goal — optimum care resulting in a dignified and peaceful death for the resident.

Debriefing

Health-care professionals generally recognise the need for debriefing, particularly following a patient's death. In the nursing home environment where many residents have been a part of the community for extensive periods of time, there is often a significant emotional impact on staff when a resident dies. As demonstrated by the story of Dr Thomas, such emotions may also be experienced by the doctor involved in the care. While recognising that the circumstances of each resident's death are unique, consideration of the doctor's feelings may also be an appropriate and humane response.

Several references have been made already to the positive outcomes resulting from staff and residents attending the funeral of a particular resident, however, it is generally believed that doctors do not have time to attend funerals. There may well be time and benefit in the doctor attending a particular patient's funeral, in order to pause and reflect, to acknowledge grief and to share the sadness. Appropriate closure prepares the way for the demands of the next resident or patient who needs care.

Case conferences

Unfortunately, as evidenced by the contrasting story of Lola, doctors are not always available to attend a case conference in the nursing home. However, time spent on a well-planned review may result in a significant reduction in time wasted on unnecessary phone calls and visits. In our experience, it is the resident who benefits from a comprehensive review clearly communicated to all concerned. Palliative care principles lead to improved quality of care when opportunities for discussion between doctor, family and staff are given high priority.

Nursing home philosophy and policies

The question of the specific skills which doctors need in order to care for residents in a nursing home is too large an issue to be addressed here in detail. However, when the focus of a resident's needs has changed to terminal or palliative care, the nursing home staff will be assisted if there are readily accessible, comprehensive guidelines to assist in the planning of that care. Doctors who visit nursing homes may find their task clarified by well-defined philosophy statements and policies outlining the particular nursing home's standards for practice. Mutual benefit also derives from the visiting doctors' involvement in formulating policies such as a drug policy or palliative care policy. For example, the situation of a doctor continuing to order medications even when a resident is refusing to take anything by mouth (as in Lola's story) highlights the need for medication review when a resident's condition is thought to be terminal. Such a policy protects the resident from unwanted or intrusive treatment because elements of care such as the prescribing of drugs are continually reviewed in accordance with the goal of care. Comprehensive policies are, therefore, removed from the realm of irrelevant theory or impractical ideals; policies become useful tools of care for the ultimate benefit of the dying resident.

Litigation

The trend towards increased litigation concerns all health-care professionals. This fear needs to be balanced with a clearly documented rationale for specific treatments, or for the withholding of certain treatments in favour of comfort and palliation. While such fears may be well founded, the rights of the resident to experience a dignified death demand a continuous review of all aspects of care.

Continuity of care

Comprehensive doctors' notes in a readily accessible form may help to overcome unhappy situations, such as the one described in this chapter. Of further concern to nursing home staff is the problem of after-hours medical attention. Here again, a well-documented medical plan of care provides guidance for an after-hours medical service in the difficult situation of a 'midnight crisis'. When the dying resident's own doctor is available after hours, the potential for reassurance and confidence both for staff and resident cannot be overestimated. The benefits derived from continuity of medical care are also apparent to nursing staff, for teamwork is made easier when each member knows the specific roles, functions and expectations of the key players.

QUALITY ISSUES FOR ENHANCED PRACTICE

The gerontic nurse

- Doctors' notes should form a comprehensive part of each resident's clinical record, providing clear information and guidance as to the goal of care. Professional nurses have the responsibility to ensure that doctors' visits, which are relatively brief in relation to the nurses' constant presence, include thorough documentation.
- Referral procedures for the involvement of palliative care personnel should ensure smooth communication between local doctor and specialists.

Management

- Doctors visiting the nursing home require comprehensive information about the nursing home's policies, including the palliative care policy. It is important to ensure that each 'new' visiting doctor receives this information.
- Doctors may also appreciate being involved in the formulating and review of such policies.
- A doctors' committee is the appropriate forum for dealing with the practical issues arising from these policies.
- Partnerships with palliative care teams may be enhanced through education sessions and information forums where staff, families and general practitioners have an opportunity to discuss issues relating to terminal care.

Indirect carers

- Wherever possible, palliative care planning is best achieved in a multidisciplinary team. Involvement of allied health professionals adds an important component to the palliative care goals and outcome.

THE CHAPLAIN: I WORE MY BEST DRESS

Not every nursing home has a formally appointed chaplain — either the need is not perceived or the framework and resources are not available. In our experience, the appointment of a chaplain who understands the nature of aged care adds a dimension to the nursing home community. Chaplains work in hospitals, in hospices, in schools and factories, so why not in nursing homes? Using examples from our experience, this section of the chapter demonstrates the benefits of such a valued team member. However, a note of caution is added from the story of Betsy who, unfortunately, was hurt and offended rather than reassured and helped by the chaplain's attention.

What is the nursing home's philosophy?

We were asked why a nursing home would need a chaplain. It was suggested that the many residents who suffer from some form of dementia wouldn't know whether there was a chaplain or not. Anyway, these people are at the end of their lives; all they require is basic nursing care. I don't remember any residents who said they had problems they'd want to discuss with a chaplain. We have such a mixture of residents, how would one person suit everybody? And anyway, what would a chaplain *do*?

If such opinions were our guide we would never have appointed a chaplain. Yet, the nursing home philosophy states clearly that we cater for the physical, emotional, psychological and spiritual needs of our residents. While several local church representatives called regularly to offer pastoral care or to give Holy Communion to selected residents, they came and went without their care being integrated in any holistic way.

The decision to appoint a chaplain is based on the nursing home's philosophy and the care best suited to local needs. While some nursing homes cater for ethno-specific groups, others are more reflective of society as a whole. Where there is a mixture of religious denominations represented, where the nursing home population reflects both the Christian and non-Christian faiths of Australian society, then a chaplain may be required who will coordinate the care from a variety of other sources. Spiritual care is considered by aged-care legislation and current Standards of Care, to be an important component of each resident's care when provided in response to assessed needs. These reflections from the chaplain's journal show some of the diversity of needs and responses.

Giving and receiving

Hughie Jones lies in bed looking out the window and asks God to take him. Every day he asks this. He believes one day God will. Meanwhile he notices the birds on the roof, the clouds racing by, the sunlight on the leaves. And he goes back over his life.

When you know life is short it's important to tie up loose ends. It's also important to know someone else cares. So Hughie and I often have a yarn. We both enjoy it.

Hughie gets depressed, his memory fails him and he wonders what purpose his life has had and why God doesn't let him die. When I hear his life's stories it amazes me that he can be positive. So much pain and injustice. This is true for many people at the nursing home.

How does chaplaincy work? Spiritual needs are not simply about going to church, humans need to interact with other people, to get a sense of their own worth and uniqueness. For nursing home residents this is particularly important. Chaplaincy is not all one way; the chaplain giving to the residents. One time I was sitting with Sarah Wilson who suffered from dementia and a constantly sore back. She would sit in a chair and cry out for hours, driving everyone crazy. Sometimes I played her music, sometimes I prayed out loud. There was little response but I believed she found comfort in my visits. But I did not realise the comfort I received until one day, while I sat holding Sarah's hand in silence, this poem came to me:

> A stately woman
> Sits silently.
> A stately woman now sits silent
> And alone.
>
> Her hand reaches constantly
> For comfort
> Another hand to hold
> A cup of tea?
> Ceaselessly her right hand moves across the table top
> Clasping nothing
> Grasping nothing
> She sighs...

> We sit together
> Silently,
> Hands together.
> We are together.
> No longer alone.
> The warmth of her hand
> Comforts me.

(This material comes from the personal journal of a former chaplain.)

I wore my best dress

When Judith was appointed as the new minister of the local church she came to visit two of our residents who were on her parish members' roll. Judith had a way with the residents, a way which did not intrude but invited a response. The staff liked her too, as she never minded helping a resident in a wheelchair or assisting another resident with a drink; she even knew how to handle the aggressive residents as well as those with dementia. To have her appointed officially as part-time chaplain seemed a natural extension of her existing role. Judith took the view that the best service she could offer the residents was to get to know them.

Getting to know Lily was not easy. She was not the most popular resident to care for. Her sharp tongue would tell anyone who came near her that they could turn around and go back where they came from. No respecter of persons, Lily was no more welcoming of the chaplain than of anyone else who approached her bed. One by one Lily's friends stopped visiting and you couldn't blame them. There were a few people who managed somehow to break through the caustic veneer to the warm and lovable person underneath. Her old friend Stan stood by her till the end; he knew what tricks this dementing illness played on her mind. He knew she didn't mean it when she called him unmentionable names, and he mourned as life seemed to gradually slip away from her.

Lily's funeral was the chaplain's first from our nursing home. She wondered what could be said about this person she hardly knew. Only three others attended the funeral but Judith, donning her chaplain's robes, resolved there would be no short cuts, this would be a proper burial. 'There is only one Lily. Her value and worth may not be immediately evident; nevertheless, she deserves our respect. So, as one mark of respect, I decided to wear my best dress.'

In the first chapter of this book, many contrasts were made between fully funded palliative care and the kind of care we offer dying residents in the nursing home.

Chaplaincy services are an integral part of formal hospice/palliative care, an acknowledgment of the commonly expressed wish to explore the spiritual depths of one's life as death approaches. Palliative care principles acknowledge that a trained counsellor or pastoral carer may help the dying person find meaning in the dying experience.

Age is no barrier to the search for meaning. When older people face death, common questions may emerge: What is the meaning of this life, now nearly over? Is there anyone who can help me make sense of what is happening? Will anyone come to visit me when I need them, or will they gradually disappear like they did when Freda was dying? Guilt and concern about the past have emerged in residents' conversations with the chaplain. One resident expressed her concern at having felt angry towards a roommate who seemed to attract all the attention. Another felt guilty at her past impatience with a resident who, accustomed to wandering, would find her way into the wrong bed or take other residents' belongings. Yet another resident was troubled by what he regarded as unforgivable wrongdoing in his youth. Fears and anxieties about approaching death are not the exclusive province of the young. Neither may it be assumed that older persons face death with wisdom and spiritual maturity. It is also commonly assumed that a nursing home resident with no particular religious affiliation has no need of a chaplain. While care and sensitivity is required to respect each resident's choice, every opportunity should be made to offer this important aspect of care.

I'm not good company today

The following account of the chaplain's encounter with Ethel highlights the positive benefits of a chaplain who does not represent staff or administration. The chaplain is, therefore, free to listen, and is able to hold in confidence those matters which come from the deeper well of the resident's being.

Ethel was described by her son as 'a real lady, the essence of good breeding and charm'. Her manner indicated she had not a problem in the world. Gracious and appreciative of all care offered to her she would greet the day with a smile, welcoming each member of staff to her bedside. Enquiries from the director of nursing on her formal rounds of the nursing home or when passing through the lounge would inevitably bring the same response: 'I'm quite well, thank you. And how are you?'

Ethel had at first politely rejected the approach of the chaplain. 'Thank you for asking but I don't feel I need to see the chaplain for any particular reason. However, you are most welcome to pop into my room whenever you are passing. I am always happy to pass the time of day with you.' On one of these visits Judith found Ethel without her customary smile and benevolent attitude. 'I feel perfectly miserable, thank you, and I think it might be wise if you were to leave now, as I am not particularly good company today.' Recognising an opportunity, Judith sat on the bed and invited Ethel to tell her a little more of the sadness she was experiencing. Without betraying specific confidences the chaplain was able to report the general nature of their conversation.

Ethel was angry. Resentful and disconsolate, she vowed she would never accept fate's cruel blow in the form of this stroke. She was sick and tired of being polite to everyone when underneath she hated living in a nursing home. 'Oh, don't misunderstand me,' she said, 'They are all wonderfully kind but I feel I've left my real self back in my own home.' Ethel was able to describe the frustration she felt at her immobility, having to depend on others for every move. She was aware that it was nobody's fault, but she had to vent her feelings. She knew it was wrong to bear so much resentment towards her bachelor son who had no alternative but to arrange nursing home accommodation. It was no use jollying her along for in this mood Ethel was adamant, 'I don't want to go on living. I wish I were dead. There, I've said it.'

No need to apologise to this chaplain for these seemingly outrageous words; here was someone who understood. Understanding did not necessarily provide resolution, for Ethel knew very well that 'Even someone as close to God as the chaplain can't hasten death's call.'

Life did not change very much for Ethel; she resumed her polite response, 'I'm very well, thank you. No, there's nothing I want, I'm perfectly happy'. She also made it quite clear to the chaplain that their conversation would not be repeated. She'd said all she wanted to say and that was that. We may never be sure whether or not this conversation helped Ethel prepare for death. It was clear, however, that Ethel did not choose any of the regular staff to confess the darker side of her emotions.

Betsy's experience — the best and the worst of pastoral care

Betsy had had a sheltered existence. When she was born in 1910 there were few community resources available for someone considered to have 'something wrong with her brain'. The doctor told Betsy's parents, 'You must take her home and care for her as best you can. She won't be able to go to school and you should not attempt to teach her too much as it will addle her brain. And, of course, she will never walk.' Betsy was protected from the outside world by her parents and, after their death, by two elderly aunts. When they became too frail to care for her, it was time for Betsy to come into the nursing home.

Betsy immersed herself in every program within the nursing home. Never having learned to read or write, somehow she knew when it was 2 o'clock and time for the bus trip, or swimming, or bingo or poetry circle and she never missed Sunday morning church in the adjacent chapel. The chaplain was keen to know about her past. 'Where did you learn to have faith in God, Betsy? Where did you go to church?' Replied the astonished Betsy, 'I've never ever been to church. I've learned all about God and Jesus from you.'

Humbled and overwhelmed by her role in Betsy's spiritual life, the chaplain pondered the power of religious symbols and rituals used in regular worship. She had often thought about the most meaningful way of communicating to a congregation of nursing home residents, many of whom had impaired cognition. She had decided to preach without 'talking down', to administer the Sacraments without trying to explain these deep mysteries of the church and, in her pastoral interactions, to include each resident unconditionally. Betsy's response reinforced for her the power of church attendance as a teacher, even for a person considered incapable of learning. The chaplain was also reminded that many unself-conscious acts bring their own profound rewards.

In contrast, another scene from Betsy's history revealed the unfortunate consequences of a thoughtless and condescending pastoral encounter. Ted, as he liked to be called, had been visiting the nursing home for so many years no-one knew how he had adopted the role of pastor. He greeted Betsy with a pat on the head, 'How are we today? Have we been a good girl this week?' An irate staff member, overhearing his comments and observing his patronising behaviour towards this woman of 89 years, immediately reported the incident to nursing administration, demanding immediate intervention.

Unfortunately, Betsy had experienced many of these infantalising and dehumanising encounters before it was reported. No-one liked to challenge the practice of this well-meaning, earnest pastor who, in spite of his own deteriorating health and increasing irritability, continued to visit the nursing home every week.

ON REFLECTION…

Policies, protocols and procedures

Chaplains are not immune from acting in consultation and with clear direction according to the nursing home's policies. Nor are chaplains immune from discipline where their practice is clearly in breach of nursing home standards of care. However, in order to be accountable, chaplains and visiting pastors require a comprehensive framework including position description, reporting structures and procedures for review. Before these parameters are acknowledged, recruitment procedures for the chaplain and/or pastoral care team need to be similar to those used for all other staff.

Chaplains are in a position to observe care given by nurses and other staff. Their unobtrusive presence may at times place them in a position of observing inappropriate care. In a climate of trust, the chaplain may report inappropriate care in the interest of resident advocacy.

Part of the team

When the chaplain's role is understood as complementary yet distinctive, the contribution to resident care will be acknowledged. For example, there is no need to report or document all the chaplain's encounters with residents. However, there may be some occasions of significance, such as the conversation with Ethel, which are worth reporting in broad detail. Nursing staff and others may then be reassured that Ethel had expressed those feelings of anger and resentment which everyone suspected were there anyway.

When the chaplain is encouraged to produce reflections on a particular episode (the text of a funeral eulogy or snippets from a personal journal), this additional documentation offers another perspective to the resident's care.

Rites, rituals and relationships

Before the chaplain's appointment it was left to nursing staff to call a minister or priest when circumstances seemed to require it — hence, Patrick had received the last rites fourteen times! Since the chaplain's appointment, areas of responsibility are more clearly defined. It is the chaplain who develops an understanding of residents' and families' spiritual needs and wishes. Now, the staff may phone the chaplain for advice about such matters, confident she may have the most comprehensive understanding of the situation. While religious rites and rituals have significance for many residents and the formal priestly presence offers an authoritative reassurance, there are others for whom the quiet presence of a person willing to listen, or just to be with them, is more appropriate. The chaplain, coming to the bedside without a task to perform, free from the time constraints placed on other staff, says in effect, 'I am here for you.'

Coordinating role

It is not expected that the chaplain will meet every resident's religious and spiritual needs — other clergy and pastoral visitors fulfil this role. The chaplain coordinates various worship services which recognise the residents' denominational variance. Staff facilitate residents' choice in this matter by placing a high priority on ensuring residents are assisted to chapel or to Mass when appropriate.

Where have all the clergy gone?

How does one approach a pastoral visit to a person who is dying and demented or unconscious following a stroke, or one whose hearing is significantly impaired? This specialist area seems to be overlooked by many clergy. Perhaps the nursing home would be an appropriate environment for student clergy to learn the art of communicating with frail, elderly persons, many of whom are inarticulate and unresponsive. Even though a significant component of clinical pastoral education depends on verbal input and response, there may be much to learn from this challenging environment.

The chapel, the funeral and the follow-up

Several of the stories in this book illustrate the important role played by the chaplain presiding at the funeral service, especially when there is a chapel adjacent to the nursing home. Here, continuity of care reaches its clear conclusion. And yet the role of a chaplain or counsellor for the purpose of bereavement follow-up seems to receive little attention. Such a service benefits not only the family of the deceased resident but also the staff and remaining residents.

Chaplains for the living as well as the dying

While intervention from a chaplain or pastor may be needed at times of crisis such as serious illness approaching death, there is also much to celebrate and rejoice in when developing relationships with residents. Having an ordinary conversation, sharing the joy of watching birds in the birdbath, seeing the chaplain perform in the nursing home concert — provide unique opportunities for residents to gain trust in the chaplain's role.

Once a relationship of trust is established, the consequences may prove of lasting benefit to other residents and staff, surprising even the chaplain.

Spiritual care and bodily care united

Much is said about holistic health care, particularly in residential aged care, where the physical, spiritual, psychological, social, emotional and cultural are not separate parts of care, but form a whole. When spiritual care is left to the chaplain, the spirit is split off from the whole person. While chaplains have a unique role, spiritual care is enacted by all who care, through touch, gesture, even hesitant and clumsy words which convey the healing gift of one person's presence to another. Spiritual care, when understood in this way, is the role of every person in the health-care team.

Spiritual assessment

Nursing staff usually have no qualms about enquiring into intimate details concerning bowel and bladder elimination but often have little understanding of assessing spirituality beyond ticking the 'religious denomination' box. Careful assessment of a resident's spiritual needs encompasses a broad range of issues, from the narrowly defined identification of denominational affiliation of the resident to a broad understanding of the resident's wishes and dreams, fear and anxieties affecting the whole of life. Spiritual needs also change over time, so that the person who confessed to no spiritual needs on admission may develop different needs throughout their life in the nursing home. While at first expressing no desire to see the chaplain, the resident may change their mind after gaining the confidence of the chaplain, or after watching the chaplain interacting with others.

The family's needs may also change; from an initial reluctance to have any involvement with the chaplain, to an increased awareness of the chaplain's role.

This may include a timely conversation with the chaplain in anticipation of a funeral. Getting to know the chaplain while the resident is living in the nursing home paves the way for meaningful pastoral care at the time of death. However, it remains important to acknowledge that some residents and families prefer not to engage in any dialogue concerning spiritual needs.

Support for the carers

When the chaplain's position is part-time, there is very little time to assist in building relationships with staff. However, one suspects that the chaplain has many informal meetings with staff which are never officially recognised as hours of work. The need for staff debriefing is acknowledged in other more high-profile areas of work but the absence of formal provision for staff counselling in nursing homes suggests it is not needed. Not all staff–chaplain encounters arise from traumatic experiences or crisis situations; they may involve the subtleties of teamwork, praise for work well done or listening to another's point of view; all of which may raise staff morale. These by-products of an effective chaplaincy service increase the potential for support within the team, as well as for the care of residents.

Reporting inappropriate care

When reporting procedures are in place, staff are encouraged to report unwelcome or intrusive care, as they would for any inappropriate care they observe. Acting as the resident's advocate, the nurse who was disturbed by and reported the pastor's treatment of Betsy assisted the pastor to move to retirement. The report was dealt with in a conversational manner which encouraged the pastor to make his own 'confession'. He admitted to feelings of frustration and increasing tiredness as he forced himself to continue his weekly visits in spite of failing health. He had wanted to give up this voluntary task he had taken on many years ago, but he felt uncertain of how to end his visits. He was reminded of changing attitudes that include residents' choice as to whether or not they want a pastor to visit them, and of the new procedures required for all care within the nursing home. He left with an acknowledgment of the positive elements of the service he had given for so many years.

QUALITY ISSUES FOR ENHANCED PRACTICE

The gerontic nurse

- Where appropriate, the chaplain may be invited to attend case conferences where a resident's total care is being reviewed, and particularly if there are significant spiritual issues.
- Resident assessment should indicate whether or not the resident wishes to have the chaplain's involvement in their care.
- The chaplain's involvement should be documented clearly. While it is not necessary or appropriate to record details of pastoral encounters, particularly where confidential matters are an issue, a simple entry which notes the chaplain's visit serves as a communication to other staff.

Management

- Each nursing home has a responsibility to provide for residents' spiritual care, and policies and practices can be formulated according to the particular nursing home context and philosophy.
- Where a chaplain is appointed, a clear role description should be made available to staff, residents and families.
- Comprehensive communication procedures may include the chaplain receiving regular updates on resident admissions and discharges, promotional material, newsletters and invitations to programs and functions.
- Regular reviews of the chaplain's role and function will assist the nursing home to evaluate the outcomes of the spiritual care provided to residents.
- There may also be mutual value in the chaplain being involved in policy making.

Indirect carers

- Even if communication is difficult with a disabled resident, the quiet presence of the chaplain may be worth a thousand words.

- More vocal contributions from the chaplain may be used for the benefit of the whole nursing home. For example, personal reflections or other contributions may find a significant place in the nursing home's newsletter or other publications.
- When the text from a eulogy is included in the resident's file after death, this provides a unique opportunity for closure.
- Chaplains have a vital role to play in resident advocacy and an accessible chaplain may also provide valuable support for staff.

THE VOLUNTEER: I LEARNED SO MUCH FROM FLORA

Patsy, the volunteer, came each week to feed Flora. What passed between them to establish such a lasting and intimate bond? This exuberant young woman with enthusiasm and commitment and this frail old lady who was unable to say anything — somehow the relationship between them had deep significance. Who was the teacher and what was the lesson, not only for other volunteers, but also for qualified professional staff? This story examines the pitfalls and highlights of Patsy's service, offering some vital clues for the use of volunteers in the care of the dying.

All Patsy knew was that she wanted to help old people. Her mother had died in a nursing home where 'the staff were run off their feet'. There was no time for any extras. When she visited her mum she would spend more time helping the others in the room, her mum being asleep most of the time anyway. She couldn't bear to see their meals go cold waiting for someone to help with cutting up or feeding. Patsy never knew these residents' names; there was nothing to indicate who they were and she never heard them called anything else but 'darling' or 'sweetie'. She wondered what the residents thought of this. Was it just one of those things, that when you live in a nursing home your name doesn't matter any more?

So, in response to an advertisement in the local paper, Patsy found her way to our nursing home. In her enthusiasm she had ignored the protocol for interview and reference checks, expecting to start then and there. 'Please give me something to do. It looks like lunch time — does anyone need help with feeding?'

Does anyone need help with feeding! 'We've got seven feeds at the moment!' one nurse complained at morning tea. 'And Flora is so slow, I nearly fall asleep feeding her.' Patsy was introduced to Flora, not that Flora could respond for she had not spoken in three years. She seemed like a tiny bird, eyes darting everywhere, mouth open to receive the teaspoon. It was such a tiny mouth, Patsy thought. How long is it going to take to get this plateful of food into it? I wonder what it is? She turned the spoon over trying to recognise in the pureed meal some distinctive flavour.

'Well, Flora, is it all right if I call you Flora? I'm Patsy. I wonder what the cook has made today? I'd say by the colour that it's pumpkin and something else. I hope you like pumpkin.' Flora made no response but it didn't matter to Patsy. 'You should see what a terrible day it is outside, Flora. I thought I'd get drenched through coming here... Now, here's something I'm sure you will like — jellied fruit. Look how pretty it is, the golden fruit in the red jelly. This is one of my favourites.'

This ritual continued every Wednesday for a whole year. Patsy would tell Flora about her day, then proceed to the guessing game, 'What's in the bowl today, Flora?' And Flora would continue to open her mouth for the next spoonful. The feeding procedure took 20 minutes but Patsy always stayed for an hour, finding extra things to do such as brushing Flora's hair, tidying her cupboards, or just sitting and chatting.

Gradually, a deep bond grew between them, evident by the way Flora's eyes concentrated on Patsy's face as she fed her, evident also by the warmth of the embrace as Patsy greeted and farewelled this old lady who never spoke a word. Sometimes they would sit holding hands in the silence.

When Flora grew weaker, the feeding took longer and she could no longer manage the plateful. She seemed to be fading away to a shadow and each Wednesday she ate less and less, until one Wednesday Patsy knew she had fed Flora her last meal. Flora's last days were restless, posing a challenge for the nursing staff. Was she in pain? Was she afraid? It was only Monday, not yet Patsy's day, but worth a try to see if she would come in. For six hours Patsy stayed by that bedside, soothing and singing, whispering and caressing until she was spent. Flora too was spent, her restless and jerky movements subsiding until she was at rest. When the night staff phoned Patsy early next morning she was not surprised.

Patsy joined the small band of staff and residents at the funeral. 'I'd like to say something,' Patsy told the chaplain. With words more eloquent than those of a professional eulogy Patsy, with charming spontaneity, spoke of how it had been for her, this relationship with Flora. 'I learned so much from her.' What could one learn from an inarticulate old lady in a relationship which centred round a weekly feeding ritual?

Patsy spoke of how it was at first, how she wondered at the intrusiveness of a complete stranger presuming to take over this most intimate of functions. How would she know if the food was too hot or too cold? How would Flora make known her preferences? Would Flora recognise her when she returned next week? Patsy regarded it a privilege to be allowed into a relationship which she kept referring to as 'intimate'. Feeding a resident — how could this be perceived as intimate? Jolted out of our complacency, those of us who had regarded this as just another chore in the daily routine of nursing home care heard of the finely balanced nuances in this gentle art of feeding another person. For those of us trained in the task of feeding, we learned more of this art from Patsy than from any textbook or clinical teacher. What Patsy taught us was what she learned from Flora. She learned patience, she learned that words were not always necessary for two people to share a relationship, she learned that the art of feeding was more than the mechanics of getting the spoon in the right place at the right time. She had to think and feel for Flora; put herself in Flora's place as it were. 'If it were me, what would please me, what would irritate me? What's it like to be so helpless you can't even place a spoon in your own mouth or hold a cup to your lips? What's it like if someone forgets to feed you or hasn't got time to give you a drink? What does it feel like to have the remains of your last meal crusted around your lips two hours later?'

Food is life. It was life that Patsy gave Flora every Wednesday for a year.

ON REFLECTION...

Feeding is not everyone's cup of tea

There have been no more 'Patsys' in our nursing home. When providing lists of tasks for new volunteers the option of assisting with feeding is seldom taken. We have learned from Patsy that it takes a special understanding and empathy to take on this role. As there are some qualified staff who have this special knowledge and some who don't, so it is with volunteers.

Food presentation

While many textbooks offer sound, practical and illustrated advice on the presentation of food for nursing home residents, scant attention is paid to the presentation of meals for residents who need help with feeding. An aesthetic appearance enhances this important part of care, both for the person feeding and for the resident being fed. Eating is also a social function, as highlighted by Patsy's experience. When the food lends itself to positive comment, the whole exercise becomes more palatable.

The art of volunteering

While much can be learned through formal training, the volunteer's role is largely intuitive. This chapter has explored only one aspect of this important component of nursing home life. Palliative care manuals emphasise specific aspects of the volunteer's role including having an appropriate volunteer at the bedside of a dying resident. Nursing homes able to recruit willing and committed volunteers are indeed fortunate. For the resident who is dying, the presence of a volunteer may enhance their quality of life in a way which complements the care of paid professional staff and the presence of relatives.

Caring for the volunteers

Every volunteer group depends on good coordination for smooth functioning. Apart from comprehensive recruitment, relevant training, sensitive support and supervision, the volunteer needs the kind of care that recognises their unique contribution and values their presence in the nursing home. While there are many ways to do this, when volunteers participate in the care of residents who are dying, they deserve special attention. When a volunteer has enjoyed a particular relationship with a resident, the volunteer may wish to be notified when that resident's condition deteriorates. The volunteer may agree to having their name included on the list of next of kin to be phoned in such a crisis and particularly when death occurs. Administrative processes need to ensure that this happens. To be avoided at all costs is the unhappy situation of a volunteer arriving to care for a resident, to find that resident died some days ago!

Volunteers and staff

'It's all very well for her! I'd love to have time to sit for six hours with a dying resident. We're the ones who do all the work and they get the glory.'

Praise of volunteers' contributions may leave staff feeling undervalued. However, when a variety of skills is required, the team approach enhances the resident's care. The staff reaction above also highlights the need for alternatives when there is no volunteer available. If every dying resident deserves someone beside them, how may this be managed with limited resources?

Relief for the carer

It would have been easy for busy staff to make assumptions that, because Patsy had chosen to sit beside Flora for so many hours, she did not require special care or relief from her post. Patsy commented that while she appreciated the domestic staff bringing her a cup of tea and a sandwich, she would have welcomed a complete break from the bedside. Torn between wanting to stay ('I promised Flora I wouldn't leave her') and the need to replenish her own emotional and physical resources, Patsy needed some direction. Had such care been taken, she may have been able to resume her vigil, coming back refreshed for another shift after an appropriate time out. Because burnout is common to volunteers and paid staff alike, every effort should be made to care for all the carers.

QUALITY ISSUES FOR ENHANCED PRACTICE

The gerontic nurse

- Professional staff have much to learn from the volunteer's encounter with the resident when the gerontic nurse encourages the sharing of information between volunteer and professional staff it can only benefit the resident.
- When a volunteer is sitting with a dying resident, the volunteer's physical and emotional comfort can be enhanced by supportive staff.
- All staff need to be encouraged to welcome the volunteer as part of the team.

Management

- Volunteers need the support of formal procedures and guidelines that are communicated to all staff.

- Volunteers may require education and guidance in the most simple of tasks, particularly if the volunteer is not familiar with the care of older people.
- Following a resident's death, debriefing may include special acknowledgment of the volunteer's care.

Indirect carers

- Although volunteers are not on the nursing home payroll, their presence is priceless to individual residents. The reward of volunteer activity is the relationship with residents and the opportunity for focused caring that is often denied to busy staff.

THE STUDENT: THERE IS LIFE IN A NURSING HOME

'What immediately comes to mind when you think of a nursing home?'

'Smells.'

'Old people.'

'Depressing.'

The orientation session provides an opportunity to hear nursing students' perceptions of residential aged care. The groundwork may then be laid for a positive outcome from clinical placement in the nursing home. When students are encouraged to express their presuppositions, expectations and/or anxieties, the field is wide open to ensure a sound learning experience. Students are challenged to change negative perceptions when they witness excellent role modelling, particularly when issues of death and dying are encountered. By contributing to students' learning in this important area of nursing, nursing homes have the potential to influence the quality of aged care in many settings.

Smells, old people, depression: these are always high on the list of student nurses' perceptions of nursing homes. On the first day of their clinical placement they were also asked to describe their most significant relationship with a person over 80 years old. Grandmothers were high on the list, most comments being favourable. However, there were descriptions of 'the funny old lady down the street who often went out in her nightgown' or 'the old man who lives in the most appalling conditions and never seems to wash'. Many studies show that when asked to rank working in a nursing home on a list of preferred health agencies, almost every student placed nursing homes last.

When the subject of death was raised, students seemed to think that, for old people, this was just a natural progression. None of the students had thought how they may respond when faced with a dying resident. However, two of the students volunteered to be assigned to Fred. Fred was barely conscious and required all the basic nursing care these students were anxious to practise. Under the careful guidance of their clinical teacher and our charge nurse, Deidre and Robert performed well. At first tentative and afraid to touch Fred's body at all, after the third day Deidre wrote in her journal:

Sat and massaged creams and oils into Fred's wasting limbs. He especially seemed to like the back massage. I think it made a difference. I hope I helped him to die peacefully.

At the end of two weeks' placement the students evaluated their experience, both for their academic requirements and for an internal nursing home audit. Many were surprised to witness only one person close to death; they seemed to assume that of the 50 residents, most would be relatively lifeless. They learned too, that death's hour could not always be predicted and that the best preparation for a resident's death was to concentrate each day on improving quality of life. They quickly responded to the idea of life review as enhancing residents' self-esteem as well as being therapeutic. For some of the students, it seemed that the residents had always been old and dependent, so it came as quite a surprise to learn of their lives before nursing home admission. 'Did you know that Mr Brown was once the mayor of a large provincial city?' 'You should see the photos of Milly dancing at the Tivoli.' Slowly, the students' perceptions were changing. These residents had a wealth of experience and an accumulation of life's wisdom unimagined by the students, who had looked on nursing home residents as beyond the pale.

While the students cared for a typical mix of nursing home residents — those with dementia, physical frailty, emotional instability, mental frailty or alertness of mind, some close to death and others relatively independent — they also witnessed residents' participation in bus outings, counter lunches at the local pub, concerts and a lively movement-to-music session. One student summed it up well: 'There is life in a nursing home!'

ON REFLECTION...

Student placement: threat or challenge?

There was an air of anticipation before the first group of students came to the nursing home. 'They needn't think that just because they go to college they know more than us!' 'I suppose they've never changed a dirty bed in their lives.' Balancing these predictable comments was the feeling that here was a challenge. Our nurses, most with many years' experience, had much to teach these students and here was a chance to act as positive role models. There was also an element of protectiveness guarding the residents' care. 'We'll have to make sure they know how to handle

Fred.' 'And look out any student who makes fun of Gertie's bear!' Much was to be gained by our staff from the students. 'What do they teach you about mouth care?' 'Could you show us how you do care plans?' 'How would you assess this resident's mobility?' Acknowledgment of the staff also came from the clinical teachers, 'How do you manage Mr Black's shower? You know him better than we do.'

Sharing the care

After initial territorial guarding, our staff were pleased that at least two of the students had the chance to care for Fred. While there was some dismay about the time spent by the students ('How will they ever manage *thirty* patients!') there was also a degree of satisfaction that Fred's hygiene would be meticulously attended. They would also have the time for that extra massage and for the regular pressure care Fred now required. There was also evidence of mutual commendation on the part of staff and students. 'You've managed to position him well. He looks so contented.' And the student's comment, 'I don't know how you manage to do all this and all the other jobs you have to do. And he hasn't even got any pressure sores.'

Reversing negative perceptions

At a time when gerontic nursing is increasing in prominence, every opportunity should be taken to positively influence students' perceptions. When aged care is seen as mere routine, straightforward, unrewarding and back breaking, skilled professional staff will not be attracted to this challenging area of practice. Positive reinforcement from committed carers, particularly in the context of student preparation for nursing, will slowly but certainly change negative attitudes. Nursing home staff have a significant role to play in this regard.

Influence beyond the nursing home

Aged care is inevitably part of general nursing, for older patients die in hospitals every day. When the care of nursing home residents at the point of death is seen as an opportunity for applying the best care, resulting in a positive nursing experience, then students' attitudes toward older patients in any setting may be enhanced. Nursing homes have the potential to make a positive contribution to aged care in other practice settings.

QUALITY ISSUES FOR ENHANCED PRACTICE

The gerontic nurse

- Staff need relevant information about the purpose of student nurses' placement, with an emphasis on staff role modelling and the potential for influencing future gerontic nursing practice. (This also applies to students from other disciplines on placement in the nursing home.)
- Permanent staff may also learn from the students. Assisting to create an atmosphere of reciprocity helps to guard against animosity and any other anxieties on the part of either group.
- Resident care is often enhanced by students' activities; their careful documentation identifies any new needs or responses.

Management

- Thorough orientation at the commencement of the students' placement assists in clarifying expectations; the way they are welcomed has a significant influence on their perception of aged care.
- A student handbook describing the nursing home philosophy and procedures which affect students is one way of ensuring the students receive relevant information.
- A thorough student evaluation and debriefing at the end of their placement period ensures questions and concerns are raised. It is a morale-boosting exercise when students' positive comments are passed on to staff; it is a learning exercise when negative comments are aired in a constructive way.
- Brief education sessions with allied health staff may assist students in gaining a holistic view of the resident.

> **Indirect carers**
>
> - It is important to introduce students to allied health professionals, offering them the opportunity of informal conversation as well as promoting the students' attendance at the various social aspects of the nursing home.

ALLIED HEALTH STAFF: MARY'S FINAL FLING

> Sandra, in reminiscence, reflects on the impact of Mary's life in the nursing home. Proudly, and with affection and sadness, she recalls Mary's response to her initiatives as activities coordinator. And she will never forget Mary's last fling. Only 12 days before Mary's death, Sandra took her to the community tea dance. At the funeral Sandra recalls this unforgettable experience, along with the other highlights of Mary's six months in the nursing home. There was certainly a lot of living being enjoyed by this frail woman with the indomitable spirit. Whenever Sandra felt that her task was a thankless one, whenever the other residents failed to respond to her programs, there was always Mary. 'What will I do without her?' This is Sandra's story.

Life intruded on death at Mary's funeral. A crying baby drowned out the chaplain's opening comments; from time to time Joe rattled his foot in the plastic bag protecting the site where his two last toes had been. And Alison sang very loudly and out of tune during Peter's sensitive guitar solo, 'One Day at a Time'. Peter had been a particular favourite amongst Mary's 'boys' (the male nurses) and this had been her favourite song.

Even so, as we sang 'Amazing Grace' and 'Abide with Me' for the second time in a week at a resident's funeral in this chapel, the uniqueness of Mary's personality was ascendant. As we sat side by side with her family and acquaintances of many years, our attention focused on memories of the diminutive lady with the big heart. On the coffin was an extravagant spray of pink flowers, reminiscent of her last days. She died peacefully in a pink ruffled nightgown that matched her pink-painted nails, offset by the subtle tint of blue in her newly permed hair. She would have been pleased with that impression of her final appearance.

After the funeral, as Alison was escorted from the chapel in her wheelchair, one of Mary's gracious family made a point of speaking with her, 'You sang that song beautifully!' Alison waved her escort on, beaming. Once round the corner she said conspiratorially, 'I'm glad she liked my singing but I was really singing for Mary. I sang up loud for her.'

That was part of Mary's impact on the nursing home. We all wanted to sing up loud for her, to praise this zest for living in the cancer-ridden and frail 84-year-old frame.

Some days later, Sandra recalled:

> Had to go away by myself after the funeral, not being able to come to grips with Mary's death. Death and funerals are not my scene really. The mixture of exhilaration and grief disturbed me but I'm glad I went. I'm really glad to have known her and I'll miss her terribly. Was it really only 12 days ago that I took her to the tea dance? I'll never forget seeing her clothes all laid out on the bed from early morning, including her brand new 'dancing shoes'. How she kicked up her heels and eyed off the men! Did she know then she was flirting with death, that this was her last dance? Was it really only a week before that Mary had stolen the show at our nursing home cocktail party with her pearls, fur stole and corsage? I'm so pleased I took those photos.
>
> I didn't want to believe it when the nurses told me about the cancer. Mary was always so happy and responsive. Although we never spoke of her physical problems I think we both knew that she wanted to make the most of the time she had left.
>
> What about the day Greg (from maintenance) brought his vintage car to the nursing home? Mary was the first to go for a ride. 'Boy, that brought back memories,' she said. 'My first boyfriend had one of these. What he couldn't do with one free hand! No seat belts and gearbox between you and your boyfriend in those days!' What will we do without her?

ON REFLECTION…

Those unfamiliar with death

We usually associate allied health staff with programs and activities, not with death. Sandra was not one for visiting the bedside of a dying resident; she felt her time was better spent with those who still had some living to do. But Mary was different. Even on Mary's occasional days in bed, Sandra received inspiration from going to see her. 'Who won at Bingo today?' Mary was always interested. When Sandra was feeling down she'd go to Mary. 'How about a stroll in the garden, Mary?' And the two would set off together, wheelchair at the ready in case Mary became tired. They formed a close bond, bridging the 50-year age gap. Mary's enthusiastic responses to outings and programs was what made the job worthwhile.

No regrets

From the time Mary entered the nursing home, social profile complete, the occupational therapist and other allied health staff took every opportunity to provide her with appropriate stimulation. Focusing on the dancing she loved, the sherry she looked forward to each evening, the latest fashion magazines or simply her reminiscences, it was no problem to fill Mary's days with a variety of activities. As well as overwhelming sadness, Sandra felt a great deal of satisfaction as she recalled her own contribution to Mary's care. While this story highlights the special contribution of one or two allied health staff members, there are many untold stories which attest to the role played by the physiotherapist, music therapist and others who assist nursing home residents to achieve a variety of experience according to their choice. Many of these staff develop special relationships with the residents and may benefit from appropriate acknowledgment and encouragement by nursing staff who are more likely to have a direct role with the resident close to death. Consider, for example, the mutual trust built up between a music therapist and a particular resident, and the potential for building on that experience when the resident's life is coming to a close. The music therapist may choose to take a prominent role in the funeral to round off their relationship.

Communication and teamwork

In mentioning specific categories of staff it is important to acknowledge the particular contribution of the podiatrist, hairdresser, dietitian, social worker or the many other staff who contribute to the residents' care. Depending on individual circumstances, each one of these carers may be involved during a resident's final weeks, days or hours. Simply notifying them of a resident's deterioration may be all that is required. No individual has the monopoly on care; a variety of skills is needed to ensure each resident has the care appropriate to his or her circumstances. Communication is the essence of this team approach.

QUALITY ISSUES FOR ENHANCED PRACTICE

The gerontic nurse

- Allied health staff have a valuable contribution to make as important members of the care team. This needs to be formalised through allied health staff's involvement in review of residents' care and in case conferences.
- Depending on their prior involvement with the resident and the specific skills allied health staff have to offer, they may provide a vital role in the care of a dying resident.
- Sharing the task of assessment with allied health staff adds to the formulation of a total care plan.

Management

- The nursing home needs to have clear means of communicating with allied health staff at the time of a resident's death. Such communication may also be the means of acknowledging their specific contribution to the resident's terminal care, where relevant.
- Information gained by allied health staff about a resident, particularly the resident's social history, is valuable for nursing staff to absorb into the total care plan. Therefore, comprehensive assessment forms provide a snapshot of the resident's life history and current dreams, fears and expectations.

Indirect carers

- Allied health staff may also have a vital role in volunteer orientation and supervision. Multi-skilling of indirect care staff results in greater flexibility and job satisfaction.
- For example, if the activities member is away, a well-prepared domestic or kitchen staff member may be able to assist with programs.

CHAPTER SIX

This chapter is about families: how they visit, when they visit and if they visit at all. The chapter opens with a discussion of the vital pre-admission visit. The stories that follow highlight the dilemma of some families when the primary reason for visiting the nursing home is gone — when the resident has died.

FAMILY RESPONSES

While Cara's story is indicative of the ageing population and the implications for carers who are also ageing and facing the challenge of finding appropriate accommodation, for residents and families the physical move is merely the outer representation of a larger adjustment.

All Trevor saw of his wife was her back as she chatted to the other visiting wives during her rare visits. Even on the day Trevor died her delayed response to our telephone call meant she arrived too late to say goodbye. In the room next to Trevor, Pat's son struggled to stay with his mother. Confused and upset by her erratic behaviour he often left after a few minutes, even though she was dying. And Joan, well no-one seemed to visit her at all now she was unresponsive.

We may never know how these residents felt about their visitors or lack of visitors — if they found the visits pleasant or unpleasant, if seeing their families was unbearably sad or if every minute was precious to them. Perhaps some even felt indifferent. Aged-care standards rightfully advocate free access of residents to visitors of their choice, but what if those visitors choose not to come? When families fail to visit, staff sometimes pass judgements such as,

'Wouldn't you think they'd visit at a time like this?' The following vignettes provide clues to possible meanings and emotions hidden behind disrupted visiting patterns and family dislocation or estrangement.

MOTHER AND DAUGHTER: OLD-OLD AND OLD

When Cara rang for the appointment to put her mother's name on our waiting list, her clear descriptions of her mother's needs, together with her precision about getting the address right, were indicative of a person eager to find the best accommodation for her mother. Her careful attention to detail also suggested careful planning and thorough investigation of nursing home options. 'I've cared for her all of my life, but the doctor tells me I must now slow down. But, I'm not just going to put her *anywhere!*'

When Cara arrived for the appointment, the receptionist was confused. 'There's a very elderly lady to see you,' she told the director of nursing, 'I think it must be the resident herself.'

Cara did not expect any confusion, as if it were the most natural thing in the world for an 85-year old to be negotiating nursing home accommodation for her mother of 105. Cara showed evidence that her own health care had been neglected as she had cared for her mother without any assistance for several years. As the social worker later explained, Cara did not want strangers coming into her house so she politely declined all community services offered. Cara's legs were roughly bandaged ('I go to the doctor's once or twice a month, or whenever I can leave Mum, to get these ulcers dressed.') and it seemed as though shopping for clothes may have been well down the list of her priorities.

Cara proceeded to list the detailed care her mother required, including continence management, medications and assistance with meals. 'I could come and show you how to do everything,' she stated with confidence. Cara's reassurance was evident as she was shown over the nursing home. Overawed by the size of the bathroom and the equipment for lifting, relieved to know all the food was cooked on site, delighted with the idea of bus trips ('Perhaps I could go with Mum on the bus?') Cara could visualise her mother being well cared for. When she saw the chapel she asked, 'Could Mum go in there sometimes, just to sit? She's a very religious woman but we haven't been able to get to church for many years.'

Cara's mother died before a nursing home bed was available. Perhaps Cara will now be better prepared and more hopeful if the time comes for her own move to a nursing home.

ON REFLECTION…

The pre-admission visit

Each nursing home has its own mechanism for managing the waiting list, facilitating referrals and negotiating with prospective residents and their families. As this is often the very first encounter with the aged-care system, it requires thoughtful and careful planning, comprehensive procedures and, most important of all, understanding and empathy for those seeking information. If it were merely information that families require, an application form could be mailed to them to secure a place on the waiting list. However, at this point in a person's life, information is not the primary need. When the pre-admission visit is conducted in a public area, or in an unprofessional manner, when the completing of forms takes precedence over conversation about the prospective resident, then society's negative attitudes towards aged care are reinforced. When the visit commences with a reassuring tone ('Tell me something about the person who is needing a nursing home bed'), when open-ended questions of feeling and attitudes take their place along with gathering of demographic data, the *person* needing full-time care becomes the central focus. Families who are encouraged to express their concerns, ('Do you have any questions or anxieties about taking this step towards nursing home admission?') may have some of their fears dispelled. 'Yes, I do have fears. I've experienced guilt, rage, resentment, horror, denial — the whole gamut of emotions. They're all still there, but being able to express them has made a difference.' Although time consuming, this kind of discussion is ultimately far more important than which labels are to be used for the resident's clothing.

The pre-admission visit is about hearing the person's story as well as giving and receiving information. While matters of time and efficiency need to be acknowledged, the very personal nature of this process needs to be undertaken with sensitivity. It is therefore important that the person responsible for this process is professionally suited to the challenge.

Promoting life in the nursing home

Managing the waiting list and facilitating unhurried discussions with prospective residents and their families is a resource problem not recognised by the current funding mechanism. However, it is vitally important not only for the resident who will ultimately gain admission to the particular nursing home, but for promoting a positive view of nursing homes in the wider community.

Professional managers, taking pride in their role, have both the privilege and the responsibility to reverse the current tide of ageism, to counter community attitudes of horror and dismay at the prospect of nursing home admission and to reverse the negative stereotypes of old age.

'You have given me hope,' said one family member, after hearing the positive emphasis placed on all aspects of living and dying in a nursing home.

THE ABSENT FAMILY: WOULDN'T YOU THINK THEY'D VISIT AT A TIME LIKE THIS?

Trevor: Is there no end to his demands?

Usually Trevor enjoyed a hearty breakfast. The day he left his tray untouched the charge nurse took one look at him and knew it was time to call his wife in quickly. Even so, she hesitated before dialling the number, recalling the many times Mrs Gill had not responded to requests for visits. Surely today would be different.

But Mrs Gill was annoyed to be woken. She was also annoyed that Trevor had chosen today to die because she had an appointment to have her hair permed. After that she had agreed to mind her niece's children. She just didn't know if she could manage to come in. 'Really!' her tone of voice seemed to say, 'Is there no end to his demands?'

In the absence of family, the staff rallied round Trevor as he died. For a man who had reputedly led his family a merry dance in his drinking days, the Trevor we knew was usually gentle, softly spoken and withdrawn. His career as an alcoholic had obviously brought marked changes to his personality, but that was past history now.

In a subtle, indirect way Mrs Gill had let us know of her endurance as Trevor's wife. By the time Trevor came to the nursing home their relationship was also 'indirect'. On her rare visits she brought a basket of special food that sat proudly on the locker saying, 'There is someone who remembers Trevor's previous appetites', but then she turned her back on Trevor to gossip with other visiting wives. She never seemed to talk to him, nor did he acknowledge her. After her visits the food looked strangely out of place to us, but Trevor still enjoyed it.

Perhaps we were unrealistic expecting her to visit the day Trevor died. In the end she did come in, but only after her own activities were complete — and that was too late for Trevor. When Mrs Gill discovered Trevor had died, she seemed annoyed. She pulled a hastily wrapped slice of cake from her basket. It was obviously meant for Trevor but she said to the nurse, 'You might as well have this.' It was like the consolation prize, but it was no consolation to us, we would rather have had Trevor back.

ON REFLECTION…

The culture of visiting

The way to visit a patient in hospital is part of our cultural knowledge, as is the behaviour expected from the patient. We disrupt our normal routine to attend the bedside with flowers and magazines and are acknowledged by the grateful patient for our friendship and thoughtful attention. Rewarded for our trouble, we pay proper attention to the patient's condition and progress, then spend the visit chatting about things of mutual interest. We are relieved if the patient's hospital stay is short, as hospital visiting is a deviation from our normal social interaction and a strain for most people. However, when the illness is prolonged, visiting may become much more difficult.

Visiting a resident in a nursing home may represent the extreme situation, often requiring long-term commitment. Visits tend to reduce in frequency, particularly when there is no reward for visiting, such as a grateful patient or satisfying conversation.

When the resident is difficult to visit, due to altered behavioural responses or a reduced ability to interact, it takes determination and intense loyalty for a family to continue regular visits. If the relationship was already strained due to unresolved past conflict, visiting the resident may be an unpleasant task which is soon put to the bottom of the list of 'things to do this week'.

For close family members who feel it their duty to visit, non-attendance or reduced visits may result in feelings of guilt. In order to forget this uncomfortable emotion, the needs of the resident may also be forgotten. This can be rationalised in many ways: 'She's getting such good care in the nursing home' or 'I only seem to upset her when I go'. Guilt may also be dealt with by symbolic acts of care, such as Mrs Gill's extravagant gifts of food.

Staff support for visitors

Sometimes staff attitudes can add to the reluctance of a relative to visit. Cool or openly hostile behaviour from staff is not conducive to repeated visits. As it is not possible to know what relationship residents and their visitors have enjoyed (or not enjoyed) in the past, we cannot hope to understand reasons for distant or abandoning behaviour. We cannot fix relationships which broke down long ago; deathbed reconciliation usually belongs in the movies. Much as we might wish, we cannot make someone else visit in a way that satisfies our need to see the resident loved, cherished or forgiven.

Sometimes families find it difficult to face a resident due to feelings of guilt, confusion about the visitor's role or lack of intimacy in the past. Staff may facilitate greater openness between resident and family by encouraging family members to talk about their feelings in an atmosphere of acceptance.

The rhythm of the resident's daily nursing home life is different from the life once shared with family. Increasing lack of response, withdrawal or altered behaviour may alienate even closest family members. Even if this occurs, residents with few visitors are rarely abandoned. As with Trevor, often the staff, other residents and volunteers form the resident's new family. When infrequent visitors do attend, all we can do is welcome them on the resident's behalf, encourage open communication and offer appropriate support.

Pat: She never used to be like this

Pat is dying slowly. Often she lies quiet and withdrawn in her bed, but at times rises up like a toothless dragon, loud and aggressive. She no longer recognises her only and devoted son, Alf, who cared for her at home for many years.

Today Alf has had a difficult visit. Pat is restless and irritable. 'Mum, I'm not Reg! I'm Alf! Dad's been dead for 20 years. Please lie down. You're disturbing the lady in the other bed.'

In response, Pat strikes him angrily with her tiny fist and Alf, embarrassed, says to the nurse: 'She never used to be like this. She was the most gentle, loving mother and a real lady. She wouldn't hurt a fly. I hate to see her like this. Nothing I say makes sense to her. I go home exhausted and then I resolve not to come in the next day. But then I feel guilty if I don't come. It's funny, some days she's quiet and gentle, just like she used to be. Then I could sit with her for hours.'

ON REFLECTION…

Educating the visitor

If Alf's conflict between the mother he remembers and the mother she's become is not resolved, he may stop visiting altogether, even when death is imminent. There are many ways staff can support and assist visitors, like Alf, who feel awkward. It is part of our role as residents' advocate to assist visitors to visit. Alf's greatest need may have been for basic information about dementia and cognitive changes to help him understand the changes in his mother and so separate the person he loves from her disease. He may also have benefited from a frank discussion about the changes foreshadowed as death approaches.

Families as a resource

Families are a great source of information and represent potential allies in the challenge of caring for unpredictable or uncommunicative residents. Once better informed about his mother's illness, Alf may become a valuable resource. Involving Alf in planning his mother's care, by explanation of her daily routine and consultation about change, may help him understand her life in the nursing home. Instead of feeling anxious and ending the visit, Alf may identify a pattern to his mother's changing cognition or even identify causes of irritable reactions that come from her past history.

Alf may also benefit from an opportunity to recall memories of his mother as she was before the onset of her disease. In compiling or updating Pat's social history he may begin to separate old from new, an essential step towards accepting Pat as she is now, rather than longing for her as she was.

The specifics of visiting

Each family is unique in the way they manage their visits to the nursing home. Some will need help and support from staff and volunteers, others will not. However there are few visitors who do not benefit from practical hints about how to visit a frail, dying resident, particularly when dementia is involved.

Behaviours that were normal and natural at home may seem inappropriate in the nursing home. Family members may need 'permission' to touch their relative; they may also need specific information about how to hold and stroke her so as not to cause pain. They may enjoy gently massaging her skin if this seems to soothe; they may also benefit from continued encouragement. They may wish to draw the curtains for a private time together or, where facilities have a small lounge, to use this for visiting rather than the public space of the main lounge. They may be delighted to bring in special music, or even sing to the resident. They need information about how she perceives the world and whether she is likely to hear their voices, even if she is unable to respond.

Just as it is difficult for staff to learn to interact with residents isolated by dementia, brain damage or depression, families need suggestions as to how to make their visits meaningful and how to maximise communication with their resident. Involving the family in the care of the resident may provide enormous satisfaction both for family and resident. When death approaches they may be able to continue that important physical communication to the last.

Joan: They used to visit often

In the early stages of Joan's dementia she continued to respond warmly and with recognition to her many visitors, even if she couldn't remember their names. As the disease progressed she became hesitant and stumbling, turning her face away even from her two daughters, preferring her own inner world to the external world of conversation. The number of visitors decreased; one daughter said she was too busy with her own family, leaving the other to visit often and to work hard at retaining a relationship with her mother. This was more often via one-sided conversations and attempts to concentrate on photo albums.

Consultations with the charge nurse centred on mother's needs — new clothes, clothing protectors for meal times, comfortable night wear and a doona to replace the weighty blankets. Emotional issues were not broached. Mother was discussed in a tone slightly removed, as if discussing some anonymous patient. But mother was patient, she just sat by her bed most of the time, sometimes singing funny little tunes from a world known only to herself.

Over time, we saw less and less of either daughter, or any other family members. Grandchildren went on with their lives, Joan went on with hers, quietly but slowly dying. When she spent most days in bed, we were not surprised that she developed pneumonia. It was difficult to contact any of the family: one daughter had moved, the other was overseas. At Christmas, we only knew Joan's family had visited by the flowers at the bedside, an open tin of sweets and a card, 'From all the family'. Even though we read it to her as we turned and changed her, it was impossible to know if she heard or understood.

Joan was still alive some months later. Although her needs seemed to have changed little it was time to formally review her care. We felt the review would not take long. As a formality the family had been notified but no-one expected them to attend; we hadn't seen them for a long time. Staff responsible for the review felt resentful that in the absence of family members they would have to assume greater responsibility for planning Joan's care. So it was to our surprise that Joan's oldest daughter, Beverley, appeared in the foyer on the morning of the review.

She was obviously on edge, never having been asked to a meeting before. Was this meeting going to be difficult? Had staff noticed she hardly ever visited these days? What if her mother was to be moved out of the nursing home? Had the funding been cut? Beverley felt acutely embarrassed that, although her mother had been in the nursing home for several years, she had never met the 'new' director of nursing or any of the other staff present.

Beverley relaxed when the purpose of the review was explained to her. No-one rebuked her for not visiting and each component of her mother's care was discussed separately to highlight concerns or ways of improving her care. Reassured and becoming more relaxed, Beverley was able to paint a brief verbal picture of the mother she knew before dementia had changed her. Staff were moved by the passionate description of her mother as an outgoing, proud and assertive women who had been a teacher, a strong advocate for women's rights and involved in political and community issues. Beverley recounted the profound grief felt by the family as they prayed their mother would not survive the stroke she suffered some years earlier.

'We couldn't bear it when she was just a shell of her former self and didn't recognise us any more. That was four years ago and we still haven't got over it. Sometimes I drive the 20 kilometres from home to visit her, reach the door of the nursing home, and, without coming in, turn and drive all the way home in tears. I worry that you think I'm uncaring but I care so much I just can't bear to visit.'

She went on to speak of her son and daughter, both in their twenties. 'They just don't know how to visit. Mum used to help them with their schoolwork (maths was her specialty) but now they don't know what to say to her. They'll never forget her. I just tell them to remember her the way she was.'

Having listened to Beverley express her sadness and confusion, staff tried gently to draw her into the present by encouraging her participation in planning her mother's care. Slowly Beverley could perceive a role for herself as the main family carer. Perhaps she could send flowers if unable to visit. Even if her mother could not understand, staff could see her tangible expression of care. Beverley said she did not feel at home in the nursing home and she had never been shown where to make herself a cup of tea, so strategies were suggested to help overcome her feelings of isolation. Perhaps she could be introduced to other families who visited? She was also reminded that families were welcome to celebrate special occasions, such as birthdays, in the nursing home, involving the resident even if that resident was not able to acknowledge the event.

As a result of Beverley's participation in her mother's review, nursing home staff learned an important lesson: it is easy to make unfair and inaccurate judgements based on assumptions. The experience of empathic listening provided a reminder that a relative's absence does not necessarily mean a lack of care.

ON REFLECTION…

When a family stops visiting

There may be many reasons why a previously attentive family stops visiting. Ageing visitors may themselves experience difficulty with mobility. If this is the case we can keep them involved and informed by regular phone contact. Not all families are devoted, or wish to continue regular visiting. In the absence of warm relational bonds it may be enough for family to know their relative is well cared for to feel their duty is done.

Sometimes family members resign themselves to the death of the older person, grieving and separating prematurely. The grief at losing a beloved person to dementia or other related disorders may be such that visiting what they perceive to be 'the shell of her former self' is unbearable, even when the resident is dying. This defence against the pain of loss has the unfortunate effect of leaving the one who is dying alone, cut off from previous emotional supports.

If family visits cease it may be appropriate for a suitably qualified staff member or chaplain to make a phone call or home visit. Appropriate assistance, such as arranging volunteer transport or discussion of grief issues, may prompt a resumption of visits. Most often we will never know the reason or combination of reasons behind cessation of visiting. All we can do in those circumstances is try to maintain contact on the resident's behalf, welcome family when they do visit and fill the gap ourselves as nursing home staff often do. Perhaps that is a part of the carer's role in a culture where the elderly are misunderstood or devalued, sometimes even by their families.

QUALITY ISSUES FOR ENHANCED PRACTICE

The gerontic nurse

- Thorough assessment of family process provides guidance to staff, particularly in identifying the implications of past relationships for continued visiting.
- Next of kin details should include whether or not family wish to be contacted immediately if the resident's condition changes or when death occurs.

Management

- A comprehensive assessment form includes expected visiting patterns by relatives and/or friends; it may also include family's responses to nursing home admission.
- Visitors' support groups may include a welcoming committee consisting of families of other residents who are prepared to welcome new families into the nursing home.

- Information books from external sources, for example the Alzheimer's Association, may be offered to relatives who need assistance in communicating and visiting.

Indirect carers

- Volunteers may play an important role in supporting visitors.
- Indirect care staff, such as domestic, cleaning and laundry staff normalise the nursing home environment. A friendly comment or a moment of conversation with a visitor while cleaning in the bedroom or lounge may be all that is needed to make an uncomfortable or lonely visitor feel welcome.

CULTURAL CONSIDERATIONS: BREAD OF LIFE

Joe's family visited every day without fail to feed him food 'from the old country'. Even though he coughed and spluttered on the soup, Joe opened his mouth every time, drinking down their devotion and love. We were puzzled by Joe's well-informed family exposing him to the risk of aspiration pneumonia, but our observations were made with the eyes of another culture.

A member of Joe's family visited every day at lunch time to feed him. They brought special food from home. In the words of Joe's son, 'There's nothing wrong with the food in the nursing home, it's just that Dad likes the way Mum makes things, like in the old country.'

This son was 40 years of age, a second-generation Australian, a professional man, and so committed to ensuring his father received family food that he even took time out from his busy schedule to take his turn ladling spoon after spoon of home-made pasta, soup or noodles into his Dad's mouth.

Dad was 80. He had been a migrant factory worker and, before that, a subsistence farmer in the old country. Following his stroke he existed in the nursing home in a chronic, passive state, not even responding to his family as far as we could tell. Except that he always opened his mouth for the next spoonful of food. Perhaps that's how he took in their love.

Day after day the family appeared. Often it was Joe's wife, who was shy and smiling and dressed in black from head to foot. We still don't know what her hair was like because it was always hidden by the black scarf she wore. Sometimes one of the eight adult children accompanied her, sometimes one of the children came alone. Always at lunch time, and always with a basket of steaming food.

At lunch time there was always a still, intent figure at the bedside, silently spooning in food. After a while we stopped saving Joe's nursing home lunch, there didn't seem much point. How he could be so inactive, eat so much and remain tiny was a mystery to his family. But, day by day, he seemed to become more wizened, until one nurse could pick him up easily and turn him without any effort. It seemed obvious to the staff that Joe's system was failing and that his death was approaching.

Joe's dysphagia seemed less of a problem when his family fed him, but he still spluttered, especially on soup. We tried to warn his wife about Joe aspirating the special soup from the old country and getting pneumonia but she just smiled. And if one of the children were with her they would say, 'He likes it so much. And look, he hardly ever chokes if we feed him.'

The day came when Joe's usually mild productive cough became a torrent. He coughed until he was cyanosed and he had a fever. The doctor confirmed what we already knew: Joe had aspiration pneumonia. Still Joe's wife came. She tried to coax him to take a little pasta or some special soup. But the pasta remained in his mouth and the soup dribbled down his old chin or sprayed out into the room during a paroxysm of coughing. The family wanted Joe to have antibiotics so he could be made well enough to be fed again. Joe's wife was frantic, his sons came in morning and night and just stood beside the bed not knowing what to do with the hands that were normally so busy feeding him. The doctor reluctantly prescribed antibiotics.

'What can I do?' he said sadly. 'I've known Joe and Maria for 40 years, since they arrived in Australia. I've cared for all the children. They talk to me in Italian and beg me to make him well again. I can't say there's no point in antibiotics because he's dying, it's a cultural thing. If I don't give him medication they'll just find another doctor who will.'

However, for Joe, pneumonia was the 'old man's friend'. Or perhaps Joe was just tired of all that chewing, tired of staying alive for his family. After an initial response to the drugs he deteriorated. Even so his wife appeared every day with a basket full of food and hope. Every day she held the spoon to his lips and cried.
The day before Joe died she didn't come in. One of the sons came early the next day, before work, 'just to check on Dad'. He came out crying. 'I've told Dad that Mum isn't going to bring in the food any more.' Joe died that afternoon.

ON REFLECTION…

Appropriate cultural knowledge is essential to holistic care

Australia is a society made of many cultural groups. It is therefore not appropriate for aged care to be based on the customs, norms and values of one group. People of different cultures hold different views on such issues as ageing and death. In more traditional cultures aged people may be afforded a special place within the family. While we admired the devotion of Joe's family, it was not until close to his death that we finally understood our own cultural bias.

Cultural diversity enriches the nursing home. Entering the world of another culture by understanding is a privilege as well as an essential ingredient of holistic care.

Spiritual issues related to death and dying

Among some cultural groups it is not acceptable to speak of death to the person who is dying. This may have some impact on the plan of care when a cognitively intact resident is diagnosed as terminally ill. However, even though different ethnic groups have distinct concerns, expecting a family to behave in a particular way because of their cultural origins is stereotyping.

As part of getting to know the family of any cultural origin (well before the crisis of impending death) inquiries should be made as to that particular family's expectations of terminal care for the resident in regard to religious or spiritual requirements.

Interpreting — who should do it?

Not speaking the dominant language of the culture may predispose the resident or the resident's family to a feeling of powerlessness and isolation. To communicate with Maria it was necessary to use an interpreter. Mostly we used Joe's adult sons.

When sensitive issues of resident care are to be discussed it may be more effective to use a professional interpreter. Family members are often too involved to be impartial, and also have a right to be fully involved in the discussion, not preoccupied with interpreting. However, some families have a strong commitment to managing their own communication and may distrust professionals. In the end the question of whether or not to use a professional interpreter is one for each family to decide.

Who should intervene?

There may be times when concerns about a resident's welfare need to be raised with family. If such negotiations are transcultural it is unfair to expect one family member to represent our concerns to a relative from another generation. Genuine concerns for the welfare of a resident are better raised by a mutually respected, non-family member.

For Joe's family, feeding Joe, despite his poor swallowing reflex, was of paramount importance. To us it fell into the realms of unacceptable risk. Provided this cultural difference is fully discussed and documented, with the nursing home's guidelines clearly directed by the doctor, then staff and families may learn to live together with their differences. A clash of culture may, in some circumstances, provide the opportunity for a mutually acceptable outcome.

How is our care perceived?

Sometimes unexpected reactions to the well-meaning care we offer may signify a misinterpretation of our words and gestures by residents and families from a different culture. Differing norms, values and cultural experience may mean an unexpected response to our professional roles. How are health-care workers regarded in the resident's country of origin? How would a dying elderly person be cared for in their own country? What do they expect of us? Our way of doing things may, at best, seem perplexingly foreign.

QUALITY ISSUES FOR ENHANCED PRACTICE

The gerontic nurse

- A comprehensive cultural assessment provides information about specific cultural values and how such values apply to the individual family.
- Specific care arising from the assessment is then included in the care plan; thus providing guidance for all staff.
- Family members may benefit from discussion with the speech pathologist who conveys the processes of assessing the resident's swallowing difficulties and offers recommendations. In some instances it may be helpful to have family present when the assessment is made.
- Discussion with families may focus on alternative means of caring for a dying resident, where a previous ritual of care, such as the daily provision of culturally specific food, is no longer appropriate.

Management

- Comprehensive in-service education for staff includes issues in transcultural care and the provision of relevant literature. Both direct and indirect carers should be encouraged to attend.
- Written policies should include what kind of ethnic mix is appropriate for the nursing home, with respect to both staff and residents.
- It may be helpful in caring for residents whose first language is not English for management to formally identify the different languages understood and/or spoken by various members of staff.

Indirect carers

- Indirect carers should attempt to familiarise themselves with residents' specific cultural requirements. Such knowledge may avoid embarrassment or offence when working in proximity of the resident's bedroom.

- If the nursing home contains a number of residents from a specific cultural group, it may be possible to provide an ethno-specific meal choice on a regular basis. Residents' families may be willing to assist with advice or traditional recipes.
- Volunteers who are fluent in languages other than English may provide an important service to residents and families who find it difficult to communicate in English.

VISITORS: I'M NOT THE ONLY ONE

After many days at Martha's bedside, Bill and Ruth were fatigued and in need of care themselves but the busy staff could only offer passing sympathy. Bill and Ruth were undemanding but clearly needed more than this. When they guiltily left Martha's bedside to join other staff and residents at Happy Hour ('just for a minute or two') they were able to return replenished to Martha and settle more comfortably to their vigil.

Alf was at his wits' end when it came to visiting his mother. Far from dying quietly and with dignity, her dementia-related behaviour meant he felt embarrassed about her rather than loving towards her most of the time he was with her. Reluctantly he agreed to attend a relatives' information session on the subject of dementia. There he gained more than just information.

In both instances, family members found what they needed in the informal community of the regular visitors to the nursing home. This valuable resource of support and solidarity is easily overlooked but can be a powerful component of holistic care.

Ruth, Bill and Martha: A little help from our friends

Ruth and Bill were farmers. They had been called 'down to town' to Bill's dying mother many times, only to return to the cows when Martha rallied. This time, after a vigil of many days, Martha was finally about to die, but she was taking her time.

Though Bill was patient and gentle with Martha, he looked out of place at the bedside, uncomfortable in the unfamiliar suit, big farmer's hands fidgeting. Inactivity didn't suit Ruth either, she looked as if she should be at home baking in her kitchen. They were people of few words. While Martha dozed comfortably thanks to good analgesia, they sat straight and silent. There were no other family members to share the waiting, or to give Bill and Ruth a break.

It was not until after five uncomfortable days of stoic and faithful attendance at Martha's bedside that they could be convinced to take a much-needed break. It was Thursday and Happy Hour had just begun on the floor above. The sound of bright music floated down the stairs. 'Where's that nice music coming from?' Bill asked a nurse wistfully. At first they said they couldn't go up there away from Martha. The nurse suggested they would not be missed for a few minutes and promised to call if Martha needed them. 'Come on, I'll introduce you,' and away they went.

At first they sat stiffly together as they had at Martha's bedside. Bill brightened visibly when he was offered a beer. Soon Ruth had a tea towel doubling as an apron at her generous waist and was busy at the sink washing up. Then they joined in the community singing and began to nod at some of the others in the room. Some of the downstairs residents recognised them and asked after Martha. One of the volunteers knew a bit about cattle. Ruth and George's wife talked knitting. Time passed.

Returning to Martha's bed they looked 20 years younger. Though they resumed the same positions beside her they seemed less out of place. After Happy Hour they looked like part of the community.

ON REFLECTION…

The untapped resource of the informal community

Regular visitors and volunteers interacting with staff and residents make up the informal community of the nursing home. When there isn't enough time for staff to care for emotionally needy families, this informal community can be a source of support. Social interaction provides access to this support, either formally at nursing home functions or informally when staff introduce visiting family members to others. One regular visitor said, 'If only we'd been introduced to another family on the day Mum was admitted I wouldn't have felt so alone.'

The normalising effect of social interaction

Prolonged visits can be stressful, as anyone who has sat by a bed day after day will know — particularly if the occupant is not responsive. Humans are social creatures. The stress reduction of social interaction for Bill and Ruth was obvious. After a few words of normal conversation about the weather or the football, they were no longer isolated sitters at a bedside but an acknowledged part of a warm and caring community. When they returned to Martha's bedside they were more able to endure the wait and were more available to her when she needed them.

Encouraging families to care for themselves

It is important that families have somewhere to retreat when they need a break; some small place visitors can call their own for a few minutes' respite. The surroundings don't have to be grand, even some chairs in the dining room or a table and chairs outside in the garden. By providing such an area, staff convey to families that taking a break when they need it is an important part of caring for themselves so they can continue to care for the one who is dying.

Networking as a practical means of support

Friendships made at the nursing home often result in practical support between families; providing transport, sharing information about resources, attendance at a resident's funeral and maintaining phone contact during bereavement.

Alf: 'I'm not the only one'

On the charge nurse's recommendation, Alf reluctantly attended a 'relatives information night' to hear the guest speaker on dementia. He was too shy to ask questions, but took some pamphlets home to read. Although attending the evening function seemed a bit strange to him at first, there were staff there he knew who made him feel at home. He met Sophie's family that evening.

Two days later they met again in the nursing home while visiting. Sophie was up and wandering around, not interested in sitting down and being visited, so Alf suggested Sophie's family might like to join him for a cup of tea in the dining room. They talked freely and without embarrassment about dementia, being more able to separate the person from the disease. Away from the residents they were struggling to visit, they all relaxed. In fact, they looked so companionable sitting around the table that Sophie stopped her wandering and sat down to tea with them for a few minutes. Alf returned to Pat's bedside, feeling supported and refreshed.

ON REFLECTION...

From the resident's point of view

Residents with dementia do not necessarily know they are in a nursing home. They do not, therefore, behave in the manner of a person sitting expectantly waiting for visiting time, and then respond as the one being visited. It may be reassuring to discuss this matter with some families who become easily offended and frustrated when their visits seem unappreciated. It may be more beneficial for the visitors to accompany a restless, wandering resident rather than expecting the resident to sit patiently. Families may also feel awkward and unsure when entering other areas of the nursing home, expecting their visits should be confined to the seating spaces in the lounge.

Nurturing relationships between regular visitors

It is in the informal nurturing of relationships that the nursing home develops as a community. Friendships can't be contrived, but opportunities can be created by: spontaneous introductions, relatives' support groups and social functions which involve both residents and families. Much can also be achieved by arranging the physical environment to create an ambience of openness and friendship. The attitude of staff and management towards the role of families is crucial to the development of informal support networks.

The solidarity and self-help of informal support networks

Because of their common concerns and problems, residents' families are able to meet each others' needs in a way staff cannot. Education, emotional and practical support and a sense of identification and solidarity through difficult times may be some of the benefits of bringing residents' families together. Staff who foster a sense of community enable families' needs to be met while decreasing families' dependence on staff.

QUALITY ISSUES FOR ENHANCED PRACTICE

The gerontic nurse

- When a new resident is admitted, a brief welcome may be arranged formally; for example, at morning or afternoon tea.
- Other family members may be asked whether they would like to take on the role of helping new visitors feel at home.
- Care and sensitivity are required when visitors spend a long time at the bedside; the offer of support and suggestion of other options may ease the tension.

Management

- Relatives appreciate being given a copy of the nursing home's activities program for the month, together with the invitation to attend any of the functions.
- A comprehensive induction/orientation program for families should include introduction to other families and residents. The induction process also includes welcoming families into specific areas of the nursing home, clearly identifying areas confined to staff.
- It may be helpful to designate to a particular person or small committee the responsibility of welcoming relatives and visitors to the nursing home.
- An institutional relationship with an agency such as the Alzheimer's Association provides families with opportunities to make use of external services' education and support, as well as access to up-to-date printed material to assist in understanding dementia.
- A welcome notice conveys the name of the new resident to the whole nursing home community and encourages families and friends to visit.

> **Indirect carers**
>
> - Volunteers may be willing to offer support to new families.
> - Activities staff may enlist the help of family members in certain activities, an involvement of equal benefit to the nursing home and the family member.

THE BEREAVEMENT VISIT: SEND MY LOVE TO ALL THE GIRLS

When Jimmy died suddenly after a fall in the nursing home it was the end of a long and close relationship between the staff and Jimmy's wife. Although all care had been exercised, staff felt guilty and upset, wishing his death could have been different. We worried about Jimmy's widow who had remained close and devoted to Jimmy, despite his confusion. We were concerned that the traumatic end to Jimmy's life might increase her distress. Although not funded, a bereavement visit was arranged to Jimmy's widow as continuation of our care.

Through the doorway she looked tiny, all shrunken with grief as if the death of her husband of 50 years had physically diminished her. The house was as spotless and white as the apron she took off as she showed me to the lounge used for entertaining guests. Matching her manner, it was a formal room and we sat carefully on the little-used 'best' furniture. I knew there would be no sharing of emotions in this room.

The conversation was stilted and polite. I expressed my sympathy, personally and on behalf of the staff, while she assessed me to see if I could be trusted with her memories. Gradually she relaxed and began to talk of Jimmy. When the tears came she made to wipe them away but allowed them to flow when she saw I accepted them.

Still she was holding back. After the first testing she took me a room deeper into her grief — the kitchen. She put the kettle on and began a tour of the house, pausing at significant places, each room a memory. 'This is where he fell over and hit his head. There was a step there, he was always so careful about it. When he fell I knew I couldn't look after him at home any more.'

That was my cue to raise the delicate matter of his fall in the nursing home, just before he died. There had been an autopsy; it had shown a fracture which had contributed to his death even though he had terminal cancer. She started justifying; remembering how hard it was for the nurses to keep him in bed when she wasn't there.

'He just wanted me there all the time. Of course I couldn't be, but I didn't worry because I knew he was being so well looked after.' Then came the bitterness and anger: 'The Coroner said I could ask for an inquest! But of course I didn't want that, all that trouble for the nursing home.' She paused for emphasis and stared at me hard. I took her point.

'It wasn't as though he wasn't well looked after. If I could only have had him here at home, I would have kept him in bed. If he'd known I was here and he was in his own bed he would have stayed there, never would have fallen. All he ever wanted was me, "Grace, Grace", he used to say, "you're the most beautiful girl in the world". And look at me now!' She laughed and blew her nose. '"Take me home," he used to say, but he knew I couldn't look after him here, not like the way you girls did at the nursing home.'

Again she paused, caught by the irony of her words. She needed to believe he'd had the best of care, better then she could give, but she believed his death was hastened by a fall he may not have had if he had been at home with her. She had wanted to care for him at home but couldn't and now she had to reconcile that with the site of care she had chosen falling short of her standards. She cried from sadness and guilt, feeling her care had not done justice to their love.

She told me the romantic story of their meeting at a country dance and how they had set off to the city to make a new life together, how they had bought this little cottage and raised their son here. Further and further back into their lives she went, telling me of his history and antecedents and hers, showing photos and treasured mementos of a life now over. The house was full of him, but sadly empty for this tiny widow on the beginning of her long journey in grief.

After a cup of tea and many more stories and tears she seemed a little lighter, less bowed by her grief and guilt. She thought she might go and visit one of the other recent widows from the nursing home. We walked up the white passage to the door and she told me she could never visit the nursing home again to see the staff she had come to know so well in sharing the care of her beloved Jimmy. 'So send my love to all the girls.' Her face clouded again and the tears welled up. 'If only I could have brought him home.'

ON REFLECTION...

Who does bereavement follow-up?

We cannot know the isolation and pain of elderly widows and widowers, cut off from society by the diminished mobility and social networks characteristic of ageing. Bereavement follow-up is regarded as an integral part of hospice care because patient and family are regarded as the unit of care. Bereavement support for family is simply an extension of the care given to the dying patient; therefore such programs as Widows' Groups are unquestionably part of the service. Nursing home funding does not provide for bereavement services, and bereavement follow-up is not recognised as part of our function. Whose is it?

How to support the bereaved without a formal program

When grieving relatives revisit the nursing home we have little time to offer them, for resident care is our funded priority. In aged care, where bereavement is concerned, it's a case of the living taking precedence over the dead.

If we are committed to providing holistic care for dying residents, innovative ways must be found to provide bereavement support for the families of recently deceased residents, ways which do not divert time and energy from the funded purpose of caring for living residents. Consider the following suggestions:

- Lend families literature about bereavement.
- If the home has a chaplain, he/she may be prepared to make a routine phone call to bereaved families and consider a home visit, if desired, as part of the pastoral role.
- In the absence of a chaplain, distressed families may be referred to local parishes, community bereavement organisations or counselling services.
- There may be times when referral of the bereaved to a doctor or counsellor is necessary. Read up about normal bereavement; learn to recognise the signs which indicate professional help is needed.
- Some family members may wish to become volunteers in the nursing home. This should preferably be delayed until after the initial stages of bereavement have passed. From experience, this type of volunteer seldom lasts out the bereavement period. However they may give valuable service during this time, while letting go of the nursing home in a legitimate and healthy manner.

- If the bereaved family wishes, they may maintain their link with the nursing home by continuing to receive copies of the newsletter. In this way they can keep up to date with news and hear about special events such as fetes, which may offer an opportunity for an informal return visit.

Families' needs

Each family is different. Some will continue visiting for a while, some will never want to return to the nursing home and will find even receiving a newsletter painful or intrusive. Part of our continuing sensitive care is to take our cue from them.

Saying goodbye to the resident's family

In most cases staff and families gradually relinquish contact once the resident, who was pivotal to their relationship, has died. Staff do not have the emotional resources to maintain contact with all the families of past residents, even though all are special in some way. Where the resident's death is unexpected, the abrupt end to the relationship may make saying goodbye more difficult for both staff and families. For Grace, losing Jimmy was compounded by the loss of friendships with staff, who had become her friends and family.

Staff need to consider how to 'finish off' without being intrusive. The need to let go does not mean our concern for these people we knew so well ceases when the resident dies. Legitimate finishing off may take the form of funeral attendance or a note of condolence to the family. It is rarely appropriate to visit families at home — the nursing home was the context of relationship and it should remain so. Unwanted intrusion by staff can be distressing for families. This being so, we need to ask whose needs are being met by such a visit?

Special circumstances

Grace's sense of loss was magnified by the circumstances of Jimmy's death. When there has been an incident which may contribute to the family's distress it is part of holistic care to follow through and give the family an opportunity to have their grievance heard. Anger and guilt are very much a part of normal bereavement, whatever the circumstances of death. Sometimes anger may be directed at staff irrationally, but then the emotions of bereavement are never rational.

Grace needed an opportunity to air her feelings about the care Jimmy received at the nursing home. Her veiled accusations were mixed with her own sense of guilt at not being able to care perfectly for him at home. To keep her guilt from being overwhelming she was unable to express anger directly to staff, needing to believe she had done the very best for her husband. An opportunity for healing was provided by the staff member listening, without judgement, to her sadness, anger and confusion.

QUALITY ISSUES FOR ENHANCED PRACTICE

The gerontic nurse

- The charge nurse is often the focus of contact for bereaved families and it is appropriate that a period of diminishing contact follows each resident's death.
- The charge nurse should have information about support groups or bereavement counselling services to offer families.
- A phone call from the charge nurse one or two days after the death may be a welcome sign of care by the family.

Management

- Where resources do not allow for a bereavement visit, a letter of condolence to the family of each deceased resident may include contact details of a community bereavement counsellor.
- Continued lobbying for resources is essential if nursing homes are to provide this important aspect of bereavement follow up.

Indirect carers

- A bereavement group may be arranged once or twice each year in which families of recently deceased residents may meet to share informally their experiences. Once such a group is initiated it may become volunteer-run, with 'recovered' widows (or widowers) taking responsibility for arranging meetings and issuing invitations.

- Where the nursing home has a chaplain, bereavement counselling becomes an important part of their role, providing sufficient resources are allocated.

COUPLES: THE MILK CARTER AND HIS WIFE

Nursing home admission may have profound, life-changing significance for a spouse, depending on the couple's history, their relationship and their expectations of separation and death. This was the case for Bob and Doris, married for 67 years and 'never ever apart, not even for one night'. The story of their unique life together challenges the kind of response required from the nursing home. Doris's attitude that this was to be their 'home away from home' reinforced her confidence that, even with this separation, they would not be apart.

Bob and Doris lived in the inner suburbs all their married life and Doris was proud of the fact they had never been apart. Bob had been a milk carter for 40 years until his retirement at the age of 65; their pattern of life never varied. Doris recalled those days as if it were yesterday. Their day started at 4 a.m. when the alarm summoned them to the breakfast table, set the night before. Doris had laid out Bob's clothes already, 'Bob cleaned his boots the night before, never missed!' When Doris waved him off to work she commenced her housework, food preparation and gardening. She also prepared food for their son and his disabled wife, who lived close by.

Now well into his eighties, Bob's emphysema and chronic pain from arthritis meant he was frail. His weight loss and difficulty in breathing made it hard to maintain his fiercely held independence. When signs of dementia appeared which Doris refused to acknowledge, the complications of incontinence and poor mobility made it apparent that Bob could no longer be managed at home. Bob's frequent falls left him covered with bruises and Doris realised after the last fall, which resulted in cracked ribs, that it was unfair to continually call their son to help at night.

On Bob's first day in the nursing home, Doris's mantra had a new audience, 'We've been married 67 years and never been apart.' She rationalised this enormous change in their lives with the confident statement: 'I don't call this being apart because I'll be here every day.' Keeping her promise, and in spite of her own health problems, Doris never missed a day in six months.

Now there was a variation in Doris's daily routine. She continued to rise at 4 a.m. 'to sweep the path and hose the front verandah'. After this, instead of sitting at the kitchen table, she lovingly ironed Bob's clean pyjamas, made her packed lunch, filled the thermos flask and was ready for the tram at 7.30 a.m. 'I like to be here to make sure he eats his breakfast.' Sitting in a comfortable chair beside Bob's bed with her knitting and the crossword, she kept a watchful eye on Bob's every movement. At 1 p.m., after she had settled Bob for his afternoon nap, Doris packed her belongings, ready for the 1.30 p.m. tram for home. What then? 'I do Bob's washing, go down the street for my messages, then make a hot thermos of soup and my sandwiches for tea, lock myself in for the night and hop into bed at five o'clock. I eat my tea while I listen to the wireless (it's good company). I'm usually asleep by seven or eight, and the alarm goes off again at 4 a.m.'

Some staff found Doris's constant presence a source of irritation. 'She sets herself up here just like it's her own place!' Others felt insecure or offended by Doris checking on all Bob's care. Some, like the cleaner, felt Bob needed more of his own space. 'I see Bob close his eyes as soon as the wife comes in. I know he's not asleep, he's just faking it. He's probably been under the thumb all these years and even now he can't get away from her!' Words of wisdom or the cleaner's imagination?

And what of Bob? It was Doris's perception that Bob had always directed her life; their closely shared history would not easily be interrupted. She described him as 'a wonderful protector' who accompanied her even to the corner shop, never let her dry a dish and was always concerned for her comfort. ' "You sit down and let me sweep the floor," he'd say.'

We never knew Bob's thoughts about Doris's reflections or his nursing home admission because he never spoke a word. The speech pathologist could give no reason for this but perhaps it was that Bob had said all he had to say and was now resigned to the last chapter of his life.

From the day of Bob's admission to the nursing home, Doris was convinced that each day would be his last. 'I don't think he's got much longer,' she would confide. When his deterioration became unmistakably rapid, Doris demanded hospital admission. 'I promised him I would never put him in an old men's home to die.' Staff at the acute hospital were sympathetic, agreeing to her wishes for intravenous fluids, treatment for his pneumonia and every possible intervention to reduce his fever. When it was evident that these measures were not life saving, negotiations commenced about his transfer back to the nursing home. Hospital doctors and staff explained the palliative measures available in the nursing home, gently convincing Doris that resuscitation measures were not advisable and not appropriate. After two days of bargaining, Doris made up her mind. However, her version of events was different from the hospital's: 'They kept waiting for me to make up my mind. They wanted to keep him at the hospital but I told them that the nurses at "the home" all loved him and wanted him back there, so they finally agreed to let him come back. I want him to be where all his things are.' All Bob's 'things' included several jars of faded plastic flowers, wedding photos, pictures cut out of magazines and some football trophies from his teen years. All these articles Doris had dusted tenderly each day, unwilling to trust them to the cleaning staff.

The nursing home had a carefully formulated palliative care policy, including the use of subcutaneous fluids in exceptional circumstances. It seemed a good palliative measure to offer for Bob because Doris could not bring herself to have the hospital's intravenous fluids 'switched off'. She was comforted by the knowledge that a continuous infusion of normal saline would meet Bob's hydration needs. At the staff team meeting, all agreed that this may bring Bob some physical comfort, while providing reassurance for Doris.

Doris showed the ambiguous feelings common to those who watch over the final days and hours of their loved ones. She hoped Bob would recover and yet she claimed to be prepared for his death. Afraid that she was not able to accept that Bob was dying, concerned staff arranged a meeting with Doris and her son to offer an opportunity for them to discuss their feelings and expectations and to describe the nursing home routine following death. The charge nurse was about to begin the discussion when Doris spoke up, 'I know it could be any hour now and while I don't want it to happen I'm prepared for it.' It was gently explained that when Bob stopped breathing, indicating his heart had stopped pumping, there would be nothing more we could do in the sense of reviving him. 'I know all that,' she said. 'They told me at the hospital they would have to pounce on his chest and I was horrified. He's already got cracked ribs. I told them Bob wouldn't want that, and neither would I.' With that cleared up, the discussion became easier. There would be many other elements of nursing care to offer him and yes, she could give him sips of lemonade.

The discussion turned to what might happen after Bob's death. There would be no hurry to remove his body, Doris was assured. She could stay and say her goodbyes until she felt ready to go, unlike what would happen in the busy hospital setting. 'Oh, yes, I know what that's like. They'd be wanting someone else in the bed even while it was still warm!' She also welcomed the reassurance that she had done everything possible to care for Bob and that his death would not be of the 'old men's home' variety she had feared.

True to her word, when Doris was notified of Bob's imminent death in the early hours of the morning, she arrived within the hour. Her visit extended to several hours following his death, her actions carefully measured, consistent with her lifestyle and with her self-expectations and what she believed Bob would have wanted. 'We've often talked about all this you know, we knew this time had to come.' Night staff offered non-intrusive care and support, leaving this last exchange between Doris and Bob to the privacy it deserved. If the cleaner had been present, he may have altered his previous judgement.

After several hours the nurses, in their desire to be helpful, were anxious to pack all Doris and Bob's belongings. 'You go home and rest, we'll see to packing all this.' However, this was an affront to Doris's housekeeping routines and to the final act of her care for Bob. Never having been apart for 67 years, never ceasing to look after his clothes and possessions, this final act was not to be hurried, nor was it to be placed in the hands of others.

The funeral service was to take place from the nursing home chapel. Doris confessed Bob was never a religious man but nevertheless he would like a decent burial and she would be glad of the chaplain's services. Having no specific religious sentiments to express, Doris was keen that the chaplain should emphasise the wonderful care she and Bob had experienced over the six months. 'Don't you forget to thank them,' she reminded the chaplain.

Thoughtful as always, Doris wanted the flowers from the funeral to be taken to 'Bob's bed' ready for the 'new man'. No longer concerned about indecent haste in filling the bed, Doris was resigned to the fact there would soon be someone else to take Bob's place.

ON REFLECTION...

Bereavement follow-up

Amid the routine busy-ness of the nursing home, there is seldom time to consider the grieving families of recently deceased residents. It was not known how Doris was coping: no more pyjamas to iron, no more breakfasts and lunches shared with her beloved Bob. What reason would there be now for her to get up at 4 a.m.? We wondered what she would do with all those hours, six hours a day for six months, that had been devoted to visiting Bob? We hoped she would come and visit. We thought we had done well to get Doris through Bob's dying and the immediate activities following his death. For some staff, this would be a fitting end to the relationship. For others, thoughts of Doris's lonely widowhood would remain.

The old men's home

Doris's attitude changed from fear of an 'old men's home' to accepting the nursing home care available. For all her complimentary remarks about the nursing home, she continued to have this euphemism in her mind until Bob's hospital admission. Hospital visiting was not quite the same. 'Oh, they're very nice and all that. But I don't feel at home; you get the feeling you're in the way and they never tell you what they're doing to Bob.' It seemed the change occurred when the palliative care team described the treatment available in the nursing home. For Doris, death in an 'old men's home' would be the death of loneliness and isolation, the slow death of dehydration, death without any pain relief, death without professional supervision, death without dignity. When it was explained the nursing home could continue to administer fluids (Doris was not bothered by the difference between intravenous and subcutaneous) as well as the morphine infusion, Doris wanted the transfer to take place without delay.

Continued relationships

It is not unknown for staff to maintain relationships with the family following a nursing home death. There are some staff who live close to Doris. Will they be planning to call in on her? Would such relationships create unhealthy dependency? Should such visiting continue with the permission of the nursing home and be documented as follow-up bereavement care? Or should it be regarded as a private, social arrangement? When such informal arrangements are made, staff may continue to visit out of a sense of duty, long after the appropriate time for closure. Nurses are not generally educated about bereavement and therefore may not be skilled in assisting Doris with her grief, nor with concluding the relationship. However, in the absence of funding for bereavement support, informal arrangements are bound to occur.

Making herself at home

Much is said about aged-care facilities offering a homelike atmosphere. Perhaps Doris had read this philosophy in the nursing home brochure? Or perhaps she had never contemplated a situation where she would be separated from Bob for most of the day. Whatever her reasons, Doris established her routine of 6 hours per day at the bedside without feeling the need to seeking anyone's advice or showing any sign that her presence may be questioned. Her place was 'never to be apart' from Bob.

Doris came to regard Room No. 7 as her second home. Her constant presence annoyed many staff, 'She can't impose her own routine on us. She should adapt to *our* routine while she's here.' Others were more sympathetic and considered her presence appropriate. 'You make yourself at home,' they said. Her way of being there certainly challenged the philosophy of the nursing home to provide a 'homelike atmosphere'. There were many indications that Doris interpreted this quite literally.

Chaplain's services

Because Bob had 'None' marked in the spot for religious denomination it had never occurred to anyone to call the nursing home chaplain prior to Bob's death. It may have been wise to offer both the chaplain and Bob, the opportunity of meeting each other at least once before the funeral. Doris also may have experienced greater continuity rather than having a stranger arrive at her house to discuss the details of the service. When assessment for spiritual care and pastoral support are defined merely by the ticking or crossing of a 'denominational box', opportunities for review may be overlooked. Such review would allow the question to be raised again as circumstances change, particularly in the context of death.

Long-term relationships

Contemporary society is characterised by short-term relationships, statistics showing a high divorce rate and a variety of relationships and living arrangements between couples. On hearing of Bob and Doris's 67-year marriage, one nurse commented, 'I'm lucky if I stay in a relationship for 67 hours!' Given the changes in society's patterns, it may become increasingly rare to find couples who have known no other relationship but the intimacy of marriage for 50 or more years. In such circumstances, it may be difficult for carers to understand the couple's distinct and unique needs. Their lifestyle as described by Doris would not easily fit all staff's frame of reference, leading to curiosity and incredulity. However, in accepting the challenge to provide Bob with holistic care in the context of his family and his previous history, staff need to try to step outside their own frame of reference. This entails a conscious effort to understand Bob's nursing home admission by 'entering the story' as told by Doris and adapting the care to meet their particular needs. Increased understanding may have led to greater consistency of staff attitudes.

'I know some of them think I'm in the way,' Doris had said.

QUALITY ISSUES FOR ENHANCED PRACTICE

The gerontic nurse

- Thorough assessment of family concerns, both on admission and regularly afterwards, should include resident and family's attitude towards hospitalisation. Open discussion may yield valuable insights to guide decision-making.
- Clear communication between hospital and nursing home, especially when the issue of palliative care arises, is enhanced by careful documentation and regular phone contact.
- When death approaches, busy nurses are usually focused on immediate procedures. Even when admission data clearly state 'no religion', the services of a chaplain may quite properly be offered in a non-coercive manner.
- To avoid inconsistency of staff attitude towards various visiting patterns, the needs of the family have a place in the care plan, thereby providing a formal plan to be followed.
- Careful and regular review of the plan in a team environment allows the opportunity to discuss difficulties as they arise and to negotiate changes as required.

Management

- Clear protocols and procedures for palliative care communicated to other health agencies greatly assists decision making, especially regarding transfer from hospital to nursing home.
- A policy regarding follow-up visits by staff may guide and assist staff who wish to continue visiting a family following death of a resident.
- Careful planning is needed to provide some means of support for relatives to mix with others if they wish, and to have space away from the bedside when visiting.

Indirect carers

- It is clear from this story that the cleaner had his own judgements about Bob and Doris. It is important such comments are not given an inappropriate status. Other stories show the very important and acceptable involvement of indirect carers; however, sensitivity is needed to place such informal comments in perspective. Some indirect carers may benefit from education about making judgements or drawing hasty conclusions.

UNFINISHED BUSINESS: COMING BACK

In nursing homes and hostels, lifelong friendships are sometimes established among residents, friends, relatives and staff. This section provides some 'snapshots' of relationships between visitors and people in the nursing home; relationships that continue after the death of a resident. It also includes an example of missed opportunities for continued friendship. Suggestions are made for a type of care that encourages communication between the nursing home community and the broader community, yielding important societal value.

He never came back

After twice-daily visits for five years, George acknowledged it would be hard to stop coming to the nursing home: 'My car automatically turns in this direction.' George had made many friends among staff, residents and other visitors. Because his mother's conversation was limited by her dementia, he found it hard to know what to say. After a few minutes with her, he would spend an hour talking to his other friends in the nursing home.

When George's mother died, he returned to the nursing home straight after the funeral with his arms full of flowers. They would bring much more joy here than in his bachelor flat. George's mother had died at a time when staff were distracted by other, seemingly more urgent, crises. The charge nurse was on leave and no-one thought about the funeral which occurred a day earlier than was expected and at 10.30 a.m., the busiest time of the morning. Although the funeral was at a church nearby, none of the staff had attended. George reflected sadly, 'There was nobody there.' We could not imagine that his mother, the Italian matriarch with her huge extended family, would have a poorly attended funeral. 'Were none of the staff able to come?' he asked. Rather feebly, we explained that we'd attempted to find the time of the funeral but that it wasn't in the paper. 'Nobody rang me to find out,' he said.

In deference to grieving families, it is not always appropriate to telephone asking for funeral details. This time we wished a call had been made, because George's disappointment left us feeling his mother's care was incomplete. We wondered if funeral attendance should be considered part of holistic care, if it might offer the resident's family an opportunity to express publicly their appreciation for the care. Disappointment was in the air and, despite his promises to return, George never came back.

ON REFLECTION…

Attending the funeral

It is not possible to know the particular expectations of every family following a resident's death. Nor is it easy to gauge staff's varied responses or to predict which funerals staff may wish to attend. On this occasion, reactions were neutral rather than sharply divided for and against attending the funeral. Staff may be reluctant to phone families during early bereavement for funeral details and, as often happens, the events of the living take precedence after a resident's death. In this instance, George may have been reassured to know we were thinking of him. We wondered if our non-attendance at the funeral had any long-term effect on George; whether he found our lack of response offensive or regrettable, a long-term irritation or merely a passing disappointment.

Formal follow-up

Some nursing homes provide a formal follow-up service where a phone call or card is sent to the family on the anniversary of the resident's death. As there is little research into this area to show how effective this procedure is, it may require thoughtful consideration when planning such follow up. Others may send a formal letter from the nursing home management, to mark the significance of the event.

Another practical means of follow-up is to send a copy of the nursing home's regular newsletter to the family of each recently deceased resident, giving them opportunity to continue to receive a copy or merely to ignore the gesture.

Personal, direct contact

While staffing structures differ widely, the person responsible for coordinating the resident's care (such as the charge nurse) is the person most appropriate when considering a follow-up phone call. Sometimes a spontaneous phone call is the best. 'How are you, George? I was just completing the filing of your mother's notes and was thinking of you, so I decided to ring to find out how you are.' While there is no particular structure for this spontaneous follow up, it may lead to arranging a structured bereavement program, or a discussion with the chaplain. Or, it may be simply resolved by inviting George back to morning tea.

She took a long time to come back

Pat promised she would return one day as a volunteer. We looked forward to her contribution because, before her father's death in the nursing home, she had worked as a volunteer coordinator in a large health-care agency. There was an unspoken hope that she might take on this role in a voluntary capacity for the nursing home. In addition, residents with whom she had formed friendships would welcome her continued visits.

Pat's father's death had been expected for several weeks; she and her sisters had been more than satisfied with their father's care. We thought Pat would manage her own grief with relative ease and return as a matter of course, so it was puzzling and then disappointing when time passed without her making any contact. 'She must have decided not to come back but she did promise,' was the conclusion of staff.

Nine months later Pat rang to arrange a starting date as volunteer. 'I've found it terribly hard to make this move. I attempted to ring several times but, for some reason, was unable to follow it through. Then I'd feel guilty and try to pull myself together. In the end I just had to wait until the time was right for me.'

The first thing she wanted to know was who occupied her father's bed now and whether there were any other changes in his room because, 'I might find it hard to go in there to begin with.'

Her next priority was to find a resident 'a bit like my dad, someone I can relate to'. This turned out to be one of the residents who remembered her as 'that nice lady who always says hello to me as she's going past'. After initial contact with a resident to whom she felt some attachment, Pat found it easier to chat with unfamiliar residents. 'I'll come every Wednesday afternoon for an hour and gradually I'll get to know everyone.' In this way, Pat found her unique level of participation as a volunteer. Although we had expected her to take a leadership role, her faithful commitment brought much joy to residents and staff for the next two years. When the opportunity came for Pat to travel overseas, her invaluable service to the nursing home was acknowledged at a special farewell session attended by residents and staff.

ON REFLECTION...

Volunteer coordinator

It is puzzling that funding does not necessarily allow for the employment of a volunteer coordinator; in the absence of a paid employee a volunteer may take on this very important role. On reflection, our need was so acute that our dreams and wishes were projected onto Pat, who had all the necessary qualifications and experience. We made assumptions about her ability and readiness, and we underestimated her grief following her father's death. We also failed to discern how her former well-structured role in another organisation would translate to a different environment. We did not appreciate that her association with the nursing home was in the private realm of her relationship with her father and that this could never be a neutral environment.

When we realised how unrealistic our expectations were, we were able to appreciate the unique qualities Pat brought to the hands-on volunteer role.

Volunteer recruitment and support

For a volunteer program to work effectively it needs to include comprehensive recruitment procedures, education and support for volunteers, and ongoing coordination. Volunteers need to be able to select the tasks most suited to them. Because their work is not always sufficiently acknowledged, structured procedures may offer reassurance. However, there are other volunteers who would prefer not to be 'locked in' by structures and procedures, preferring a more casual relationship. It is a challenge to actively recruit volunteer support, while guarding against inappropriate coercion. Acknowledgment needs also be given to volunteers that they should feel free to 'retire' at any time.

She was back the next day

Ada had cared for Tom at home for eight years before agreeing to have him admitted to the nursing home. They had no children and, with a history of 60 years of marriage, their lives were grafted together. Ada became a daily visitor, staying for several hours each day, helping with the morning teas and assisting other residents, especially when Tom was non-communicative or dismissive of her.

After Tom's death, Ada promised, 'I'll be back' and it didn't take long for her to return. With some self-consciousness she was back the next day. 'I made the funeral arrangements and then the house seemed so empty and lonely I decided to come back here. I stood outside for a while. Then I took a deep breath and decided I must go straight down to Tom's room and get it over with. This is still my home,' she added, asking about the other residents. 'I think of them all every day. Sometimes I remember someone I had forgotten to think about, so I quickly add their name to my list.'

With her lack of pretension and innate humility Ada did not disclose that she prayed for the residents every day. She had no desire to be known as a 'religious fanatic'.

Later she confided her prayer life to a staff member whom she felt would understand. 'I believe in the power of prayer, but I know many who regard it as superstition.'

It is impossible to measure the impact of Ada's daily prayers on the nursing home community but her regular presence remained unobtrusive and of incalculable benefit. Among her many other activities in the nursing home, Ada would make sure she had morning tea with Freda, a resident whose complex psychiatric history made her social life extremely difficult. Ada related normally to Freda and succeeded where other volunteers and staff had failed. Freda had regarded all attempts to 'match' her with a specially appointed volunteer as one more institutional ploy for her to oppose, whereas Ada was accepted as Tom's widow.

Never wishing to register formally as a volunteer, Ada saw her service as nothing extraordinary; she would certainly not consider it therapy for her grief. She merely returned to her second home.

ON REFLECTION…

Fulfilling a need

Ada regarded the nursing home community as her family and her second home. This response was fostered by including her in her husband's care from the outset. Having cared for his every physical and emotional need for eight years prior to his admission, Ada was reluctant to relinquish her caring role. Staff, through careful assessment, understood Ada wished to be involved in washing and turning Tom whenever she was present. She had no wish to intrude on the nurses' professional care; however, she had a wealth of wisdom unique to her personal nursing experience. 'I don't know if I did things the right way, but I seemed able to get him comfortable.' She was also grateful for respite when his demands on her seemed relentless. 'I can see I was becoming exhausted having to care for him 24 hours every day.'

Official and unofficial volunteers

'The only time we've been apart was during the war,' she told us. Having lived a fairly closed existence, and happy in their 60-year marriage to be together for each other, Ada now faced a separation too terrifying to contemplate. Continuing her role at the nursing home was an extension of her care for Tom. She called herself 'just a helper' and wanted no fuss.

Some may have regarded this relationship as an unhealthy dependence on Ada's part. 'She should be getting used to being on her own more,' was her brother's opinion. For our part, we needed to watch our dependence on Ada. It became so easy to leave small tasks for her to do. 'Ada will be in at 10. She'll collect the cups.' Or, 'We'll ask Ada to sit with Freda. She's usually able to calm her down.' Ada may have felt compelled to continue some of these tasks in return for the hospitality she enjoyed during her daily visits. It occurred to us that we had never asked Ada's opinion on these matters; we expected she would always be there.

Opportunity for review

When volunteers are not part of a structured program, important opportunities for review may be missed. What did we know of Ada's responses to her helping role? Was she coming because she felt she had to? How was her own health? Did she need assistance with transport? Would she have welcomed a few weeks off? She may have wanted a holiday but felt she'd be letting the nursing home down. Ada may well have fitted the 'willing helper syndrome', wishing to continue as she always had. Without asking, we would never know.

He resigned after four years

Arthur adapted quickly to the nursing home routine following the admission of his older sister. 'I'm all she's got, so I'll be here as often as I can.' True to his word, he never missed a day's visiting. When his sister died unexpectedly three months after her admission, we assumed Arthur would merely resume his former life. His offer to be a volunteer was totally unexpected. 'I'll be in next week to help with the pub lunch. Estelle used to enjoy it so much, and I know they're short of volunteers.' Over the next few years, Arthur took on more and more, visiting the nursing home three times a week to assist with the leisure program, always phoning in advance if he was unable to attend.

His letter of resignation was formal and to the point. He was becoming tired, had suffered health problems and decided it was time to 'retire from active service'. We had grown accustomed to Arthur's presence; his 'resignation' had the effect of the resignation of a valued permanent staff member.

ON REFLECTION...

Unconditional giving

Arthur saw a practical need and fulfilled it, to the advantage of the whole nursing home. His physical strength was a tremendous asset, particularly in steering wheelchairs along the rocky footpath to the local hotel which the residents visit each fortnight. This provided Arthur the opportunity to share a meal with those he had come to regard as his friends. 'It beats my home cooking,' he confessed. The allied health staff had come to rely on Arthur as an indispensable part of the team; he had his regular tasks and would offer extra time for special occasions. It is impossible to fully compensate volunteers like Arthur, for their significant contribution to the life of the nursing home. All we could offer was a formal, public acknowledgment of his retirement, together with a token gift.

Formal acknowledgment

A regular letter to volunteers with a tear-off slip indicating their desire to continue or their desire to retire from voluntary service is one way of providing an opportunity for review. This kind of letters doubles as a 'thank you' letter, as well as ascertaining the volunteer's wishes for the future.

The memorial service when more than 40 came back

Some nursing homes have a long-held tradition of regular memorial services when the lives of those who have died in the preceding months are remembered through both formal and informal ritual.

It had taken us quite a long time to plan for our first memorial service. Questions about leadership, style, symbols, language, venue, staff involvement and invitation lists did not lend themselves to quick decisions. The chaplain's draft outline for the proceedings was agreed upon with minor changes. Symbols of water, light and life were depicted in a large transparent bowl with water lilies and floating candles; appropriate symbols for the passage of time from birth to death, as well as for hope and new possibilities.

Each person representing a deceased resident was invited to light a candle as the name was read out; the candles signifying the eternal flame of memory and the reading of the names signifying the lasting place of these residents in the nursing home's history. Space was allowed in a brief period of silence for memories to come to the surface. Music provided a sense of calm and the bright display of coloured flowers lifted the atmosphere with a focus on new life and growth.

A family of six adults had brought flowers and greeted staff warmly, overwhelming in their generous praise of the care given to their relative. Mr Abbott had died over a year previously, after only two days in the nursing home. The senior nurse on duty at the time had since transferred and very few other staff recalled any contact at all with this family. It fell to the director of nursing to make further enquiries and to have her own memory jogged. The Abbott family had been extremely distressed at the cursory manner with which their father had been treated at the acute hospital. They knew he was dying and did not wish him to be moved. They were not reassured by the hospital's prediction that Mr Abbott may have many months to live; nevertheless they were instructed to find a nursing home. Unable to win what they termed 'the battle of the system' they resigned themselves to the inevitable. They knew their father's wishes and their unspoken prediction came true; he did not want to be moved again and had no desire to settle into a nursing home. He wanted his own familiar bed. When the unmistakable symptoms of pneumonia emerged the family wanted to discuss the treatment options. They all agreed with the offer of palliative care; they were delighted this would not involve another move for their father, either to hospital or to a hospice. Without inappropriate intrusion they formed their own roster to keep a bedside vigil for the next two days and nights. When Mr Abbott died they were grateful to have the lounge facilities at their disposal; so while the family were together, the necessary funeral arrangements could be made. Seldom had we seen a family so united in their determination to 'see this through to the end'. It also seemed as though they felt 'at home' in this short space of time between their father's admission and his death. In the life of a busy nursing home, the 'Abbott story' was quickly forgotten. We were quite taken by surprise to see the entire family again, at the memorial service. What to us had seemed a fairly insignificant, brief episode of care, had lasting positive memories for this family, as indicated by the statement, 'We just wanted to come back to say thank you.'

The senior nurse at the time of Mr Abbott's death was a qualified palliative care consultant; she led the family through all the care options with sensitivity and patience, allowing them to make their own judgement after being furnished with the appropriate information. When so much of their father's care at the hospital had seemed to them to be imposed without proper consultation, this family were grateful to be allowed emotional and physical space to make their own decisions. 'I'll never forget that nurse,' said one of the sons, 'she told us what the nursing home could offer, then left us to talk amongst ourselves and make our own decision. She told us this may be one of the most important decisions we would ever make for our father, but she didn't impose her views.' This family welcomed the opportunity to tell their story, at the service of remembrance.

Two other strangers appeared, unknown to any staff or other families present. On introduction over a cup of tea they described themselves. 'You won't remember us. We're sisters of Emily Smith who died here last year. She was only here one week and we only "found her" on the last day.' It transpired that these two women were sisters who had only recently become aware of each other's existence and of a third sister, Emily. Each having been adopted, they had found each other through an adoption reunion program. By the time they found Emily, they had the opportunity for a brief visit only, the day before she died. Not wishing to intrude on Emily's other family at such a time, they had made a quick and unobtrusive visit, leaving without saying who they were. Somehow, they had managed to see our invitation to the service of remembrance. 'I hope you don't mind us being here. This has meant so much to us; it has rounded off our relationship with Emily. We lit a candle for her, and told her we'll be joining her one day, all together at last.'

We were very surprised to see Frank at the service. He had paid only fleeting visits to his mother during her two years in the nursing home, and we had assumed their relationship was not close. With tears in his eyes he thanked us for arranging the service. 'This was better than the funeral,' he said. 'I arranged the funeral so quickly, I wanted to get it over and done with and yet it never felt finished. This has given me the chance to round it all off. I feel I've said my proper goodbyes to mum.'

After the names of the deceased residents were read out, and a candle lit for each one, the opportunity was then given for any other person to light a candle for a person they wished to remember. Staff assisted residents to light their candles, some lighting their own as well. Other family members came forward to light another candle, perhaps for family or friends who had died some time ago. 'I lit a candle for my husband who died 30 years ago,' Lillian said with satisfaction. 'Mum died only three months ago, but it's Charlie I remember as if it were yesterday.'

We learned a little more of the complex lives of some of our current residents. 'Who was your candle for, Ruby?' 'For my baby boy,' Ruby replied. The chaplain happened to be close by and was able to comfort Ruby as she recalled her grief of 60 years ago, at the loss of her only son. She had come to the service of remembrance, along with several other residents, to pay her respects to other residents who had died. Ruby had not expected to recall her own unique tragedy. She felt it had helped the healing process. 'It's painful to remember,' she said, 'but I can never forget.'

Perhaps most of the healing and debriefing took place informally over drinks and snacks following the memorial service. Here, relatives greeted one another as those who had smiled across the corridor or met in the foyer. For others it was a reminder of deep, shared sadness originating when each watched over their relative's last days and hours in an adjacent or nearby room.

ON REFLECTION...

Unexpected gratitude

Nurses and other staff may not always know the lasting impression made by their care of dying residents and their families. To be given space for emotional reactions, as well as for physical comfort, was important for the Abbott family and possibly for most families in this situation. With the best intention of 'advising' families from the wealth of their past experience, carers often neglect to provide this space for families to come to their own decision, freely and without imposition.

Such encounters at the memorial service gave carers a salutary reminder that while their actions may have profound significance for the person who is dying, their attitudes live long in the memory of families.

Who prepares the service?

Preparing for a service of remembrance takes time and sensitivity. Who is to be invited? Have we missed anyone? What should be the theme? How do we acknowledge the pluralist society reflected in most nursing home populations, and design a service of remembrance that will be inclusive? Should the service be religious or secular? Should it reflect the Christian faith or take a multi-faith approach? These questions can only be resolved by the individual nursing home, considering factors such as philosophy, past practices, availability of the chaplain and the wishes of the residents and their families. Planning is best done by a small group or committee, to ensure that practical matters as well as the more deeply philosophical matters are considered. What has worked well in our situation is to have an ecumenical approach, with both Protestant and Catholic representation, and leadership which involves staff and current residents where possible. Matters of detail, such as name tags, are small but important factors to assist smooth functioning of the program. We have also found that each year we have made adjustments and improvements to the program.

Staff involvement

In our experience, very few staff have attended these functions. It is acknowledged that busy staff may not wish to attend a function 'out of hours', they may also wish to have no further involvement with families once the resident has died. However, the staff who have attended have voiced their deep satisfaction with the event. Acting as a welcoming presence, they have given out copies of the program, assisted with name tags, assisted with the lighting of candles and helped with refreshments. Families have generally been delighted to renew acquaintances with staff.

QUALITY ISSUES FOR ENHANCED PRACTICE

The gerontic nurse

- Nurses require sensitivity and expertise in the assessment phase to gauge the level of involvement desired by family members in the care of their relative. This needs to be documented clearly and reviewed regularly.
- When evaluating a resident's care, it is important to acknowledge significant input from family members.
- Following a resident's death, it may become part of the charge nurse's routine to make a phone call to the family to check on funeral details and to offer condolences, as well as mentioning anticipated staff attendance or non-attendance at the funeral.

Management

- Clear guidelines for staff in relation to funeral attendance and follow-up contact with families may prevent the communication difficulties experienced with George.
- Clear guidelines for recruitment, support, education and evaluation of volunteer programs provide helpful checks and balances on this important volunteer workforce.
- Regular, public acknowledgment of volunteers' services offers a great deal of support and encouragement, even for those who 'want no fuss'.
- It may also help volunteers if management has a formal way of reviewing their services, providing the opportunity for the volunteer to either renew their commitment or to withdraw their services without feeling guilty.
- Instituting the practice of regular memorial services provides a significant opportunity for another stage in the grieving process for families.

Indirect carers

- Those who return as volunteers have a variety of expectations. It is important for volunteers to talk about their expectations and to receive reassurance. An opportunity to discontinue service gracefully, when appropriate, may prevent volunteers feeling they must continue at great cost to themselves.

CHAPTER SEVEN

This chapter shows some gaps in the care of dying residents. Reflection on these episodes of care highlights the importance of clear communication among all carers.

SUDDEN DEATH: NO TIME TO SAY GOODBYE

When Alex collapsed without warning there was some doubt expressed by the nurse as to the action taken. Did I do the right thing? Was my reading of the situation accurate? Staff who witnessed the crisis and those who heard about it afterwards expressed mixed reactions. Criticism, anger, resentment and hasty judgements left little room for praise and understanding for the swift action by the nurse who arranged Alex's transfer to hospital. In dealing with their own shock and sadness at Alex's death many staff reacted with the 'If only...' syndrome. In order to avoid lasting negative consequences following such a crisis it is important to encourage expression of feelings. Although it is not easy to admit mistakes, it must be considered that, given the same situation again, some factors may have been addressed differently. Or would they?

'Dianne, get Robert! I think he's in Room 3. Alex has collapsed.' Alex was a survivor — a survivor of wars, the one survivor of his nine brothers and sisters, a survivor of alcoholism and lung cancer, and a survivor of one amputation and then another, until he joked about his two very short legs which provided a continuing challenge for the surgeon: 'There's not much left to chop off.' Continuing his chain-smoking habits and with little regard for his prescribed diet, Alex was not concerned with his poor circulation or his diabetes. Non-compliant to the extent of pretence at medication time, Alex would grin roguishly when his tablets were discovered in the oddest of places. At these times his failing eyesight would provide him with a sound defence. Independent to the point of risking danger, he would rise early to complete yet another excursion in his battery-operated wheelchair. For all his eccentricities, Alex won the affection of staff with his cheery, uncomplaining attitude to life and unceasing gratitude for their attention. He was regarded with some disdain by his fellow residents whom he would bypass in the passageways, displaying a distinct lack of judgement about the distance between his wheelchair and their walking frames.

Accustomed to many sudden trips to hospital, Alex was noted for his resilience and philosophical outlook. 'What will be will be, love. I know you have to do your best with this rickety old body of mine. I suppose that one day it will just splutter to a halt like a burned-out motor. Then you can just dump it in the rubbish bin.' From every hospital episode he would return, full of renewed compliments for the nursing home food and knowing that, if the right nurse was on, he'd get his whisky nightcap.

This episode was, however, quite different. There was no indication of unstable diabetes, no telltale dark spots on his amputation site, not even the signs of urinary retention which Alex would treat with customary nonchalance, 'I think you'd better get me to casualty, love.' This time, Alex was making no suggestions at all. His abdomen was tense and distended, his respirations were rapid and shallow, his pulse was thready and racing, his skin was pale and there was no response from his clammy hand. 'Lie him down gently while I call the doctor,' Robert said in an authoritative, calm voice which belied his worst fears. By now Alex had rallied a little, but staff were overwhelmed to see him in so much pain. No jokes this time, not even about keeping the bed warm for him while he went to hospital. The course of action was clear, 'Send him to hospital as soon as possible,' advised the doctor by phone. It was all over in an hour. The thoughtful admitting officer rang from casualty stating Alex had stopped breathing before he could be properly assessed.

It doesn't take long for news like this to filter through the nursing home. Reactions of shock, horror and disbelief were followed by anger, recriminations and guilt. Why did he have to go to hospital? Why didn't someone go with him? If only we'd had the chance to say goodbye. 'I'd have gone with him if someone had called me,' was the frequently heard protest.

The circumstances of Alex's death appear at first glance to be less than ideal. What about the planned approach to terminal care we recommend? What happened to our philosophy of careful consideration of all options? Were Alex's wishes known or considered? What other action could we have taken? Would things have turned out differently if the local doctor were to have left her surgery to assess Alex in his own bed?

In summary, Alex's story illustrates the point that it is impossible to prescribe perfect care in advance, especially crisis care. However, lessons may be learned by careful evaluation after the event.

ON REFLECTION...

Swift, decisive action

It was a valuable exercise to consider all the care Alex did receive in those few short minutes. In the nurse's professional judgement the nursing home was not the appropriate place to address the obvious symptoms of an 'acute abdomen'. With no doctor at hand and no narcotic pain medication, Robert knew the symptoms were beyond Alex's customary tolerance. Within the space of a few minutes an ambulance was called, an accurate description of Alex's signs and symptoms given to the doctor by telephone, a brief but comprehensive transfer form completed for the hospital admitting officer and a phone call made to alert Alex's official advocate. Unfortunately, the advocate was unable to go to the hospital and in the absence of any family members there was no-one else to contact. With the wisdom of hindsight a nurse may have been spared to accompany Alex to hospital, but this crisis occurred at the busiest time of the morning. Weighing up the situation, staff assured themselves that Alex would be adequately cared for by the skilled ambulance officers. Alex had faced these trips to hospital and back many times, often claiming that the hospital was his second home.

'If only...'

Staff attitudes conveyed more of their own grief and shock than was at first acknowledged. In these circumstances it is not uncommon for issues of blame to surface, giving rise to the 'If only...' syndrome. When these factors cloud rational thought, it is easy to lose sight of objective facts. It is also easy to lay blame rather than to express solidarity with the staff who acted according to their best judgement at the time.

One prescription to fit all?

In another situation it may have been wise to arrange for a nurse to accompany the resident to hospital, particularly if that resident was clearly anxious about the transfer and afraid of facing the unknown. For Alex, whose preferred approach was 'toughing it out', the need to have a trusted friend beside him as he died may not have been of paramount importance. However, in the absence of any clear direction from Alex, we will never be certain if this was the case.

Assessment by previous patterns

Alex was not unaccustomed to hospital trips alone in the ambulance. He had many times referred to the hospital as his second home, having confidence in knowing his long-standing medical records would be readily accessible. He had also, not long before this crisis, alluded to his imminent death and he had always wanted to spare the nursing home staff extra trouble. So, we could rationalise, sending him to hospital alone would not have been a disappointment or shock for him. However, because this occasion was his very last trip, he may have welcomed company. We may also offer the defence that he was unconscious before the ambulance arrived at the hospital, so he did not know he was alone — or did he?

Dealing with staff reactions

Some staff were vocal in their objections to the circumstances surrounding Alex's death, but others kept their opinions to themselves. For those who verbalised their anger or frustration, the matter may have been over and done with. However, the feelings of others may only be resolved over time, while a number of staff will keep the feelings buried forever. While it is not possible for all feelings to be acknowledged and aired, it is useful to develop strategies that invite staff to discuss their concerns.

Objective facts or subjective opinion

It is a fact of life that those who were not present at the time of a particular crisis will presume to know best what course of action should have been followed. On the other hand, staff who know the nursing home philosophy, principles and policies concerning residents whose death is imminent, may offer valuable comments after carefully considering all factors. Such constructive evaluation may promote a clear course of action for future occasions of crisis.

Advocacy

In the absence of family members, a formally appointed advocate is able to make decisions on the resident's behalf. Fortunately, the nurse on duty knew Alex had an advocate and that the advocate should be notified of this crisis. Given other circumstances, the advocate may have then played a decisive role in clarifying a decision regarding hospitalisation. In this instance, there was no time for that ideal to be realised.

Mixed feelings

Staff welcomed the advocate's suggestion that the funeral be held in the chapel adjacent to the nursing home. The advocate also thoughtfully arranged for afternoon tea to be catered for, after confirming that staff would welcome the opportunity to meet in the lounge where Alex had so often been the centre of attention. Laughter and tears were shared as the advocate told some of his stories about Alex. It was a time of 'rounding off' for him too.

Would we do anything differently next time?

Once immediate reactions have been aired and doubts and criticisms dealt with, reflection provides a significant forum for learning. Would we do anything differently next time? In evaluating Alex's crisis there was no clear indication of an alternative course of action. It was therefore resolved by leaving the matter unresolved, not as an insoluble problem but as one of those situations where the best judgement is recognised as the judgement made at the time.

QUALITY ISSUES FOR ENHANCED PRACTICE

The gerontic nurse

- Each resident, on admission, should have a nominated person to be included in decision making wherever possible.
- When a hasty decision needs to be made, documentation should include the reason for the decision, as well as evaluating the outcome.
- Good documentation is the cornerstone to communication, so that other staff come to rely on good problem solving rather than subjective opinions.

Management

- When designing assessment forms, a question relating to the resident's attitude towards hospitalisation may be included. This provides valuable guidance when a hasty decision needs to be made.
- Management has the important role of supporting senior nursing staff, especially when a crisis demands swift decision making.

Indirect carers

- Allied health staff, a particular volunteer or a chaplain may assist in diffusing grief, shock and rumour after a resident is taken to hospital and subsequently dies.
- Other residents may require support and the chance to vocalise their feelings in a carefully facilitated small group or individual conversation. A particular volunteer may, at times, be available to accompany a resident to hospital.

SITE OF CARE: COULDN'T I COME BACK HOME?

No sooner had Esmae won her way into our hearts than she was gone. In just three short weeks her impact on the nursing home community was quite remarkable. Here was the case of a younger person, aged 45 years, physically frail but mentally alert, whose immediate access to 24-hour nursing care gave her increased independence, at least for a short period of time. Esmae actually *wanted* to live in a nursing home. Even an acute hospital admission for a serious medical crisis failed to change that desire. 'Couldn't I come back home?' she pleaded.

Esmae's admission to the nursing home was a rare example of planned, resident-centred decision making, initiated and followed through by the resident herself. Left partly paralysed from a road accident, Esmae had struggled to live independently for as long as she could. Even though Jan, her only daughter, lived nextdoor, after weighing up the consequences Esmae made her own decisions and then announced them to Jan. Such was the case with her decision to enter a nursing home.

Bravely, she came alone in a taxi, accustomed to manoeuvring her wheelchair in unknown territory. Having inspected the mandatory number of nursing homes, ours was chosen as the one closest to her circle of friends. 'This is where I'll see my days out,' she said confidently. 'Jan will be able to call in after work and catch the tram home while it's still daylight.' Personal notes kept by the charge nurse at the time of Esmae's admission capture Esmae's settling-in period:

> It took Esmae only a couple of days before she was participating in all the nursing home activities: bus trips, pub lunches, videos — things she had not been able to do when she was living on her own. We managed to repair a motorised scooter which gave her more mobility than her wheelchair. Up the street she would go to see the local chemist, to put her bets on at the TAB, to do little bits of shopping for herself. It seems she had to pack so many things into a very limited time, almost having to keep an appointment book of all the things that had to be done. Meal times became lively events as football, horses and the day's activities were discussed around the table with Jack, Mary and Eileen, who quickly became her friends.

'I'm happy here and very thankful I got a bed so quickly,' Esmae told the director of nursing. And we were happy to have her living with us. Always cheery, she made it her business to get to know everyone. Without intruding, she would tour the nursing home each morning, greeting the kitchen and laundry staff, inquiring after this nurse or that very ill resident, asking if there were any letters to be posted. A nursing home and yet independence, a combination never dreamed of in her wildest imagination. Esmae's disabilities meant she often required urgent assistance. Many a time at home she had been so distressed that she struggled for enough breath to call the ambulance, but still managed without worrying her daughter, 'Jan's got enough to do with her own family and getting herself to work.' So it was that after her first night, Esmae declared, 'That was the best sleep I've had for three years.' And after three weeks she commented, 'I've done more things in these three weeks than I've done in years.'

She knew that on her good days she could achieve most of her goals. Volunteering her services for the residents' committee, she asked which residents were without families and friends. 'I see myself as being so fortunate. There must be something I can do for those who are lonely and isolated.' It didn't take long for the nurses to realise Esmae's value in sitting beside a restless resident or in reading the headlines to Jim who was blind. Esmae won her way into the heart of the nursing home community. However, we did not realise her own heart was failing rapidly.

'It's just one of my attacks,' she told the night staff, but when her breathing became more distressed she agreed that hospital was the place she should be. 'They'll fix me up with a drip for a few days and then I'll be back.' Esmae took this medical emergency in her stride, the same way she viewed all events in her life. The way she spoke of 'home' during her hospital admission formalities, the staff thought she must have lived at the nursing home for years rather than just three weeks. When phone messages from the hospital ward seemed less hopeful each day, the director of nursing decided to see for herself.

Esmae was gravely ill, her cheery face now clouded with anxiety and fear. Intravenous drips, oxygen, complex medication did not seem to be reversing the crisis. 'All I want in all the world is to come home. Couldn't I come home?' she managed to whisper. Nonplussed for a minute or two, the director of nursing thought Esmae meant her own home. All she could offer inadequately in reply was an assurance to Esmae that the staff and residents sent their love and were thinking of her.

'She must be someone pretty special,' said the hospital nurse in answering yet another phone query about Esmae's progress. For several days, the notes in Esmae's nursing home record told of her condition, the visits by several staff members and the messages Esmae relayed. Then came the word that Esmae's struggle was over. There was no reversing this attack; there were no more messages to be relayed. Word spread quickly round the nursing home, with residents and staff comforted by the family's arrangements to hold the funeral in our chapel. Yes, of course we would make the lounge available for afternoon tea, a fitting farewell for someone who had entered our lives for such a brief period. Esmae was unique.

ON REFLECTION…

Coming home

Esmae's question about coming home was never really addressed. Surrounded by what seemed like absolutely essential technology, Esmae's hospital bed brought her neither comfort nor security. Having tasted the atmosphere of her new home and resolving to die there, Esmae was not prepared for this latest crisis. Neither were we. In order to explore the option of returning home, Esmae and her carers would have to confront complex ethical issues. When her body failed to respond in the usual manner, Esmae knew she was dying. Perhaps these thoughts prompted her request to the director of nursing. 'Why bother with tubes and drugs and all those fluids, why continue to force air into these diseased lungs? Why can't I just come home to die peacefully, surrounded by my very dear friends? The nursing home staff will look after me.' Sadly, Esmae was never consulted by the hospital staff about where she would prefer to die. We didn't speak out because we thought they knew best.

Liaison between nursing home and hospital

Hospital doctors are always busy and it is often difficult to find the one person responsible for a patient's care. Who was responsible for considering other options such as whether essential technological intervention could be managed in the nursing home with advice and supervision from the hospital? If the doctors considered Esmae's death was imminent, what factors would influence whether or not she should be moved, and why was there no liaison with her primary carers?

Esmae's choice

Esmae was younger than the average nursing home resident and far more accustomed to making decisions about her own health care than most residents. She managed her own medications before transfer to the nursing home and we saw no reason to take this responsibility from her. Esmae decided when she needed oxygen, when she needed a day in bed and assured us that she would know when she needed to go to hospital. We were just beginning to learn about her complex medical conditions and were anxious for her to retain control over her health care. Should we have intervened earlier and not relied on Esmae's judgement? There is a fine line between issues of self-determination and professional intervention. In relation to her admission to hospital and in relation to her death in hospital, our judgement may have been out of balance.

Having experienced dozens of emergency admissions from her own home to hospital, Esmae knew the signs and symptoms well. Living in a nursing home, however, meant there was no need to crawl from armchair to phone and then wait, counting the minutes until the ambulance arrived. This time she had professional nurses to monitor her symptoms and decide when action was required, so she was not impatient to get to hospital. Hoping against hope, she had played her own private wait-and-see game. This time, the stakes were too high and she lost.

Progress notes

When used as a communication tool, clear and comprehensive documentation in the resident's progress notes indicate to all concerned, the progress or health status of a resident even when the resident is in hospital. Relying on the accuracy of the documentation, staff are freed from speculation and rumour. The progress notes tell the story of the continued care offered by staff through phone calls and visits, as well as communication from the hospital.

Impact on other residents

Esmae's presence changed the nursing home atmosphere quite remarkably. Always cheerful, face carefully made-up, attentive to her clothes, she was particularly admired by Peggy who, although 30 years older, was also careful with her appearance. Peggy went to the funeral and did not hesitate to wheel herself towards the open coffin. 'Doesn't she look beautiful?' Those of us who know Peggy were aware of her unspoken thought, 'I hope they will say that about me.'

Given the average length of stay for nursing home residents is a little less than one year, Esmae's stay was prematurely ended by the medical crisis. What went through the minds of those residents whom she had so quickly befriended? She represented a sign of comparative youth and vitality. Then she was gone. It was important for those residents who wished to, to attend the funeral and/or the afternoon tea in the nursing home lounge. Proper respect was paid, and thoughtful expression given to their emotions.

The younger disabled person

One of the most serious gaps in the health system is suitable accommodation for the younger disabled person who requires access to 24-hour nursing care. Where do such persons fit? Esmae was not at all offended by living with residents twice her age. Potentially she expected to live in this, her new home, for many years. What kind of considerations need to be made for the nursing home resident who may face 30 or 40 years in the same place? And what happens when the younger resident is not so comfortable with the nursing home environment? These issues are too complex to be discussed here, but reflecting on a different outcome for Esmae raises many questions about the most appropriate site of care.

QUALITY ISSUES FOR ENHANCED PRACTICE

The gerontic nurse

- Careful assessment on admission is essential for gauging the resident's perception about hospital admission and treatment in a crisis.
- A clear plan of care should then be drawn up, identifying as far as possible the indicators for hospital admission.
- A comprehensive letter of transfer may include the resident's wishes, for example 'If death is imminent, Esmae has expressed a wish to return to the nursing home.'

Management

- Management plays a role as the resident's advocate when the resident is transferred to an acute hospital. This may include arranging a meeting with hospital personnel to clarify goals and provide information as to what care the nursing home is able to provide.
- Where resources allow, the senior gerontic nurse may be encouraged to attend the hospital to discuss with hospital staff the options for care, including palliative care.

Indirect carers

- Family and friends may respond to the invitation to host an informal gathering within the nursing home, to provide staff and other residents with the opportunity to acknowledge the sudden death of a resident, particularly where the resident's death occurs away from the nursing home.

ACUTE CARE: KEEPING PACE

When frail-but-independent Laura was transferred from hostel to hospital after a series of falls, the outcome of her care should have been a success. She could afford the best of acute care and, with two senior, registered nurses in her committed family, few residents could have such confident and assertive support. However, key hospital staff seemed to have an agenda different from listening to Laura's wishes. Rendered helpless by the monolithic operation of the acute-care system, the family watched Laura's admission become a disaster, the outcome of which, by chance, was 'redeemed' by a 'good' nursing home facilitating Laura's 'good' death.

In this story, questions are raised about the nature of aged-care advocacy in its widest context (the acute-care system). The acute-care nurse is enlisted as a resident advocate amid the insistence of acute care's medicalisation of old age. Acute-care nurses are reminded of the duty so many already conscientiously pursue: to listen to the patient or the patient's family; to plan collaborative, individualised care within the health-care team; and to assist frail, aged voices to be heard above the busy hum of the acute-care 'system' when they (or their family advocates) express wishes and choices about end-of-life care.

When Laura's ambulance arrived from the acute-care private hospital we were glad there was a quiet room available. This frail 90-year old was obviously dehydrated and showed signs of being in the last days of her life. A brief call was made by the acting charge nurse to Laura's niece. Because we were busy that day and the family would not be in until after work, once Laura was comfortably settled in her bed the admission formalities were postponed.

When Laura's nieces (both registered nurses) arrived they told us about the events that brought Laura to the nursing home. Laura's story is repeated here, as it was told, because it raises issues of great importance for gerontic nurses in the wider context of the health-care system as they work with frail, aged persons.

The nieces' story

Our aunt, a dignified, independent woman, was bundled off to hospital one night from the hostel where she had lived for five years. After a fall, she was no longer able to walk. The family was not informed about her fall. We learned our aunt was at the emergency department of a large acute-care hospital when she did not answer her phone and we rang the hostel manager. Hospital investigations revealed our aunt had a fractured pelvis, so she was admitted to their care for a short rest which was to be followed by gradual mobilisation.

The days following our aunt's admission went as expected, so we were shocked when an intensive care physician rang one of us at work. He said he had been asked to see her and that she had 'taken a turn for the worse'. They had put in a drip. Could we come straight away? And did we want her admitted to intensive care?

Take the drip out. Yes, we're on our way. And no! She's 90 years old, for goodness sake. That's what we thought, but all we said was, 'Thank you for ringing, doctor.'

That night, our aunt's own consultant physician ceased the intravenous antibiotics, at our request. Again at our request, he ensured the nurses started giving her the morphine he had ordered some 10 hours previously. We were lucky, he understood our wish for this wonderful lady to have a good death. The nurses hadn't wanted to give the morphine 'in case it finished her off'. They looked at us with raised eyebrows as if what we wanted for her was not the best of care. The morphine calmed our aunt's respiratory distress while the nurses aspirated the copious brown liquid from her lungs which we were told was probably inhaled coffee. When we left at midnight she was deeply unconscious. However the phone did not ring and in the morning we discovered she had survived the night.

During the next few days we felt as though we were on emotional seesaw while having to make big decisions on her behalf. When she was stronger we asked for the drip to be removed. The doctor was unhappy about this. He felt she still could not swallow enough to maintain her fluid balance or take her medications. Of course she was on a powerful diuretic now, one drug among 12. When she came into hospital she took only two medications regularly.

She was often 'confused' which the staff told us was the result of a stroke. However, she had experienced many room changes in a few days, as she was shuffled round the ward from one place to another. Nobody considered these changes were significant to her loss of locality but gradually she regained her reason.

Frustrated because our aunt's care varied according to the nurse on duty, and wanting to make plans for her immediate future, we requested a family meeting with her physician. He agreed readily. The night before the meeting we had our own family meeting and discussed what we wanted for our aunt: remove the drip, give her morphine if she became distressed and no more antibiotics. We thought the drip would be the problem, as they had started her on thickened fluids which were not to her liking. She asked continually for 'just a glass of water' or 'a lovely cup of tea'. At our request the kitchen made her thickened coffee but she found this quite disgusting — 'like eating hot jelly', she said.

The drip problem was solved by our aunt. During the night she removed it herself. On the morning of the meeting she greeted us with, 'Now can I have a cup of tea?' She did not listen to our explanations, as she had not listened to the doctor's or the nurses' or the speech pathologist who assessed her. Her point of view was simple: if I can't have a cup of tea I may as well be dead.

At the beginning of the meeting the consultant's body language was closed and defensive. I wondered if he was worried about litigation over the inhaled coffee. We weren't interested in blame, we just wanted the best for our aunt. We were surprised there was no nurse present. How would the people who performed our aunt's daily care know what had been decided? Both the oxygen nasal-prongs and mask distressed her. The consultant said she should have the oxygen only when necessary; if she didn't want it, that was fine. Subsequently, every well-meaning nurse who cared for our aunt repeatedly replaced the hated apparatus; despite our protests, despite her protests, despite what was agreed at the meeting.

The doctor said that although our aunt's prognosis was poor, morphine was unnecessary now, and while he understood our position about antibiotics, he would be the judge of when they were needed. He said this in the nicest possible way — and despite her medical power of attorney being present.

Well, couldn't she have a cup of tea, a sip of tea, even if she coughed on it? Definitely not. Not ever? Probably not. As he asserted his authority his body relaxed. Soon he seemed to be towering over us and speaking from a great height. As if offering a precious gift he said our aunt might benefit from a pacemaker, and really it was such a simple procedure these days, just a little wire into the heart. He smiled confidently. Would we like him to arrange that?

Hearing our aunt's voice saying she would rather die than never have another cup of tea we shook our heads: no thank you.

As days went by and no cup of tea or glass of water arrived, our aunt often said that she wanted to die. We noticed her name with 'ACAT' (aged care assessment team) scrawled beside it on a whiteboard in the passage outside her room. The nurse told us the hostel staff believed our aunt was too frail to return there. Although they were right, we felt betrayed that there had been no direct communication from the hostel staff with whom we had a long-standing relationship. We felt they had abandoned her. Perhaps they felt guilty for not notifying us about her fall and the transfer to hospital. What was a simple lack of communication made us feel that things were being done behind our backs, that our aunt and her power of attorney were being disempowered and excluded from decision making.

Again by chance, despite a phone call to the ACAT requesting a family member be present at our aunt's assessment, we learned the geriatrician had been to see her. She said he asked her who the Prime Minister was and to count backwards from 10. She was astonished by this and wondered if he was mad. He gently tried to make her stand but of course her legs gave way. You have to prove you need a nursing home by falling, her sister said, grimly.

Our aunt knew things had changed: she would not return to her home and friends at the hostel, and no-one would give her a glass of water or a cup of tea. Fretful, querulous she said again and again, 'I wish I could die.' But still she held on.

The evening after the geriatrician's visit the physician came and shouted at her from six feet up at the end of the bed. He listened to her chest and repeated the words 'nursing home' loudly, several times. She shut her eyes in response and, when he'd gone, asked, 'Who was that man?'

While we were waiting for a nursing home bed we slipped her a sip of water, against orders, feeling guilty and torn between what was good for her and what was right for her.

After transfer to the nursing home she never regained her sense of locality. For a woman who, three weeks before, knew where she was 100 per cent of the time, five room moves in the acute hospital, and now a transfer to the nursing home were too much. Even though her possessions were still unpacked when we arrived eight hours after her transfer; even though we had to tell each shift that she would only eat ice cream; even though no admission nursing history had been taken, it was a relief to know she was being cared for in a place where ageing was considered normal, and pneumonia may still be 'the old man's friend'. At meal times the hated thickened fluids appeared on her tray, but she had lost her interest in anything other than a cup of tea. The staff, while aware of the 'swallowing guidelines', turned a blind eye to the odd sip from a cup of tea as her satisfaction was so genuine and deep — and her closeness to death so apparent.

> Once she reached the nursing home she was not moved from her lovely quiet room. She did not need morphine in the end. Given sensible physical care by confident, kindly staff, she visibly relaxed. She chose to die alone, but died quietly in a calm room, surrounded by family photos and her most comforting possessions. Common sense and good aged care prevailed, and she did not die thirsting for a cup of tea.

ON REFLECTION...

From hostel to nursing home

This book is about nursing home care; however, this story highlights the importance of good communication when a person needs a higher level of care than the hostel is able to provide. It would be helpful to all concerned for hostels to have guidelines and procedures for such an event, including transfer forms to enable the nursing home to have some knowledge of the resident's previous history (social, nursing and medical), routine, preferences and dislikes.

From hostel to hospital

While we may comment on deficiencies in nursing home communication when a resident is admitted to hospital, this story raises the issue of public relations and ordinary human interaction when a resident of some years' length of stay is suddenly admitted to hospital. Hostels generally do not have the level of qualified nursing staff found in nursing homes. For this reason, protocols and guidelines would be helpful to guide the person in charge of the hostel or other delegated staff in such circumstances.

Other hostel residents

What is communicated to other hostel residents when a long-term resident is suddenly no longer there; room packed up and cleared out, with nothing remaining to recall that person's life among them? Hostel staff also need the opportunity to farewell a resident for whom they have cared. The financial imperative to 'fill the bed' need not deny the existence of relationships. In this instance, communication was not given a high priority and one can only guess what was conveyed to other residents.

Assessment for higher level care

Government guidelines are clear about re-assessment procedures, but they do not ensure the important aspect of communication with the family. A foreshadowed move precipitates a life crisis for many older persons. When the resident is frail and seriously ill, communication about care arrangements should continue with the resident's family, or a nominated representative, and occur at an early stage in order to avoid misunderstandings. Communicating with family about assessment indicates a willingness to involve them in every step of decision making.

Gerontic qualifications are appropriate for all nurses

With the high proportion of aged people among in-patients in acute hospitals, it is important that acute-care nurses have an interest in and basic knowledge of gerontology, if not gerontic qualifications. For example, a gerontic nurse may have interpreted Laura's 'confusion' as loss of locality due to frequent change of environment, or as the result of her recent acute illness.

Decisions in hospital

Who was Laura's advocate when she was suddenly thrust into the impersonal hospital system? From the time it was decided to send her to hospital it was vital that someone was available to make her frail voice heard. Was she considered a 'placement problem' or an inmate of an institution and therefore with reduced rights and autonomy? This family, including two nurses with administrative and aged-care experience, were articulate enough to arrange a meeting, yet even they had to fight hard to make their aunt's wishes known. In the end they had to resort to the subterfuge of allowing occasional, covert sips of fluid — in so doing, upholding her autonomy, supporting her choice and promoting her comfort.

It is difficult for family members, articulate or not, to make their views apparent in a system so hierarchically structured, where the doctor's voice is law. The absence of a hospital nurse at the family meeting resulted, as the family feared, in the decisions made not being integrated into Laura's daily care. Even in the private hospital system where the patient's relationship with their doctor is promoted, the nurse's contribution to planning care is vital, just as, after this meeting, the nurse was clearly pivotal in implementing that care. Had a gerontic nurse been included in formal or informal planning of Laura's care, the seemingly bizarre suggestion of implanting a pacemaker into a dying elderly person's heart may have been challenged.

Welcome to the nursing home

Things did not immediately improve once Laura was admitted to a place purported to give higher level care. Regardless of how busy staff were on the day of her admission, someone must have been responsible for developing a plan of care immediately, even acknowledging the plan was provisional until a full assessment was made. The family were dismayed to find Laura's hastily packed possessions still crammed into bags after many hours, giving the accommodation a temporary and unwelcoming appearance. First impressions are important, suggesting the type of care a family can expect for their resident.

The fact that this was Laura's last move and that her life ended peacefully and with dignity had a healing effect on this family. Although they would long remember the needless suffering and frustration of the previous weeks, in the supportive environment of the nursing home they were able to farewell this cherished family member, freed from the perceived need to scrutinise every aspect of her care. They believed that Laura's eventual 'good death' was in no small part due to the reduction in her anxiety and theirs.

QUALITY ISSUES FOR ENHANCED PRACTICE

The gerontic nurse

- When transferring a resident from one facility to another, the gerontic nurse has the responsibility to forward comprehensive details, including a brief social history, to guide staff who will be assuming the resident's care.
- The gerontic nurse also has the responsibility of communicating with the family, arranging a meeting wherever possible, in anticipation of an accommodation move.
- The issue of multiple medications, decision making regarding thickened fluids and other factors in the resident's care need to be fully discussed with the resident, doctor and family to arrive at an agreed goal of care.
- Where such decisions may be in conflict with expert medical or allied health professional opinion, clear documentation provides the rationale for care, especially where the resident's wishes are accurately assessed and recorded.
- When a resident is admitted, it is important to check with the family regarding unpacking of clothes and other belongings. Some families prefer to do this themselves; however, the simple courtesy of asking may avoid misunderstandings.

Management

- Management of both low-care facilities and high-care facilities have the responsibility to ensure adequate protocols are in place for accommodation transfer.
- In the absence of suitably qualified staff, management may need to assume the role of communicating with the hospital and the family to ensure the resident's voice is also heard.
- A routine, simple welcoming gesture, such as a small vase of flowers and a written, personalised greeting in the form of a name card, reassures new residents and their families that the nursing home is committed to upholding the resident's identity.

Indirect carers

- There may be an opportunity for a chaplain, pastoral care worker or volunteer to be given responsibility for follow-up when a long-term resident is transferred to another facility. Whether this communication is by phone, letter or personal visit, such communication would reassure the resident and family they have not been forgotten.
- In circumstances where a resident has specific dietary needs, careful adherence to a diet plan and quality control checking of collected trays for food that is returned untouched may improve that resident's enjoyment of this vital aspect of life. Liaising with family members soon after the resident's admission about the resident's satisfaction with the meals may avoid the frustration and waste of inappropriate meals being repeatedly provided.

CHAPTER EIGHT

This chapter demonstrates the importance of recognising each resident in their unique, historical, cultural context. The stories also reveal the place of ritual in encouraging residents to celebrate life in its fullness.

THE FUNERAL: FLORA BENSON'S SPANNER

The funeral director advised against the expense of placing a death notice in the paper, 'She's got no family,' he said. Who then was the lone stranger, the man from Flora's past who arrived at the funeral with a spanner to authenticate his presence? Not wishing to abandon Flora to a lonely burial out in the sticks with no mourners, a homely and informal service in our chapel had been arranged. Through the volunteer's eloquent eulogy, the completion of a past relationship and the solidarity of shared grief, Flora's seemingly insignificant life and death was assured a place in the recorded history of the nursing home. This story conveys the unexpected consequences of publicly acknowledging Flora's death.

When Flora died, her 'next of kin' (a government official) was unavailable, so the funeral was delayed. Flora had entered the nursing home four years earlier with no family, no past, it seemed. There was no-one to tell us who Flora had been, and she was beyond remembering. In her last years at home, Flora had been so isolated that a trusted council worker had been able to methodically misappropriate Flora's life savings. At least Flora's mental frailty had spared her that knowledge, but it meant there was not much money for her funeral. The funeral director did his best to arrange a low-cost funeral. Anticipating the absence of graveside mourners he pondered the wisdom of a death notice in the paper, deciding against it because there was so little money and no relatives or friends outside the nursing home. However, at the request of the director of nursing, the funeral notice was published, and it did not go unseen.

Not wanting Flora to be sent off alone, a small group of six staff, a volunteer (Patsy), four residents and one stranger joined in the simple service in the nursing home chapel. With little pomp and ceremony Flora's death was acknowledged by Patsy, nursing administration, the chaplain, domestic staff, funeral director and residents. Last-minute preoccupations such as 'Who will play the organ?' and 'Couldn't we get some flowers from somewhere?' fell into place in this simple yet fitting farewell. The hymn, 'All Things Bright and Beautiful', celebrated Flora's bright nature; while Fluffy, her budgie, pirouetted in his cage beside the coffin.

The first speaker was Patsy who had been introduced to Flora a few months earlier, even though Flora seemed to be beyond the reach of ordinary social interaction. Eloquently, Patsy spoke of the remarkable bond that had grown between them; evidence of a genuine relationship. She spoke of learning from the silent Flora: 'She just crept into my heart,' she said. Regularly feeding Flora at meal times, Patsy sat for many hours with Flora firmly gripping her hand. Greatly affected by this intimate encounter with a seemingly unresponsive woman, Patsy wondered what it all meant. Although lacking words, their communication was tangible. This relationship culminated in Patsy sitting at the bedside for several hours when Flora's death was imminent. On this profoundly personal and final encounter Patsy offered no commentary.

Then the stranger took his place at the lectern by the coffin. Alerted by the funeral notice, Harry had arrived early and introduced himself to the chaplain as someone who had known Flora many years ago. 'I would like to say a few words, if I may?' We all listened intently, eager to hear what light he might shed on Flora's past. 'I hear you referring to her as Flora,' he began. 'We only ever knew her as Mrs Bensen. She was quite strict about that! Incidentally, you have spelled her surname incorrectly too. It was Bensen not Benson.' He recalled memories of the Mrs Bensen he had known for 45 years, an energetic worker in his father's factory, who had kindly but firmly supervised a group of female employees and personally tested each piece of equipment before it left the factory floor. 'And this is her spanner,' Harry said, holding high the sparkling and treasured tool clearly labelled 'Mrs Bensen'.

Harry recalled the kindly interest his father had taken in Mrs Bensen's wellbeing when she was widowed, and how his first suit had been one of Mrs Bensen's husband's, altered to fit. It seemed Mrs Bensen had been part of his growing up. After his father's death Harry had lost touch with Mrs Bensen but he had wondered what had become of her and watched the death and funeral notices daily for 20 years, looking for 'Bensen'. By attending the funeral, it was clear that Harry completed some unfinished business. He also completed for us the untold story of Flora's life. There was satisfaction for those who had nursed her, hearing of this other Flora who had a place in the world so different from what we might have imagined, but was still unmistakably the woman we knew.

The third and final speaker was a nurse who had known Flora since her admission. She spoke with some sadness and ambivalence about the change in the bright, 'sparky' and often difficult Flora, to someone silent and seemingly unreachable as her disease and the ageing process took their toll. As she spoke she observed a remarkable unity in the diverse group of mourners. In the front row Harry was drawn into the circle of care as he strained to hear our telling of the Flora he had lost. Behind him Flora's two roommates sat side by side, one shifting restlessly, the other straight and composed. Fluffy danced on his perch. The eyes of the director of nursing filled with tears, remembering. A nurse and a resident shared a box of tissues, while one of the domestic staff comforted her friend, the volunteer. Even the straight-backed funeral director seemed to lean forward into the circle. For that was what Flora had created around her; a community of care. Though it might seem to the world she had no-one, in the end we had become her family.

Flora's two roommates, Bessie and Doris, had watched over Flora, ending a relationship developed over many months. Despite the absence of words, they knew and loved Flora. Bessie had listened intently to every word at the funeral, later saying to a nurse, 'When I die I want a funeral just like that!' We may not be able to measure the reassurance Bessie received from the nurse. We hope, however, that her trust will not be misplaced and that when her time comes she will be appropriately remembered.

A spontaneous gesture by the chaplain made a very fitting end to this eventful day. Doris was moved to tears when the chaplain gave her the flowers from the coffin. Here was a tangible acknowledgment of Doris's grief. 'But you should have them,' Doris indicated to the director of nursing as if she, a mere resident, had no right to the one and only floral tribute.

ON REFLECTION…

What's in a name?

Nursing home standards require that we respect the dignity of each resident by using their preferred name. Had anyone asked Flora on admission whether she was comfortable with first-name terms? Or did she suffer in silence while her most basic point of reference was assaulted? Clearly, the man from the past who attended the funeral was quite astounded to hear the familiarity of our address. How do we ensure that staff convenience and contemporary cultural presuppositions do not override the resident's choice in this important matter? As demonstrated in the narrative, careful attention to the correct spelling of a resident's name is also important.

Learning from volunteers

What does the relationship between a volunteer and a totally dependent resident have to teach the professional carer? Through Patsy we learned that there are ways of communication that one does not learn from a textbook. While feeding a resident may be regarded by the professional nurse as a mundane routine ('a feed'), for the volunteer it was an intimate encounter.

Who knows what passed between Patsy and Flora during those final hours? What we did know was that, in the close, tactile presence of a trusted friend, Flora's restlessness subsided as she gradually and peacefully succumbed to death's call. Such 'treatment' may, in many situations, be a viable alternative to the administration of drugs.

Roommates share their grief

What encouragement is given for other residents to express their grief when a roommate dies? Attending the funeral may not always be possible or desired. However, sensitive staff will, if possible, give residents the option of involvement in this rite to mark the death of someone with whom they have shared part of their lives. Death is no stranger to older people, for they will have attended many funerals. Afterwards it will be natural for those residents who attended the funeral to talk about it, providing opportunity for those who were not present to share their grief also. In this instance, the chaplain's thoughtful gesture in giving the flowers to Doris provided an acknowledgment of Doris's grief and a tangible memento of a significant event. By participating in a roommate's funeral, other residents may be reassured that they will not be forgotten when they die.

Acknowledging the negative as well as the positive

In the three brief eulogies Flora's life was reviewed in its imperfection, she was not held up as a saint. Consequently, the mourners were able to recall her as they knew her, a mixture of a lovable, pleasant lady and a cantankerous, rebellious, fiery spirit.

Impact on the community beyond the nursing home

Funeral directors' comments sometimes convey the attitude, 'It's only a nursing home job', reflecting the pervasive community attitude that the nursing home is the end of the road, where death is inevitable. At this particular funeral some misconceptions were changed, illustrated by the funeral director's comment, 'That was a most moving service. I wish we could have a few more like that!' Perhaps the funeral director saw that dignity and respect and love are not dependent on popularity and the number of mourners at the funeral.

Accurate documentation

Unintended consequences arose from lack of direction about Flora's funeral arrangements. First, the funeral was delayed pending advice from the government official, making appropriate communication to interested staff quite difficult. Secondly, another resident was made anxious by the delay. Would it happen to her too? Mrs Brown wanted to ensure her funeral details were well documented in order to avoid what she perceived as a 'most unseemly' delay between death and burial. Who ensures that these vital details are kept up to date?

The informal interdisciplinary team

With little time to arrange funeral formalities, a team was quickly welded together, with offers of help coming from unexpected quarters. This experience served as a reminder that, in the absence of 'experts', the nursing home community responds with unconditional generosity.

Those who did not attend the funeral

How do we allow for the grief of other staff and residents to be shared? 'I didn't know when the funeral was on, I really wanted to be there,' said one of the nurses. Opportunity for other residents and staff to be informed of the death and to offer condolences is an important aspect of communication in the nursing home.

Tears are permitted

It the director of nursing can shed a tear then so may other staff. The solidarity of shared feelings manifests itself in a team spirit that has no hierarchy. The tears that flowed at Flora's funeral defy rational explanation. Somehow, the inarticulate Flora, with no family or close friends to cry for her, tapped a well deep in our hearts.

The resident, our teacher

Flora's seemingly insignificant life and death raised many issues; in her living and dying she was indeed our teacher.

QUALITY ISSUES FOR ENHANCED PRACTICE

The gerontic nurse

- Professional care requires accuracy of all admission details, including correct spelling of all names, and the resident's preferred name. Referral details are not always correct, so it is important to double check on admission.
- When a death occurs, other residents may be asked if they wish to attend the funeral, especially if it is on site.
- When involved as part of the team of care, volunteers should be included in the care planning whenever appropriate.

Management

- Developing clear procedures about public notification when death occurs is one way of ensuring a significant event is communicated in a timely manner.
- With scarce resources it may not be possible to permit staff to attend funerals in paid work time. However, with flexible rostering and good will, it may be possible to accommodate those who wish to attend.
- It is important to acknowledge the contribution of volunteers and, particularly after a resident's death, debriefing may be needed.

Indirect carers

- Following a significant long-term relationship with a resident, a volunteer may require a break before resuming visits to other residents. Caring for volunteers and learning from them adds to the rich network of relationships within the nursing home.
- Funeral attendance is an important part of the caring relationship, not only enabling the volunteer to 'close' the relationship in an appropriate manner, but also giving the whole community an opportunity to benefit from the insights and knowledge gained from that special friendship.

WRAPPING IT UP: I'VE SEEN THE ANGELS

At the closing stage of life there are often things to be 'wrapped up' so that life's disparate elements may be integrated. In preparing for death, nursing home residents are fortunate if they can rely on staff or family to assist them in this 'tying up of the ends'. In reflecting on this process, three stories have emerged. The first deals with confession; not the professional, religious confession, which of course has its place, but a significant nurse–resident encounter in which each acknowledges that everything has not always been perfect. The second relates the story of Jack. All Jack needed to know was that he was 'here' in a safe environment rather than 'there' in an impersonal place. The third story recounts the common theme of separation prior to integration, when an older person longs for things as they used to be. Finally, after revisiting significant areas of the past, and with the help of her daughter, Estelle was 'ready to go now'.

Confessions

Mr Philip Smith had forecast his death two days before; he'd 'seen the angels'. He called for his family, thanked everyone for looking after him so well and begged us not to send him to hospital. As long as he had the oxygen mask he would be okay. The astute evening nurse was well aware that this was no time for fobbing him off with a trite comment like, 'Don't be silly, Philip, you'll be as right as rain after a good night's sleep!' Instead, she savoured the moments he had chosen to speak to her about such personal matters. Caught up in the dialogue, yet wanting to do things correctly, she suggested he might like a priest to visit. 'No thanks.' Always a man to call a spade a spade he told Meg, 'I've been through the war, I've seen my own son die and I've survived a few scrapes, all without the help of a priest, so why would I want one now!' And he proceeded to use this trusted nurse and friend as confessor: 'I've done a few wrong things but I haven't lived a totally bad life.'

Meg also had some things to confess. 'We've had some battles, you and I. You haven't always been an angel to look after; there have been times when I could cheerfully have sent you to hospital!' Meg recalled to herself the times when she had hated this man who was so resistant to change. He always knew better than anyone else — 'This is the best angle for the oxygen mask.' Evenings seemed to be his worst times. 'Was it his fear of death?' Meg now wondered. He would pre-empt staff actions by demanding instant attention to those small but important items of detail. 'Don't forget my pills, and you haven't straightened my legs yet.' 'You should know by now I have two pillows under this arm.' The acknowledgment that death was close provided understanding, turning Meg's exasperation into empathy.

Philip's physical changes also presented a challenge. He would drift into semiconsciousness, then rouse himself to make sure he hadn't been sent to hospital. His frequent attacks of breathlessness made us wonder if we could keep him comfortable. Should we intervene and call the doctor? However, there were adequate medication orders for us to see this through with him, and Philip had made it clear that he did not want the doctor called. Philip had been well served by his doctor who had attended that morning. A comprehensive plan of care had been decided between Philip, the doctor and the nurse, including what to do in the event of increased breathing difficulties. Soon, relaxed and peaceful, he lay back, opening his eyes only to nod approvingly when his wife arrived, trusting that the nurse would not let him down.

When he died, his wife of 60 years was perplexed, 'Are you sure he's gone? I've never seen anyone gone before. We've been married 60 years in March next year. What do I have to do now? I suppose there's nothing more to do here.' Do, do, do. 'There's no need to hurry,' explained the nurse, 'We are all sad, we loved him too.' Reassured, Mrs Smith promptly sat down. We had no desire to bustle Philip's body out of the building. And yet it seemed as though this widow was waiting for further instructions. There was plenty of information we could give her but she had just lost a mate of 60 years. What did we know of that?

ON REFLECTION…

Being rather than doing

If nurses know anything at all they know what to do when death is near. What does it convey to the dying person to be the centre of flurried activity? Mr Smith had made it quite clear what he wanted from the nurse — her calming presence was sufficient to see him through. And for Mrs Smith? She may have thought she would be in the way after Philip died, but, guided and reassured by the unhurried nurse, she was able to take her own time to ponder this mystery, 'Has he gone?'

Certifying the death

Is it necessary to ring the doctor within the first five minutes after death? Convention of former years required the nurse not to make any assumptions. 'Respirations appear to have ceased and I can feel no pulse,' was the appropriate message. Mr Smith specifically asked that the doctor not be called prior to his death and one may assume he would see no need immediately after! There are no rules which adequately cover all situations, for in other circumstances it has been the presence of the doctor which has provided the necessary reassurance.

Calling a priest

Religious rites and rituals have their place but in the nursing home environment we have the responsibility of knowing the residents' individual needs. Mr Smith had some things he wanted to 'get off his chest' but he chose his own confessor. Meg had seen him through enough crises to prove her worth as his trusted nurse and friend. Much of what passed between them in his last hours is beyond words. Meg helped him draw his life together and 'wrap it up'.

Seeing it through

It was important for Meg, the nurse, to see this through with Mr Smith. Although it was a busy time of the evening, her colleagues understood that, for Mr Smith, the best and most appropriate care was through Meg's reassuring presence. She knew just how to massage his back to make his breathing easier. She had explained the action of the morphine and the limited benefits the oxygen would now produce. She knew there were things on his mind, things he couldn't even discuss with his wife. It was also important for Meg to accept the challenge of staying with him rather than calling an ambulance. When she had done all the appropriate tasks there was nothing more to do but to be with him, and yet, that was everything.

We loved him too

There is a legitimate place to speak of the affection of staff for residents. Mrs Smith was heard to tell her son, 'Do you know what she said? She said how much they all loved him here.' Small consolation compared with her own love and devotion of 60 years, but a fitting end to the relationship with the nursing home.

Here or there

Jack was one of those 'problems' who had been in a hospice unit for three months but had not died. Rather than try to find suitable accommodation for this friendless bachelor it seemed easier to transfer him to a nursing home. It suited Jack, who seldom spoke but appeared to be content in familiar surroundings. His homelessness and social isolation at 60 years of age were a consequence of chronic alcoholism. However, when living in a structured environment, Jack was completely self-caring. Following his daily routine of shower and shave he settled into his chair in the lounge with his book and cigarettes; he knew the rules and always went outside to smoke. Nobody ever saw Jack turn a page of that book; nor did he ever initiate any conversation. He was the 'perfect, undemanding resident'.

When there was no sign of the cancer returning, Jack's place in a nursing home was unjustified and he was transferred to supported community accommodation. Taken by the welfare worker to make his selection, he agreed it would be best to make the move before Christmas. With staff promising, 'We'll come and visit you Jack' and the assurance that his own doctor would continue to visit, Jack left our care.

It was three years before the doctor advised us of Jack's deterioration and his need for 24-hour nursing care. Staff who remembered Jack were pleased to welcome him back and extra pleased that he was to take Tom's bed. Tom, who had died suddenly, had left such a gap in our working lives. Appearing confused and quite overwhelmed by staff greetings, Jack asked many times where he was. 'They sent me to the other place because they couldn't keep me here. Am I back here now?'

'Yes, Jack, you are back here now. This is your home for the rest of your life.'

'And I don't have to go back there? I can stay here?'

After a few days of repeated reassurances that he was 'here' rather than 'there', Jack decided to stay in bed, curled up like a contented child, glazed eyes appearing above the bedclothes, until he no longer needed to see where he was. He was 'here'!

ON REFLECTION…

Individual choice

Jack had lost the ability to understand such concepts as setting short-term and long-term goals. He offered no resistance when moved back into the community and it didn't seem fair at the time to talk about the possibility of his return to our nursing home. He didn't seem to understand about the cancer either. From the staff at his previous accommodation we heard that Jack was no trouble, seldom communicating with anyone, continuing his daily ritual with cigarettes and book. When it was finally observed that he needed nursing home care there was a long wait for a bed. As far as we know Jack never articulated his choice concerning accommodation. In the end, what brought contentment was the difference between 'here' and 'there'.

Preparation for death and dying

Exploring the meaning of life, explaining the increasing effects of the cancer, advising Jack of his options for treatment seemed outside the parameters of Jack's life experience. When the chaplain approached him some weeks before his death, she was unsure if he had understood the purpose of her visit. Because Jack was a man of few words it was difficult to explore these issues with him. Perhaps it was sufficient for him to know that he was among people who cared about him.

Wrapping it up

Jack's admission to the hospice may have been inappropriate in the first place and his move from the hospice unit to a nursing home bed may have been ill-considered. As time drifted on we knew he should not be occupying a nursing home bed more suited to a person needing 24-hour nursing care. 'Where will he go?' 'Who will tell him?' We had the distinct feeling that Jack now had to pay for poor professional judgement. Whether to salve our consciences or not, we reassured ourselves that one day we would make it right for Jack. We would have him back when he needed our care. By readmitting him we felt we had wrapped it all up. We had brought Jack home to die.

'I'm ready now'

Estelle's devoted daughter Joan had struggled with the decision to 'put Mum away'. She knew that was not an appropriate expression for nursing home accommodation but 'putting her in a home' or 'having her placed' were apt descriptions of what she believed she was doing. Believing previous accommodation to be below standard, Joan had already moved her mother twice. Estelle, suffering a lack of insight due to the effects of a stroke, asked repeatedly, 'Why can't you take me home?' This did little to reassure Joan that she had made the right decision.

Occasionally Estelle had flashes of coherent thought. 'Of course I'll walk again. I'll be up and moving normally by next week!' At these times, she would recall her rose garden, her working days as a stenographer for a government official, her fighting attitude to her early widowhood. She would also mourn the loss of 'this defiant arm which just lies there like a log' and express an understanding attitude to her situation. 'I tell Joan not to bother coming in every night. She's so busy with her work.'

When Estelle had a heart attack, Joan was aware that her mother's life would probably be shortened. Having always enjoyed a close relationship, Joan asked her mother what she would like to do before she died. 'I'd love to go to the cathedral one more time and... oh!... do you think I could see the spring flowers in the botanic gardens? And of course, you know, dear, that what I want most of all is to go home.' Also high on the list was an 'afternoon tea with my old girlfriends'. This last, most difficult request was tackled first. Having discussed all these plans with the evening nurse, Joan was delighted with the staff's idea of having the afternoon tea in the nursing home. Joan collected a tablecloth, china teacups, a silver tea service and linen napkins from her mother's home, and arranged for a catering firm to deliver sandwiches and cakes; the nursing home had only to provide the room. Onlookers were overcome by the poignancy of the scene — Estelle 'entertaining' as though she had made all the preparations herself, speaking of the past as though it were the present. 'Yes, I made the scones this morning, and aren't the roses lovely, I picked them very early.' Of course, the 'girlfriends' cooperated in playing out this charade, but they displayed mixed emotions. All the effort was rewarded when Estelle, in a rare moment of insight, told the night nurse, 'That will be the last time I'll see those friends. Life has been good to me. You can't put a price on the richness of friends, can you?' And Estelle slept well.

Arranging for Estelle to see her own home before it was sold was slightly more difficult. Joan arranged a taxi which could transport her mother in the wheelchair, but did not bargain for the difficulties in manoeuvring the chair over the landscaped garden and up the steps. This excursion only seemed to make Estelle more confused. 'It wasn't worth the effort,' Joan concluded.

Two volunteers agreed to take Estelle to the cathedral and then to the gardens on the same morning. Packing a flask of tea and some sandwiches, they provided physical and emotional support for each other, not knowing what to expect from Estelle. The day was perfect, the transport efficient and they said that Estelle's reaction had to be seen to be believed. She asked to be left alone for a few minutes in the cathedral, emerging subdued and thoughtful, agreeing that morning tea in the gardens would be 'splendid, thank you'.

Photos of that morning's excursion proved a valuable memento for Estelle. The volunteers felt privileged to assist her in achieving one of her last ambitions. In discussing the event with Joan, Estelle concluded, 'Well, Joan, I am ready to die now.' And, having done all in her power to assist her mother to live life to the full, Joan was now ready to let her go.

ON REFLECTION…

The resident's last wish

What is the best way of gaining information about a resident's last wishes? The right moment may come at a point of insight about impending death. Or in a regular review of the resident's care the question may be raised in a matter-of-fact tone, 'If you had one wish to fulfil before you die, what would it be?' For another resident it may be more appropriate to offer choices, 'While you are still able to manage a wheelchair, is there anywhere you would like to go for a visit?' For some this will mean a bus trip to a children's playground or to see the city lights, or to the beach, or to see the street where they lived. For others, it will be to a church which holds memories, or a shopping expedition or a meal in a restaurant. The trouble is, if we never ask we may never know!

Individual in community

Such 'wrapping up' is not achieved in isolation but in community with others. Staff and volunteers, as well as relatives, have much to offer in assisting residents to draw their lives to a close. The question asked of the resident may also be asked of staff and relatives: 'What more may we do to improve this resident's quality of life? Is there a difference I can make towards a satisfying conclusion to this resident's life? What would I like to achieve for this resident before she or he dies?'

Joan's readiness

We may only guess at the value of such ordered preparation for death. But we do know that the grief and loss of relatives may be assisted by being ready to let go. Initially, Joan was not ready for her mother to die, continually feeling she had to do something more. Burdened by guilt at transferring her mother into residential care, it took Joan several months to come to terms with the decision. The process was assisted by staff who encouraged her to talk. Joan was also ready to receive compliments about how well she had cared for her mother, and was reminded that her caring did not stop once her mother entered the nursing home. Her diligence in visiting and her involvement in discussions of all aspects of her mother's care were appreciated by staff. 'Congratulations on a job well done' were not empty words but a sincere acknowledgment by staff of this daughter's care of her mother.

QUALITY ISSUES FOR ENHANCED PRACTICE

The gerontic nurse

- Access to a palliative care specialist allows for a comprehensive care plan to be developed, especially for appropriate treatment with end-stage airways disease.
- Careful planning may obviate the need to send a resident to hospital, providing satisfaction for the professional nurse in achieving the goal of skilled and appropriate care throughout the dying process.
- Discussion with a dying resident may elicit what their last wish might be; arranging for fulfilment of such wishes makes for very rewarding nursing.

Management

- Establishing and maintaining contact with palliative care consultants leads to a comprehensive referral system and guidelines for palliative care.
- Comprehensive assessment forms may be developed to include items such as the resident's final wishes.

Indirect carers

- When it is apparent that a resident has a 'last wish' to visit a significant friend or place, the contribution of volunteers or other staff may help to achieve that goal. Volunteers may also be invited to record such an event by taking photographs.

ANNIVERSARIES: IT'S THREE YEARS TOMORROW

Recognition of significant events such as anniversaries is not the sole province of the elderly. We all like to remember and we all like others to remember. At a time of life when each year might bring the last opportunity to share the anniversary of a birthday, wedding anniversary, or date of admission to the nursing home, it is important for families and staff to honour the past on behalf of those whose minds are not attuned to dates. However, certain sensitivity is required, for as these examples show, our idea of celebrating special events may not be the same as the resident's. With increased age, painful as well as pleasant memories may surface to help prepare for that very final date with death, which none of us can predict.

It's three years tomorrow

Mary could see George was slipping away. She increased her visits to four hours every day 'except for Fridays. George knows Friday is my shopping and cleaning day'. At 87 she still took great pride in her appearance and on this occasion she looked so pretty. 'George bought me this red dress for my 80th birthday. It was always his favourite, that's why I wore it today. I thought he might just open his eyes and see it.' Remembering that today marked the third anniversary of George's admission to the nursing home, Mary reminded Heather, one of the nurses, 'Remember, it was you who met us at the front door. I'll never forget how kind you were to us. You made me a cup of tea while George was settling in. You've always been one of George's favourites too.' Unspoken was the thought that it would be nice if Heather could also be with them on George's last day.

Introducing Mr Mervyn Black, aged 80 years

Brian knew that next week would be Mervyn's birthday; although for Mervyn one day was the same as any other. Belligerent and discontented, he began each day with a fight:

a fight with the nurses over his tea (too much milk, too little sugar), a fight with the cleaner about the mess on the floor ('I didn't put it there!'), a fight over the need for a shower ('That's all you know how to do — wash people, whether they need it or not!').

As Mervyn's favourite nurse, Brian had seen him through many emotional and physical crises; he wanted to do something special for Mervyn's 80th birthday. Mervyn, in a quieter mood, would tell Brian about his rough but happy memories of 'the good old days', on the railways or in northern Victoria. When he was in the mood, he'd get his photos down and show them to Brian as if for the first time. That was what gave Brian the idea. He began by writing down Mervyn's stories and offered to get some of the photos restored.

Mervyn's 80th birthday gift from Brian was an illustrated history of Mervyn's life, pieced together with the help of Mervyn's distant cousin. The book included an 'anonymous' poem, although everyone knew Brian had written it. Mervyn carried this album, called *Life History of Mr Mervyn Black*, everywhere he went, but only for two weeks. A short time after the significant milestone, which would have passed without acknowledgment had it not been for the ingenuity of this one nurse, Mervyn died.

Postscript: We would have liked to keep the *Life History of Mervyn Black* as part of our nursing home history and in memory of Mervyn, but a family member who had never shown any interest in his later years turned up and claimed it!

The reluctant birthday girl

'You'll be 92 tomorrow! What a great age!' says the nurse.

'I can't hear you. I don't want to hear you. Don't shout, my ears are turned off. It's not really me you're talking to. I stopped living a long time ago. Now I'm just waiting to die. If I really am 92, and I'm not sure if I believe you, I'd just as soon forget. Thank the Lord I won't have to put on a party frock.

'Mother always makes me wear the white starched voile with the blue satin sash handed down from Bea. It's never fitted properly and the collar scratches my neck raw. I'm afraid

I'll get it dirty.

'Dirty, dirty... who made this mess in the bed? Not me!

'It's my birthday and Will has bought me some pretty hair ribbons. I'll keep them and use them for the baby's clothes. He is an old silly. I wish he wouldn't spend money like that, there's so many bills to pay and another baby on the way.

'That was only last year. What has happened to me since then? Whose hands are these on my arms, all wrinkled and clawed? She's wearing my wedding ring. Get it off, get it off and give it back to me! That's all I have left of my Will. Oh, how I loved him! Surely he died only yesterday, the pain is so sharp... Will, Will, where are you? Who are all these people round my bed singing 'Happy Birthday' with fire in their hands? It's not my birthday. Oh, please don't make a fuss. I only want to watch the trees and wait for Will.'

Christmas: The universal festivities

It's Christmas morning. Ruth and the others in her room are washed earlier than usual so that some staff can get home to Christmas dinner. Before these four residents are properly awake they are up and dressed in unfamiliar 'good' outfits with tinsel in their hair and parked against the wall in the garishly decorated lounge. Ruth's eyes are dazzled by the flashing lights on the Christmas tree. 'Jingle Bells' is playing loudly on the stereo beside her chair. Caught in a memory lapse she worries about not having presents ready for the children. A breakfast tray is slapped down in front of her, jolting her into the present. Ruth eats her cereal numbly, pushing back the tears that go with remembering the past and knowing the present. Her family have long since gone, the family home of happy Christmas memories a blur; a wave of loneliness washes over her and she feels as if her heart will break. Suddenly tired after being wakened so early, she wishes she could stay in bed today and forget Christmas until it's over. She's done no shopping, no baking, has no family to greet. Yes, Christmas is in the past. Her angina's been so bad she knows it will be her last Christmas. Secretly she is glad.

'What a pity you'll miss sitting round the Christmas dinner table,' says the resentful nurse who puts Ruth back to bed after one of her 'heart turns'.

'Christmas means nothing when you've nothing to give,' murmurs Ruth as the bedrail is slammed into place.

ON REFLECTION…

Memories both pleasant and painful

These episodes signify a variety of responses to anniversaries and festivities. For the inner world of the resident whose memory is fading, these old anniversaries may be meaningless. For the resident who longs for death, the celebration of another birthday may bring sadness, not joy. For the resident who fears death, another anniversary may be an unwelcome reminder of mortality.

Appropriate celebrations

Who is the celebration for — the resident, the family or the staff? Sometimes it's for everyone and joyous occasions are fitting rituals. However, the challenge is to know what the resident really wants and when enough is enough. When the resident says, 'Don't make a fuss', is she really saying, 'Please don't forget my birthday' or 'Too much stimulation makes me exhausted'?

For some residents, birthdays are the most important anniversaries. For others, the anniversary of a spouse's death is more important, or the anniversary of their admission date. Some will remember the date when a roommate died, while others will not disclose their more secret anniversaries.

Private or public

Some residents may prefer to have a quiet birthday celebration or mark some other special occasion without any staff involvement at all. In circumstances where the resident is unable to go out, a hospitable environment would welcome family or a small group of friends into the nursing home to plan and enjoy their own occasion. While it is not easy to provide private space in a public place, lateral thinking and imagination may produce a workable option. Where a small lounge is available, families may be invited to book the room in advance, bringing their own provisions for a private party.

Christmas

Christmas brings many different responses from the community as a whole, depending on cultural and religious beliefs, family practices and former memories. Within each nursing home there will also be a diversity of feeling about Christmas. Residents may receive greater understanding if they were asked, 'What are your memories of Christmas? Is there any particular way you would like to celebrate Christmas day? Would you like to give any cards or gifts?' In the spirit of generosity, many staff and relatives endeavour to shower gifts upon residents at this time of year. Some residents may welcome assistance with purchasing gifts for family and friends. In this way, the joy of giving as well as receiving enhances their self-worth.

Individual assessment

Ideally, the question would be asked of each resident, either on admission or during a subsequent review of care, 'What events in your life are most significant? Which anniversaries are the most important to you? Would you like us to remind you of any special dates?'

We may not always fully understand the importance of particular dates for particular residents. Of one thing we may be sure, the key to one resident's unique treasury of memories will not necessarily unlock the memories of other residents.

QUALITY ISSUES FOR ENHANCED PRACTICE

The gerontic nurse

- Assumptions may be tested by careful questioning when acknowledging a resident's birthday or other significant anniversary; some residents may prefer no public announcement, while others may appreciate some special attention.
- Careful assessment elicits information about what the significant anniversaries are for each resident.
- It then becomes the responsibility of the nurse in charge on the day to ensure the appropriate response is made.
- Opportunities for the giving as well as receiving of gifts is facilitated by discussion with residents and offering assistance to purchase gifts and cards.

Management

- Formulating a comprehensive assessment form, which captures the resident's beliefs, attitudes and perceptions about anniversaries, leads to more responsive care.
- Establishing a small committee, with the involvement of residents' families, may lead to innovative practice for Christmas celebrations.
- Cultural factors for particular residents are also to be considered, and provision made for culturally specific festivities as appropriate.
- Space may be made available for families to have their own personal celebrations, without staff involvement or added expense or inconvenience to the nursing home.

Indirect carers

- The involvement of activities staff, volunteers and families adds much to special occasions, such as Christmas.

CHAPTER NINE

This chapter wrestles with the complexity of documentation; the official record is discussed, both as narrative and as a communication tool. Also explored is the issue of appropriate resources being provided to enhance the dying resident's care.

DOCUMENTATION: CONVEYING THE STORY AS WELL AS THE TASKS

How is dignity measured and recorded? What is it about death and dying that makes documentation so difficult that staff record little of the skilled and compassionate care they provide for the dying resident? Examples from residents' files illustrate how accurate and compassionate documentation benefits the resident and how the absence of comprehensive recording undermines care. Reflection on practice is facilitated by accurate documentation, paving the way for research which, in turn, leads to best practice.

It is a strange phenomenon that when a resident's life is drawing to a close the written record often reflects detailed physical symptoms but very little of psycho-emotional or spiritual factors, communication matters or family dynamics. It appears that, when the resident is no longer able to move about, interact with others, eat or drink or respond to the daily round of nursing home life, anything worthy of documenting is deemed to have vanished. At this time of greatest change, the care plan is rarely revised to reflect a changed goal of care, leaving nothing to evaluate and no outcome to indicate whether the care given was effective.

The official record of a resident's life and death can reflect adequately the volume and quality of care. Reassessing the resident's needs in order to establish a current goal of care, identifying the planned interventions and evaluating the outcome may be something done as a matter of routine. However, if the formal record does not reflect this, it is difficult to establish consistency and find a basis to justify the funding required to give such care. Far from being designed solely to give busy staff more work, adequate, accurate documentation provides a comprehensive record that is of significant benefit to the resident.

A detailed plan of care for the resident who is dying becomes a living instrument when it accurately reflects the resident's carefully assessed needs. The official record assumes vital importance when it is used as a communication tool and is based on thorough discussion with resident, family, doctor and relevant carers. Such a record is the resource for staff in doubt; the place to find a current and true record of the resident's wishes, notes on important family issues and details of changes as they occur. This is the guide which signposts the resident's expressed desire for classical music, a bed in the sunshine, a foot massage, a favourite drink or any other comfort measures. Ongoing assessment may also identify factors such as a fear of hospitalisation, a wish to die alone or anxiety about a will. Final wishes may be recorded, such as reconciliation with a family member, specific instructions about the funeral or bequeathing of belongings.

If holistic care is given, then the documentation will reflect spiritual, emotional and psychological, as well as physical, care. Without unnecessarily lengthy notes, significant interactions may also be recorded, such as, 'Lucy called me to her bedside and asked me to thank all the staff who have cared for her' or 'Please tell my neighbour that I'd rather she didn't come in to see me any more' or 'I'm afraid of pain. You won't let me suffer, will you?'

As well as the resident's statements, it is appropriate for staff to record their own conversations or significant interactions with a dying resident. For example, a member of staff may wish to say goodbye to a resident who is close to death, perhaps with a simple statement such as, 'David and I shared a special moment together as we said goodbye, recognising it may be the last time.' These 'interventions' are equally as important as any technical care.

The same applies to medical care. Where necessary, a comprehensive medical plan will also include a contingency plan for such elements of care as pain relief. While the nursing home is not a hospital with 24-hour medical staff, a dying resident may still require specific symptom control at any time of the day or night. While in many instances the death of a nursing home resident follows a predictably crisis-free path, it is a wise medical practitioner who ensures an appropriate plan of action should a crisis occur. It is the plan, clearly documented and communicated, which ensures the resident receives care specific to assessed needs.

Nowhere is reflection on practice more important than in the area of death and dying — without it, how do we know whether the goal of care was reached? If the staff attitude is to regard documentation for a dying resident as unimportant, a valuable learning opportunity is lost, as are the benefits of improved care for residents, based on past experience. While there is great benefit in staff sharing opinions and feelings following a resident's death, so too is there benefit in formal, objective documentation-based reflection on practice. Such evaluation invites constructive questions: 'Was our care appropriate to this resident's needs?' Or 'What was the source of the relatives' criticisms?'

When does appropriate documentation begin?

It has been stated elsewhere that care of the dying resident begins from the day that admission is confirmed. Accurate admission details provide a most important guide to communication with relatives or next of kin. Many of these details can be gathered and recorded in the pre-admission period. A thorough waiting list file facilitates smooth admission procedures; however, this information must be kept up to date and accurate by regular review of important data, such as relevant phone numbers backed up by personal communication with family members. This type of information may be revealed only by regular meetings with relevant next of kin. For example, does a very frail, elderly spouse wish to be woken in the middle of the night when they have already been alerted to the resident's deteriorating condition? Although this spouse may be the next of kin, is there someone else to phone first with news of death? Comprehensive documentation about such a point may be critical to a healthy grieving process.

The following three selections of documentation show some commonly recorded notes under broad headings, and alternatives are offered that present a more comprehensive picture of the care these residents actually received.

Examples of commonly encountered notes

General	Behaviour	Notes recorded at the time of death
All attempts at feeding have failed today	Resisted all attempts at feeding	Respirations ceased at 0100 hrs
Poor fluid intake	Lashing out and punching	Died peacefully. Doctor and family notified
Reaching for imaginary things	Kept pushing the glass away	Unable to record pulse or blood pressure
Antibiotics given with difficulty	Continues to push staff away	Doctor certified death at 0200 hrs
Pressure care attended	Objected to mouth care	Resident deceased 0315 hrs
Urinary output poor	Clamps his mouth shut	
	Praying loudly, disturbing others	
	Very irritable when disturbed	
	Refused medications	
	She is very peaceful and does not appear to be in pain	
	Seems depressed	
	Calling out frequently through the night	
	Family visiting	

These examples constitute a variety of entries in the notes of residents approaching death. It is interesting that, while the final entry is made in the daily notes, there is seldom any comment in the evaluation section of the care plan.

Alternative, more comprehensive notes

By way of contrast the following headings and comments are descriptions of care that encourage evaluation, reflection and research. These notes, when clearly dated, also constitute a guide for all carers.

Terminal care wishes: *Following a telephone conversation with Dr James, Dora wished to reiterate her wish that her mother not be hospitalised under any circumstances. In case of a crisis, Dora will come in to sit with her mother while appropriate medication is arranged to ensure her mother is not in pain.*

Palliative care: *Doctor confirmed the goal of care is now to maximise comfort. Medications reviewed; cease all drugs except analgesics. Plan of care discussed and agreed upon by family, staff and doctor.*

Family processes: *Husband and daughter attended review meeting — a frank discussion re Mary's prognosis. Clarry and Jean plan to take turns in visiting. They are to be telephoned at any hour of the night should Mary's condition deteriorate further.*

Spiritual: *Tom calling out continually and praying loudly. Disturbing others. Settled after visit from priest. Father O'Connor will call each morning and evening.*

Communication: *Mary expressed fear of dying alone. Reassured that family or staff would make every effort to be with her at the end. Clock placed within reach. Hand bell to be used in preference to buzzer.*

Nutrition and hydration: *Refusing all intake. Doctor aware of dehydration. After discussion with family and staff it is agreed that no intrusive or invasive treatment is appropriate. Continue to offer small amounts frequently, but do not force. Family now aware that nutritional needs are not a high priority.*

Pain: *Morphine (continuous subcutaneous dose according to drug sheet). Continue pain management chart. Explanation to resident and family about morphine administration.*

Comfort measures: *Music therapist has left George's favourite tapes at bedside. Wheel bed into sunshine for half-hour intervals if desired by the resident.*

Social: *Ailsa and Freda wanted to say their goodbyes. Ailsa sat in wheelchair beside Mary's bed for two hours this evening.*

Basic nursing care: *Mouth care, pressure care, continence management as per care plan.*

Hospitalisation: *Frank's wish is to be respected — he has asked not to be hospitalised under any circumstances. 'I want to die in my own bed.' Doctor and family are comfortable with revised plan of care.*

Family involvement: *Doris's daughters wish to be involved in all physical care when they are visiting. They wish to be shown how to turn her and attend to pressure care. Staff to intervene only if requested by family; offer assistance, be readily available, but do not intrude.* (It should be noted that in other instances the family may have no desire for such involvement, preferring to leave the room while the resident's care is attended.)

Emotional distress: *Family, resident and chaplain met in privacy to discuss Bertha's constant tears. Family reported it was two hours well spent, some feelings were resolved.*

The final entry

When important issues of palliative care are outlined in the care plan, the final entry takes on new significance, as the following examples indicate:

Bertha's death occurred at 1900 hours with volunteer beside her, and her favourite tape playing. Family have no wish to come in. They feel they have said their goodbyes. Dignified and pain-free death. Dr Martin thanked all the staff for excellent care. Ailsa and Freda wished to 'pay their respects'. Other residents to be told in the morning. Notification of all relevant personnel as per procedures.

Annie appears to have died between 1100 and 1130 hrs. Annie's sister commented that Annie had always wanted to die alone. She never wanted a fuss made, and so it appears she achieved her wish.

James seemed very restless and anxious prior to death; staff and family unable to comfort him. Perhaps the offer of a priest may have been appropriate.

Suzanne, the volunteer, expressed her thanks for the privilege of being asked to come and sit with Jack. She had never been close to death before and appreciated support from staff.

Dr Spring phoned to check if the morphine had alleviated Jack's restlessness. I was able to tell her Jack had just died. Letter of thanks to be written to the doctor for her availability and assistance especially during the last 24 hours.

Mary had expressed the wish not to die alone. In family's absence, staff were rostered for four hours continuously until her death.

Gertie's family were satisfied they cared for their mother until death, wishing to be left alone to tend their mother's body after death.

Despite Freda's multiple medical problems we have been able to provide her with the best care she could have received in her final weeks of life. Freda died very peacefully, free of any uncomfortable symptoms, and with complete trust in her carers.

John died peacefully with his trusted friend, Alec, sitting with him.

Joan, the volunteer, remained with Amy until the end, reading her favourite poems.

Staff may well feel satisfied that the residents' assessed needs were matched by appropriate goals and the holistic planned action was continually reviewed.

ON REFLECTION...

Advice to families

Some of the stories have already alluded to the benefit of showing relatives, and residents where appropriate, the detailed planned approach to care. Residents and families may be reassured to know, for example, that the doctor has prescribed an appropriate drug for symptom management, including prn (when necessary) orders in case medical advice is not immediately available. The documented word then becomes a realistic avenue of reassurance and support.

Coordination, continuity and consistency of caregivers

Each nursing home develops its own method of sharing responsibility regarding documentation. It is important that all carers know who is responsible for the plan of care; that they have access to the documentation and are made aware of changes. It is not helpful to the resident or the team of carers if one nurse decides, 'I don't think he needs his morphine', while, unless there are contra-indications, the next nurse gives the medication according to the plan. Such inconsistency may be bewildering for the resident and confusing for the family, whether related to pain control or any other aspect of care. As an adjunct to the doctor's authorising prescription, it is useful to include the use of narcotics in the care plan, so the goal can be articulated together with the planned action, followed by evaluation and review.

Documentation is a guide, not a foolproof solution

While verbal communication is an important adjunct to documentation, when dealing with the issue of death it is important that the objective, printed words become the basis for communication. When staff opinion is divided over an issue of terminal care wishes, for example, best practice points to the latest entry in the official record of care as the guide for decision making.

However, even the most exemplary care plan does not guarantee good care. A written plan and the delivery of care go hand in hand; the human factor links the two. Documentation may be an obstacle to care, unless supported by clear communication and a genuine attempt to understand the resident's and family's needs. This provides the key to excellence in the holistic care of residents who are dying.

Changing course

Regular review and reassessment facilitates a living plan of care which is changed to suit the resident's changing needs. For one resident, the plan may remain relevant and therefore unchanged throughout the dying process. For another resident, symptoms and reactions may change frequently, indicating further review is needed. Flexibility is the guide, both in style of documentation and attitude towards the written record. 'Damn, I've just completed a beautiful care plan!' may well be the nurse's reaction, but the beauty of the care plan does the resident little good. In design, brevity and clarity, the documentation tool must lend itself to change.

Fewer words with more impact

The aim of comprehensive documentation is not for busy care staff to spend even more time writing; rather, it is to convey, in concise terms, the main components of the dying process as experienced by the resident. For example, to include a direct quote from a resident may convey far more than a lengthy description of the carer's observations.

Further research

A wealth of insight is to be gained from further research into this area. It is not necessarily more documentation that is required; rather it is knowing how to write effectively about resident care. Comprehensive research into documentation, specifically in relation to the death and dying of nursing home residents, can only enhance future practice.

QUALITY ISSUES FOR ENHANCED PRACTICE

The gerontic nurse

- When documentation is accurate and comprehensive it can be trusted, leading gerontic nurses to 'look in the notes' rather than guessing.
- Rather than the nurse on each shift having to make unilateral judgements about care, the documented plan provides consistency and continuity.
- Where symptoms indicate, a clearly set-out crisis plan provides practical guidance for carers.
- Evaluating the care of a resident following death brings satisfaction, especially if the goals have been achieved.
- Clearly documented consultation with relatives at every point of terminal care brings reassurance and potentially saves distressing repercussions later.
- Regular liaison is necessary with allied health staff (such as physiotherapist, music therapist and staff who provide leisure activities) so that their valuable contribution can be acknowledged.

Management

- A system of auditing the final entry and the care plan evaluation for each deceased resident promotes, in turn, continuous quality improvement.
- Clear policies determining access to documentation are a useful guide, especially when family members wish to see what has been written.
- Non-nursing staff need guidance from management, reinforced by clear policies and procedures, regarding writing in residents' records.

Indirect carers

- Indirect carers may have unique opportunities to participate in documenting care, depending on the facility's policies and procedures.

- In the kitchen, practices such as recording food preferences and requested meal sizes are important.
- When laundry staff provide an accurate record of whose washing is taken home and whose is laundered on site, they contribute to the family members' sense of security, particularly when unfamiliar or agency staff are involved.

ENVIRONMENTAL FACTORS: MORE THAN BRICKS AND MORTAR

There is more to the dying resident's environment than the building. Perhaps the most important aspect of the dying resident's environment is the care that staff provide. Responsive, interactive care builds this vital element into the bricks and mortar. We provided Arthur with an appropriate physical environment to match what we perceived were his needs. Arthur was not pleased to be alive and told us so frequently and in many different ways. Even so, we failed to recognise his approaching death and missed our opportunity to provide him with an optimum environment of care.

From the day Arthur arrived, he let us know of his dissatisfaction with life. When asked if moving to the nursing home was hard, he looked at the director of nursing with scorn and said, 'I'll say it's hard, hard as bloody concrete!'

At 92, each day brought fresh misery and he spent most waking hours in a chair by his bed, head in hands, oblivious to the beautiful garden outside and completely ignoring his concerned roommates. He resisted attention, alienating well-meaning staff with cutting, hurtful comments or a tirade of abuse.

Some days, and most nights, his thoughts were in the past, returning time and again to the same painful memories and delusions. When life was too hard to bear, he would recite the 23rd psalm (Arthur's own version) or call out loudly to his personal, punishing god for mercy. Even so, he rejected the chaplain's gentle offers of companionship and sent other pastoral carers away with curses.

Surely no-one could continue to live in such misery but, wish as he might, Arthur's death was slow in coming. He ate so little there was no flesh on his arthritic bones and he was plagued by constipation. For a long time he seemed to hover halfway between living and dying. It's hard to remember if his cries, 'Leave me alone, I just want to die!' continued to increase, but it was noticed that he seemed to be staying in bed more often. 'I'm just a tired old man. Oh, leave me in bed for god's sake!' There was nothing new about these protests; we'd heard them repeated time and again. He was so difficult to manage we often went to him in pairs, both for moral support and to get his care over and done with as quickly as possible.

Even in retrospect, it's hard to tell when he began to die, whether it was when he consistently refused fluids, or after the third course of antibiotics for his chest infection. He was very frail, but he had been wanting to die for so long that when the moment came it was unclear who was more surprised, Arthur or the staff. Evaluating his care, we were made aware of the many inconsistencies in his care. With the best intentions in the world, some staff had been coaxing and tricking him to take fluids and medication right up to the week of his death. That was clearly not his wish. Why had we tried to prolong the life of this man who was so ready to die?

He had turned his back on the world long ago, despite the offer of congenial company and a comfortable home. He had never noticed the garden or appreciated the view from his window. In spite of his sheepskin and special mattress his bed was a torment. He sent his attractive, appetising meals back untouched day after day. All he wanted to do was die; it must have seemed to him we could only provide an appropriate environment for those who wished to live.

ON REFLECTION…

What is the dying resident's environment?

The word 'environment' (as a variety of dictionaries show) has a rich complexity of meaning which is relevant to holistic care in the context of dying. Synonyms and interpretations of the word 'environment' include: surrounding objects or circumstances; the act of surrounding; that which encompasses; factors; situation; milieu; state of life; social surroundings; predicament; state of affairs; appearance; rapport; context; background; setting; scene.

These words are reminiscent of a theoretical framework for holistic care, where dying residents are acknowledged as the centre of their immediate social, physical, spiritual and emotional surrounds.

For care to be truly resident-centred we must know what the resident requires and/or expects from this last environment or context of care. What are the resident's wishes, desires and priorities? This idea is reinforced when staff attempt to put into practice the essence of palliative care, that is, involving the resident in decision making about the site of care. It is important that this information is obtained early in the resident's admission, recorded in the resident's history, checked and updated regularly.

Resident focus

Resident-centred care demands that we are aware of what it is the resident wishes for now, today, not three weeks, months or years ago. Such vital information can best be obtained by regular discussion of options with the resident or the resident's representative. If, like Arthur, the resident is unable to speak to us clearly of his or her wishes, we must be alert to interpret non-verbal clues. In this way, when death is imminent, we may be in a position to offer the knowledge-based advocacy which was missing for Arthur.

Security of tenure

Providing residents with security in their last days or months involves reassuring them about the security of their accommodation. While issues such as bed position or tenure in the nursing home are of vital importance for the security of all residents, when a resident is dying, our concerns in meeting these issues may be harder to define. What could have made Arthur's situation secure? He didn't seem to appreciate the warm drinks, the clean sheets or the buzzer pinned to his pillow. Was he just ungrateful, or had we missed giving him the intangible security he craved? This may have been achieved by empathy, understanding and listening that little bit harder to someone who found it hard to communicate, but nonetheless needed to be heard.

Talking to residents about their death

Confronting one's own impending death is one of the tasks of old age. When is the right time to approach this with residents? Is it our reluctance or theirs which prevents early discussion? As the survivors of their generation, residents may be more comfortable with the thought of death than staff. Perhaps it was our discomfort about Arthur's eagerness for death which prevented us from recognising his closeness to it and communicating clearly with him. Or perhaps Arthur was one of those who deliberately choose not to discuss their impending death; for whatever reason.

What do dying residents want from their carers?

A study in which elderly patients dying at home were surveyed (Arblaster et al., 1990) may provide some answers to this question.

The study defined the most desirable and helpful nursing behaviours in the areas of physical and psycho-emotional care, demonstrating that preferred care was care offered and derived from the needs and wishes of the patient. The authors suggest this responsive care can originate only from careful assessment. This implies acknowledging and respecting the lifetime of experience and wisdom patients have accumulated by including them and/or their representative in planning their terminal care.

Other results included:
- The nurses' behaviour and attitudes were as important to patients as any of their words and tasks.
- The patients desired recognition of their independence and continuity of current level of autonomy.
- The patients desired to remain at home, in the context of everyday life, for as long as possible.
- The patients wished to be treated with dignity and respect.
- The patients wished for normalcy.
- The patients expressed a need for a sense of partnership with the carers, so that decisions about their care were made jointly, not imposed.

These research findings offer a reminder that, in terminal care as in everyday life, nursing home residents have a right to care tailored to their individual needs and expressed wishes.

The holistic environment of care

We may have missed the opportunity to provide Arthur with the kind of care important to him in his unique circumstances. By reflecting on his care, the suggestions outlined below show how the next 'Arthur' may benefit.

Social environment:
- Calm, non-officious staff providing unhurried care in the bedroom the resident is accustomed to, with the usual life of the nursing home continuing around them. This is normalcy.
- Relaxed visiting hours facilitating the companionship of family, friends, other residents and staff, if desired. Courtesy and support from staff towards visitors — but also protection from visitors whose presence may be an intrusion for the resident who prefers to be alone.
- Communication between resident and doctor, or between family and doctor, facilitated by staff when necessary.

Physical environment:
- Something that feels like home — a rug, a special cushion, a bedspread; their bedside belongings kept with the least possible disturbance; ascertaining which personal possessions are to be prominent.
- Personal possessions at the bedside not displaced by medical paraphernalia.
- An easily managed method of summoning staff: a call bell, a hand bell, or even a walking stick to thump on the floor if that is the method best suited to the resident (and without its causing undue disturbance to others).
- Comfortable chairs for visitors; pillows and blankets available if a family member or friend is to stay beside the resident at night.
- Bedrails or not, according to thorough assessment, with all issues of restraint carefully identified.
- A clear view of the nursing home activities outside the bedroom, but access to privacy if desired.

Nursing/personal care environment:
- No intrusive treatment, no interminable checking of vital signs, no injections unless necessary and agreed upon for symptom relief.
- Explanations and choices about medical and nursing care.
- Careful planning of meals, including preferred size and frequency, together with a documented care plan which takes account of refused meals.
- Sensitive planning and frequent review regarding daily hygiene, dressing in day clothes, remaining in bed or getting up.

- Thorough attention to all skin care regardless of the imminence of death.
- Careful assessment and review of bowel and bladder elimination.
- Family involvement in nursing and personal care if desired.

Change of bed position or room:

Careful consideration is required before any proposed change of bed position, for example moving to a single room. The question of the appropriateness of a special room for the resident who is dying is an issue for each nursing home to consider. Factors which may influence this decision are:

- the stated preference of resident, family, and other residents
- the isolation of dying in a single room
- fears expressed by the resident, such as 'Don't take me to that room'
- holistic care in a familiar environment — even when death is imminent
- disturbance caused by a noisy, restless resident (such factors may be better addressed by good symptom control for that resident)
- consideration for other residents who may never see the dying resident again
- careful weighing up of whose needs are paramount
- the unnecessary, imposed separation of the dying from the living
- residents' security of accommodation to be clarified well before death is imminent.

Holistic concerns indicate there can be no prescriptive rules about privacy at the time of death. Whether or not the screens should be drawn or the resident moved to a single room or the body moved immediately after death are factors which call for careful assessment and evaluation. As each situation is unique, there needs to be flexibility at work within the broad nursing home policy framework when considering such matters. Thorough knowledge of the resident, ongoing communication with the family and careful assessment at the time will provide the basis for deciding such important environmental factors.

Emotional environment:

Loneliness is a most painful experience and may occur even in the midst of a group when a sense of relationship is absent. Even if the dying resident is withdrawn or unable to converse there are other ways to maintain relationship:

- Rather than someone being at the bedside constantly (unless the resident requests it), making regular brief visits to check on the resident or quietly offering sips of fluid may bring sufficient reassurance.
- Emotional as well as physical care can be maintained by the attitude of the nurse who attends the resident, if that nurse focuses intentionally on the resident, explaining each procedure thoroughly.

- When visits to the resident's bedside are made at times other than for task intervention, an opportunity to relate on a normal level is offered. An enormous amount of reassurance is given by approaching the resident merely to say, 'How are you, Arthur?'
- It is important to remain alert for and open to residents' emotional expressions, for example, in gesture, sighing, facial expression or words. Deep and meaningful conversations may not be possible or required. Simple, accepting acknowledgment of the resident's emotional state, however unexpected or whatever the mode of communication, can be the most nourishing care at the point of death.

Spiritual environment:

When a resident is dying, practices relating to their religious or cultural beliefs are to be observed. However, these matters can be addressed only if thorough assessment has revealed the resident's preferences and expectations. As well as facilitating spiritual care when required, staff must also uphold the right of a resident to refuse any formalised pastoral/spiritual care if that is their preference. Remembering that spiritual care embraces more than mere formal religious practices, the following assessment points are of significance:

- ascertaining what or who provides the greatest spiritual support to the resident
- identifying whether or not formal visits are required by the resident's pastoral carer of choice
- identifying any rituals which have meaning for the resident, such as praying, scripture reading, visual symbols, religious (or other) music
- assessing, where possible, any fears and anxieties relating to death
- clarifying any 'last wishes' which may be realistically achieved before death.

After death:

Matters of dignity include care of and attention to the body after the death, as well as maintaining the memory of each deceased resident. Occasionally, staff may need to intervene on behalf of the deceased resident to ensure dignified handling of the body by funeral personnel. The memory of the resident lives on in the conversation of staff and other residents, as well as in carefully formulated procedures and policies which ensure the resident's unique place in the history of the nursing home will not be lost.

QUALITY ISSUES FOR ENHANCED PRACTICE

The gerontic nurse

- Pre-admission details, when comprehensively recorded, inform the gerontic nurse of the resident's feelings about nursing home entry.
- Careful assessment relating to spiritual care needs to be communicated in the written record for all carers.
- Gerontic nurses set an example to others when thoughtfully approaching residents for matters other than tasks, taking time to meet the resident's holistic needs.

Management

- Pre-admission forms need careful attention to their content. Matters other than demographic details are important for establishing the resident's and family members' feelings about nursing home entry.
- A comprehensive Terminal Care Wishes Form provides the opportunity for important details to be recorded and reviewed.
- A Spiritual Care Assessment Form is necessary for ascertaining residents' wishes and concerns, or appropriate questions can be incorporated into another assessment form.
- Continuous assessment and review takes into account the resident's changing patterns and responses, which may emerge over time.

Indirect carers

- Indirect care staff may be taken into a resident's confidence. While being careful not to betray trust, carers other than nurses have an important role to play in providing information about how a resident is really feeling.
- Indirect care staff are often in a position to observe small changes in behaviour that may not be noticed by others. For instance, the chef or kitchen hand may notice that the favourite meal returns uneaten, or a cleaner may be unable to engage a resident in a previously enjoyed topic of conversation.

STANDARDS: A MEASURE OF DIGNITY

It has been argued that documentation is a valuable tool for evaluating the care of a dying resident. The discussion now turns to the way in which dignity is measured and recorded. The story of Mr Papandreou provides, in one simple statement, a clue to the measure of his dignity. Sadly, this was not identified at the time. Reflection on this resident's life and death in the nursing home leads us to ask where on a rating scale would his dignity be placed? A variety of references from contemporary literature and a forgotten century provide further clues which may help us to grasp this elusive quality called dignity.

Dignity is a subjective matter. One nurse may assume a particular resident is dying a dignified death because the resident is quiet, accepting and presents no problem behaviours; the measure of dignity being the amount of trouble caused to staff. Another nurse's concept of dignity in death may be aligned with perceptions of death itself. Three illustrations from contemporary literature illustrate a variety of attitudes people have towards death. First there's Kingsley Amis:

> Death has got something to be said for it:
> There's no need to get out of bed for it;
> Wherever you may be,
> They bring it to you, free.

Then there's Woody Allen:

> I'm not afraid to die. I just don't want to be there when it happens.

And finally, from Dylan Thomas:

> Do not go gentle into that good night,
> Old age should burn and rave at close of day;
> Rage, rage against the dying of the light.

The first quote deals with death's inevitability, a philosophical standpoint evident in the voices of age and wisdom within our nursing homes and hostels.

The second quote reveals the ambivalence of denial counterbalancing overwhelming fear.

Dylan Thomas's poem is sometimes perceived as a comment on the experience of a young person who fights death all the way. Old people may also fight death. It is not necessarily any easier for them to let go of life. Why does this thought make us uncomfortable? As carers, we have watched dying patients rebel against this most unwelcome of enemies. This kind of rebellion may be evident in the clinical syndrome known in palliative care as 'terminal restlessness'. And the remedy? Usually tranquillisers, because we regard our inability to settle a patient or resident who is 'raging against the dying of the light' as failure. Rather than perceiving such distress as a struggle against death itself, it is likely to be recorded as agitation, anxiety or restlessness. We do not respect a resident's dignity when we apply a chemical panacea for genuine feelings of anxiety and fear related to the experience of dying.

Many residents in nursing homes have spent their lives ensuring that dignity and respect is accorded to others; that a feeling of belonging and a sense of worth is conveyed to their children, friends, neighbours and employees. For many, dignity has been gained through autonomy and control over their own circumstances; through the ordinary decisions of daily existence such as: what time to get up, whether to open the curtains or leave them closed, what to wear, or when to eat. Their unique rhythm of life was set by their chosen routine. Once the older person has entered a nursing home, control over their life (and dignity) may be lost. Dignity issues may be apparent in unspoken questions such as: How will I know what's happening to me when I can't remember who I am? How will I be able to tell them what I want when they don't seem to understand me? Who will make sure I'm well treated when I can no longer speak for myself? Will anyone remember me after I've gone?

Dignity in death is not always easily identifiable, and the achievement of this goal can hardly be proved by satisfaction questionnaires from those who have died! However, there are some indicators. Consistency brings its own measure of comfort and dignity to the resident when frequent close attention is paid to them, rather than checking from the doorway. Emphasis on skilled, thorough and integrated care from nurses and allied health staff cannot be stressed too much. From the carer's perspective, dignity may be signified by the 'do not disturb' syndrome. Nurses have been heard to say, 'We didn't turn her (or do her dressing, or attend to pressure care) through the night. We didn't want to disturb her.' While, in some instances, this may be appropriate, it is important to ensure this is the resident's wish rather than the nurse's assumption. There may be personal factors to consider here, such as fear that the resident might die at the very moment staff provide the care. Although this staff member's fear may be based in reality, the resident's need for frequent, close contact should be paramount. Compassion may be conveyed by the tender, tactile communication and close presence of a carer. When a resident is left alone 'because he seems so comfortable' he may be longing for human contact. One of nursing's great teachers, Florence Nightingale, suggests, 'Apprehension, uncertainty, waiting, expectation, fear of surprise, do a patient more harm than any exertion.'

When the resident is no longer able to communicate clearly, thoroughly documented attention to all care says in effect: 'You will not be deserted now you are dying. You may not be able to tell us what you want but we will come back in half an hour. Our close presence with you is intended to bring reassurance and to allay any anxiety you may be experiencing. Writing about what we do provides a calculable measure of the dignity we accord to you.' Family members and other visitors will be reassured also by consistent attention, satisfied that, up to the precise moment of death, dignity is maintained.

Dignity comes in many guises. What may appear professionally undignified in one instance may be a harmless, humorous exchange between carer and resident who know each other well, for example, in the friendly exchange: 'Will you miss me when I'm gone?' 'Of course not, Charlie. We can't wait to be rid of you.' In another instance a resident's dignity will be evident through a shared poem, reading or song. For one resident, dying may be a very private experience, a withdrawal from familiar contacts; for another, constant visits including visits from other residents are a welcome acknowledgement that dying occurs within a community of the living.

Of course, we will never achieve perfection; reflecting on our practice may, however, ensure that glaring mistakes are not repeated. Through the story of Mr Papandreou the reader may be stimulated to reflect on practice, asking the questions: Did we accord this resident the dignity appropriate to his situation? If not, where did we go wrong? What were the positive factors? How may we now improve our practice?

Mr Papandreou: A dignified death?

'What's wrong with the man in the third bed?'

'Oh, nothing much, but lately he's always complaining.'

The agency nurse looks at the chart. 'Diagnosis: Frailty. IDC.' She wonders why he has an indwelling catheter, and what the diagnosis 'frailty' means. As the diagnosis section is undated she assumes the data is from the date of admission. If he was frail when he was admitted four years ago, the nurse wonders what his current diagnosis is! By this time, handover is finished and the agency nurse discusses the issues with one of the nurses who knows the resident well. Another care attendant shakes her head. 'I don't think he's got a catheter, he's never had one since I've been here, and that's three years.'

Flicking through the resident's past notes, the agency nurse in charge discovers a reference to 'heart attacks', thyroid deficiency and osteoarthritis. Turning to the drug chart, trying to gain a holistic picture of the resident, she notes a variety of cardiac drugs as well as anti-Parkinson drugs. Someone says, 'Yes, I think he's got Parkinson's.' Another nurse comments that he always screams out when he's touched or turned, and they've all decided he's mainly a 'behaviour problem'. 'I might scream if I had osteoarthritis, Parkinson's, contracted limbs and the anxiety of chest pain,' says the agency nurse to herself.

Mr Papandreou did have increasingly severe chest pain. An ambulance was called by the agency nurse on advice from a locum medical officer who had never met him before. Mr Papandreou died alone in the hospital emergency department.

One week later, Jim arrived for his regular Tuesday evening nursing shift. Tucked under his arm was the Greek newspaper he brought each week for Mr Papandreou.

'Where's Angelos?' he asked, puzzled by the unfamiliar resident in bed three.

'Oh, he's gone,' said Jo from the next bed.

'Where to?' asked Jim.

'I don't know,' said Jo. 'The night staff didn't say.'

The night staff knew exactly where Mr Papandreou had gone — to the hospital mortuary.

ON REFLECTION...

Loss of dignity

Euphemisms for death are often used as an alternative to stating the clear fact of death. There is little dignity in death when there is this kind of cover-up. The elderly residents in our nursing homes know about death. They do not need us to protect them. They know, too, that their death might be next. When death is not taken seriously and the resident is not given the dignity of a truthful statement, the dignity of the living resident who has shared his room for these past four years is also affected. No-one told Jim of Mr Papandreou's death; and he was one of the few staff who had a positive relationship with him. Sadly, the potential for death with dignity was seriously compromised.

Jim knew that Mr Papandreou had pleaded with him only the previous week to make sure that he was not taken to hospital. 'I want to die here,' he told Jim. Had that statement of confidence and trust been taken seriously and recorded in the care plan, Mr Papandreou may have been afforded greater dignity. We do not respect a resident's dignity when we toss to one side their most telling comments such as, 'I probably won't be here when you come back from holidays.' A flippant reply such as, 'Don't be silly, of course you will!' may help to restore the nurse's equilibrium but does little to ensure the resident has been heard and understood.

Diagnosis

One important way of conferring dignity is to know the residents well; not only by their medical diagnoses, but also by the care issues they regard as most important. Knowing residents thoroughly in terms of accurate medical diagnosis, behavioural changes and reasons for medication is no longer the sole province of medical personnel. Well-educated nurses and other carers have no excuse for negligence in this area. After several years, it appeared that few staff really knew about Mr Papandreou in the context of his major medical diagnoses as well as his psycho-emotional needs. Nobody had sought to understand what dignity meant to him.

The resident, our teacher

By trying to enter Mr Papandreou's experience, we are opening ourselves to new learning. Here, we are not the teachers. We may know everything there is to know about pressure care, giving injections, incontinence, calling ambulances, even recognising a cardiac crisis but, in this case, we have the opportunity to learn other lessons. Reflecting on the gaps in Mr Papandreou's care may increase our awareness and so lead to better care for others. As long as we label residents as difficult, demanding or hard to understand, we will not allow ourselves to be affected by the whole person in the context of their environment. Mr Papandreou was more than the sum of his symptoms and the unlovable exterior shown by his demanding and irritating habits. Jim came close to experiencing another side to him but, unfortunately, this knowledge was not shared; for Jim was not understood either. 'It beats me why Jim spends so much time with that Greek man. They don't even speak the same language.'

There are actions that might have altered Mr Papandreou's experience of death significantly. Using this episode of care as an example, a meeting of concerned staff might have looked at:
- what factors impeded the agency nurse's knowledge of the resident
- whether there was an alternative to calling an ambulance
- how Jim's feelings could have been taken into account by other staff
- whether staff are encouraged to record and report such significant interactions as Jim had experienced with Mr Papandreou.

The measuring tool

Measuring dignity has less to do with facts and figures than the nature of experience itself.
- Who is this person whose life is ebbing away?
- What does this person mean to me?
- What do I contribute to the quality of this person's living and dying?
- What does dignity mean to this resident in the context of family, staff and the homelike environment we are encouraged to foster?
- How can we promote a partnership of care in which each resident's dignity is paramount?
- Have we considered that dignity is a gift we bestow on another person, rather than a set of rules to obey?

To ask such questions is to focus on the person as more than just the number of heart beats per minute, irregular respiration, skin colour or the site of a tumour. That is not to say that facts and figures and vital signs are irrelevant in pursuing our goal of dignity for the resident who is dying. It does, however, emphasise the intensive nature of terminal care. This replaces the 'high-tech' care of the intensive care unit with the 'high-touch' care offered by staff, volunteers and families. This kind of touch is intuitive; involving response to a hunch or a feeling that something is not quite right. In long-term care, there are opportunities to develop a close partnership with a resident who is dying. In this partnership, something else is at work that will never be recorded through the stethoscope or the blood pressure machine. The vital signs of such a relationship may, however, be life giving.

Measuring quality

The notion of continuous quality improvement and its associated audits will not be addressed in detail here, except to alert the reader to some specific measures of dignity. For example, in a residents and relatives committee meeting, this remark was made by a resident, 'It was so lovely to see the care they gave Phyllis. I watched their every move. I hope that when my time comes they will care for me like that, too.' A relative commented, 'I think it's marvellous the way they get Betty up and dressed each day, even though she may not have long to live.' And a further comment: 'Phyllis looked very peaceful. I saw her just after she died. The nurses were so gentle; they made her look really dignified.' These comments serve as a useful guide to quality and a measure of dignity.

Regular review

As already indicated, when a resident's death is imminent it is unwise to assume that information given on admission is current. Dignity is enhanced by accurate documentation based on accuracy of diagnosis, as well as by reviewing all aspects of the resident's care in a non-threatening and conversational manner. Quality of dying depends on the quality of life leading up to that death. It is hard for a resident to be reassured about facing death if they have found a lack of trust and lack of reassurance during the previous months or years. Regular reviews may assist in establishing, and then continuing, this level of trust and reassurance. Each nursing home will develop its own method for formalising this concept. It may be possible to set aside a fixed hour of the week in which one resident's total care is reviewed. A holistic focus requires the presence of the resident (where appropriate), family or carer, doctor and a representative number of interdisciplinary staff. In order to cover all aspects of care, a standard agenda, focusing on the various standards of care required, is useful. Alternatively, the care plan may be used as a means by which all aspects of care are reviewed. Accurate recording of the review meeting, together with follow-up and communication of changes, are important elements in the review process.

'How do we get time to do this?' is a common objection. In measuring dignity one may add up all the informal conversations, expressions of opinion, time and frustration spent on many phone calls to family, and inconsistencies resulting from the lack of a comprehensive plan, and ask whether, in fairness to the resident, all this time results in better care. Spending one hour, well planned, with key personnel present, achieves a more efficient framework for measuring the outcome of care.

Important ingredients for measuring dignity include: an appropriate knowledge base, current information, continual assessment, agreed goals and a comprehensive plan of action. Naturally, if circumstances change, further review will be needed. Again, revising some points in the plan will prove more efficient than dealing with negative consequences of inconsistent care. Residents and families are often empowered by the opportunity to be involved in planning the care; dignity is then matched to their expectations rather than staff presumptions. Professional carers are not the sole arbiters of dignity.

When measuring dignity sometimes the most basic elements of care are the most significant, as Bozza's story indicates.

Bozza: What's in a name?

He is always curled up in a little ball in the middle of the bed, as if asleep. Although he is tiny and never moves spontaneously, the bedrails are always raised. You can tell when he wakes up, by his repetitive chin movements. No-one can remember him being any different; he was like this when admitted. His difficult, unfamiliar name is not Anglo-Saxon. Because few staff know how to pronounce his first name, his surname is shortened for convenience. There is a religious amulet pinned over his bed but no-one knows who put it there.

ON REFLECTION...

What's in a name?

The example of 'Bozza' is an important reminder of this most tangible measure of dignity. When there seems little else to go by, attention to correct details of spelling and pronunciation of a resident's name is an important yardstick. Staff should ask themselves, 'How important it is to me that others get my name right?'

Identity: does anybody know who this person is?

Holistic care of residents with dementia includes acknowledging their social identity. This may be drawn from a comprehensive social history, an important adjunct to a carefully documented record of the resident's disease process. When residents themselves are unable to provide significant details, families may willingly share their knowledge of the resident's personality and life before entering the nursing home. Families may also provide photographs of special people in this resident's life history, together with mementos of the most special person of all — this particular resident.

The family

Some residents' special worth is acknowledged by their families or close friends. In the absence of family or friends, we are the only ones able to speak for these residents, and to tell their unique stories. Even when we have no details of the resident's former life, the care we provide defines the resident's value. The value of even the most socially isolated resident is demonstrated when:

- that resident's cupboards and drawers are kept tidy, clean and well stocked with personal items
- the laundry staff carefully hang or fold laundered garments
- staff regularly pause by the bed to give a personalised greeting
- birthdays are celebrated
- special care is taken to turn the resident gently and with love, even if it is the only touch to be felt for the next few hours
- staff know exactly how the resident's tea is to be sweetened
- the kitchen staff know of special likes and dislikes.

Then the resident is treated with respect and dignity.

Assumptions are often made of a non-communicative resident. Is it really necessary to have the bedrails raised at all times? Discussion among the staff, verified by clear instructions in the care plan, may result in the sides being removed and other measures taken to maximise safety. Communication is the key. Families may need to be acquainted with the latest research which shows the risks associated with bedrails. Some families will need reassurance and explanation, so will some staff.

Who measures dignity?

Dignity is measured by those responsible for the care of the resident; by those who consider the resident in the holistic context of their family and the nursing home environment; and by those families or carers who watch and wait. How is dignity measured? By knowing in advance what dignity means to this particular resident; by measuring care against the legislative standards and nursing home policies; by adding appropriate, individualised interventions to increase the quality of living and dying for each resident in our care.

First impressions

Reference has been made already to the significance of pre-admission communication, where accurate formal details are recorded and other, less tangible, information about the resident's life may give important clues for measuring dignity. Preparation for death with dignity begins from the date of the resident's admission, and only by appropriate evaluation after the death can an accurate outcome be demonstrated. A clear statement to prospective residents and their families assures them of the best care for the remainder of the resident's life. For most residents this is their final move, their last home. For many, thoughts of death may not be far from their mind. From their first contact with the nursing home, prospective residents and their families gain an impression of the measure of dignity they may expect.

Learning from 'Bozza'

The very small segment from 'Bozza's' story told above has highlighted a significant number of points for reflection, signifying once again how much there is to learn from each resident. In pausing to reflect on practice, many issues have emerged, showing there was much more to 'Bozza' than this brief description conveys. In asking, 'Who is this person in the context of his past history and present experience?' we may begin to delve more deeply into what it means to care holistically. In trying to penetrate beneath the surface, we may begin to understand the experience of dying from the perspective of the resident. To do this is to learn about our own humanity.

QUALITY ISSUES FOR ENHANCED PRACTICE

The gerontic nurse

- Accurate diagnostic detail, updated regularly and clearly accessible in the resident's record, provides important data for all nursing and allied health staff.
- Regular checking of basic data, in collaboration with the doctor, is one way of ensuring the resident's diagnosis is accurately recorded.
- Recording what may be perceived as a flippant, trivial comment may provide deep insight into the resident's feelings about impending death. When such a comment is recorded in the resident's own words, no interpretation is required; it may have profound significance in some circumstances and not in others.
- A 'history summary' which records major crises and episodes in the resident's recent care provides instant information to staff unfamiliar with the resident's care, as well as a quick reference for all staff. As with all documentation, regular review is essential.
- Team members, including indirect carers, welcome the reassurance that comments made to them by residents will be treated professionally and documented accurately.

Management

- Ongoing education sessions are necessary to sharpen documentation practice.
- Audits of clinical records are useful in establishing where deficits are located.

Indirect carers

- When indirect carers pass information on to the other members of the care team, the clinical record of care will be improved.

ECONOMIC/POLITICAL ISSUES: WE MUST FILL THE BED TODAY

Many of the stories have highlighted the need for appropriate funding to support the care needed by residents who are facing death. This section identifies some of the funding implications arising from holistic care (which includes the care of families, other residents and staff), indicating the need for greater flexibility in the way funding is apportioned to the care of nursing home residents.

When economic pressures take precedence over the need for holistic care, it is the residents who miss out. In a society oriented to youth, where the spirit of individualism rather than the spirit of community is paramount, the death of a nursing home resident fails to attract a priority rating. Nursing home residents are not expendable products to be disposed of as if they have no value. However, seldom does the care of dying residents attract funds needed to enhance their care.

Appropriate equipment

While many of the stories in this book highlight the importance of a change in focus or attitude on the part of the carers, factors identified as lacking in the care of dying residents also originate in the failure to secure adequate resources. One of the more tangible resources not specifically highlighted in the stories is appropriate equipment. In order to provide maximum comfort to a dying resident, equipment such as specialised bedding may prevent the unnecessary suffering associated with pressure sores. Ironically, the cost (in staff time and other resources) of dealing with such suffering often outweighs the cost of the preventive equipment. Similarly, specialist equipment is available for lifting, bathing and toileting a dying resident; all marketed with the goal of enhanced comfort. There are no justifiable reasons to deny nursing home residents items of comfort readily available in other areas of the health industry. From simple protective bedding to the most efficient means of drug administration, nursing home residents will benefit by access to appropriate physical resources. When calculating the cost of such equipment, less tangible factors, such as staff stress, inefficient use of staff time and potential for staff injuries all need to be considered.

Cultural resources

Cultural considerations have been addressed in other chapters, where the importance of staff education is emphasised. Provision of culturally sensitive, holistic care depends on access to educational material, translation and interpreter services, appropriate food services, and support networks. Additional resources may be required in anticipation of a resident's death, so that specific cultural needs can be clarified. Such advance planning is reassuring to the resident and family, and is likely to produce a satisfactory outcome rather than disappointment about gaps in care.

Volunteers

As is evident from the stories in this book, volunteers are a highly valuable part of the team. Nevertheless, for those nursing homes fortunate to have volunteers, the problem of recruitment, coordination, education, support and evaluation of their services often remains unresolved. Because volunteers are not rewarded financially, incentive and recognition of their work may be gained by supportive supervision and reimbursement of travel and phone expenses. As many volunteers will attest, it takes special skill to relate to a nursing home resident whose death is imminent. Given adequate training and supervision, such volunteers have the potential to be a cost-effective means of complementing professional care. Failure to provide support may result in volunteers suffering burnout, or merely failing to maintain attendance. Without the opportunity for explanation or discussion, important reflections on practice are denied; both staff and volunteers lose a valuable learning opportunity. Most importantly, without adequate follow-up, the volunteer's contribution may pass without acknowledgment. However, with staffing resources already severely constrained by inadequate funding, the luxury of employing a paid volunteer coordinator is one that many nursing homes are not able to afford.

The individual in community

Many of the stories in this book have focused on the resident as a unique individual who is also dependent on a community. When a sense of community is fostered, formally and informally, the potential exists for nursing home life in all its various aspects to flourish and thrive. The informal network, illustrated by the narratives which tell of friendships fostered, requires very little in the way of funding resources. However, as noted in other stories, the provision of adequate privacy for small groups to meet and talk offers an extra dimension which, in turn, assists the network of carers. Education and support sessions for this informal community are not provided for in the current funding mechanism; however, additional resources would acknowledge their support of the dying resident, enhancing this immeasurable asset.

Pre-admission coordination

When the care of the resident commences prior to admission, as illustrated by many of the stories, a relationship of trust is fostered and lines of communication are clarified. Appropriate pre-admission visits and discussions concerning issues of death and dying may ultimately save many phone calls and discussions by professional staff. It is apparent from some of our stories, that when the care is coordinated from the beginning, the response is likely to be more in tune with the resident's needs and much time is saved at a later stage. Appropriate resources for such pre-admission contact would be a worthy addition to funding a dying resident's care.

Chaplaincy services

This chapter highlights the lack of resources for providing responsive, best practice care for the dying resident. Many of the stories in this book alert us to the importance of assisting each resident to draw their life to a close in a dignified manner, bringing fulfilment and satisfaction in the resident's last days. We have also acknowledged the importance of the chaplain's role in this process. If chaplains and chapels are accepted as an important part of many hospitals and other community services, and if the funding of such services is considered vital for hospice and palliative care programs, the same should be true of nursing homes. Residents do not suddenly cease to need these services once they are accommodated in a nursing home. The provision of an on-site chapel is not always possible. However, with forward planning, the provision of space for such services can be fulfilled. There are many other practical alternatives, such as the setting aside of one room of the nursing home for a flexible meeting and conference room which also serves as a chapel. As shown in some of these stories, there is great advantage when funeral services are not isolated from the community in which the deceased has been most involved.

Bereavement follow-up

Bereavement counselling may not be needed or appropriate for the families of every deceased nursing home resident. However, our examples show there are some families for whom this service may mean the difference between healthy grieving and a pathological response to death. Many of the family members of deceased residents are themselves frail and elderly; holistic care of the resident includes appropriate bereavement support. There is a significant injustice in the funding of follow-up bereavement counselling for hospice in-patients and palliative care patients in the community, but not for those who die in the nursing home.

Support for staff

Staff issues have been given a prominent place in this book. The importance of a stable staff population with high morale has enormous benefits for dying residents and their families. However, staff may also require support as they grieve for a dying or deceased resident. When the bed has to be filled with such haste, and concentration brought to bear on the new resident, overall care may be compromised by insufficient support being given to staff. A simple means of providing such support may be through flexible staffing arrangements which allow for funeral attendance, or by allowing time for debriefing following a traumatic episode or incident. While these suggestions do not amount to large-scale changes, increased flexibility in funding would facilitate staff satisfaction and, in turn, benefit the care of all residents.

Specialist palliative care staff

Further inequity is apparent when hospice/palliative care services are funded to attract specialist staff who are appropriately educated in this area. While there remains a disproportionate rate of pay for these nurses in comparison with aged-care nurses, the care of residents and their families will suffer. When the nursing home is adequately resourced by well-qualified nurses, the incidence of hospital admission is reduced, resulting in significant saving in the general health budget. Nursing home residents who are dying, and their families who are grieving, deserve to receive the same kind of care offered to others.

Funding

While current funding procedures make some allowances for a resident's palliative care needs, more research is needed into the adequacy of the funding tool for measuring the resident's requirements at this significant point in their lives. Issues such as adequate staffing levels, appropriately qualified staff, specialist equipment, a coordinated volunteer service, spiritual care and bereavement follow-up have been discussed throughout this book. However, the statistics of the ageing population, cancer rates, foreshadowed increase in dementia and chronic degenerative diseases, all point to the urgent need for adequately funded nursing home palliative care.

Dignity

We have also addressed the concept of dignity within the economic constraint of filling the bed left vacant by the deceased resident, noting some of the unintended consequences of filling the bed with undue haste. While there is, at present, some flexibility that allows a resident extra time before leaving their former home or hospital to enter a nursing home, this does not meet the prospective resident's need in all instances. More effective (including cost-effective) and efficient care can be given to a new resident when time is allowed for a dignified farewell to the former, deceased resident. Adequate preparation for admission of the new resident will, in turn, affect the quality of care when that resident also reaches the point of death.

QUALITY ISSUES FOR ENHANCED PRACTICE

The gerontic nurse

- Gerontic nurses with knowledge of palliative care are responsible for the careful and thorough assessment of equipment, making recommendations for appropriate capital expenditure funding.
- Gerontic nurses with current information concerning relevant resources for palliative care will ensure aged people in nursing homes have access to appropriate holistic care.
- If nurses establish and maintain their own links with specialist groups, such as gerontic nursing and palliative care nursing, resident care will be enhanced.

Management

- Creative ways to obtain palliative equipment, such as battery-operated syringe pumps for delivering narcotics, may include writing to drug companies or equipment manufacturers for financial assistance.
- Relatives may be willing to hire equipment for short-term use.
- Special fundraising may result in procurement of other material resources for palliative care.
- Where other resource options exist, scholarships or study leave may be offered to nurses willing to pursue study in palliative care.

Indirect carers

- The experience of indirect carers may provide creative options for equipment purchase and other material resources.
- Volunteers may be willing to assist with an informal bereavement support group for grieving families, while local communities may offer access to a chapel, pastoral care and bereavement follow up.

THE LAST WORD: A SHARED WORLD

This concluding chapter documents an encounter with the old-old. Centenarians are no longer a novelty; those living beyond 100 years are extending the demographic predictions and becoming a visible sign of the ageing society. Those who were called the pre-old, the young-old, and who are now the old-old or super-old may need a new 'label' as they surpass the elitist-old, outliving current expectations of longevity. Because of this, it becomes difficult to define those who are the middle-aged. And who are the not-old? Those younger than 40 or 50 or 60? The presence of Gracie in our nursing home has challenged our ideas of what it means to grow old, and challenged us to re-think the way we care for those who have lived not only for three-score years and ten, but longer. Gracie's questions and conversations at the age of 102 signify her search for meaning; a common human quest, at any age.

THE OLD-OLD: BRIDGING THE GAP

Tap, tap, tap on the wooden arm of the chair, 'Yoo-hoo, is anyone there?'

The nurse quickly responded to Gracie's call, 'Yes, Gracie. What do you want?'

'I don't want anything!' Gracie replied.

'Well, why are you calling out all the time?' persisted the nurse.

'I just want to know whether I'm a human being or a lump of wood.'

Searching round for someone else who may be better equipped to interpret Gracie's question, the nurse beckoned to a colleague.

'Do you feel more like a lump of wood than a person?' asked the second nurse.

'Well, I'm not sure,' replied Gracie, 'I sometimes feel like I'm a lump of wood. I don't mean I'm treated badly or roughly, but I don't feel really treated like a person.'

'What makes you feel like a person?' continued the enquiring nurse.

'When I can talk to somebody,' Gracie replied.

Gracie's many physical difficulties and deficits were easily attended to. Carers in nursing homes know how to deal with incontinence, poor mobility, impaired vision and increasing frailty; but Gracie's independent spirit and philosophical outlook challenged a deeper core, demanding a personal response.

'Tell me about some of your early life as a teenager,' prompted the nurse. No further encouragement was needed. Gracie began speaking of her love of books, asking the nurse whether she had any favourites among Dickens' characters. Next came the description of her long voyage to England by ship, a tale of romance and adventure, including her visit to London 'to see the Queen', naming the royal occupants of Buckingham Palace in 1913. Then she described the war years when affluence gave way to hardship. Having found that the nurse also lived in the inner city, Gracie discovered some common ground in their knowledge of the inner suburbs. The nurse was delighted by Gracie's description of her walks to the city before the tram lines were installed. Finally, when the nurse's other duties called her away, Gracie concluded, 'Thanks, my dear, thanks so much for listening. I feel so much better.' And, of course, the tap, tap, tapping stopped for a while.

Gracie's responses were not always congenial or gracious; she could be curt and sarcastic, quick-witted and critical, leaving some staff wishing she would keep her demands to the manageable requests for toileting or drinks. Gracie had no qualms about correcting another person's pronunciation; she delighted in exploring the meanings of words, and would not be pacified by trite explanations.

'Come on Gracie, it's hairdressing day.'

'What do I want a hairdresser for?'

'So your hair will look clean and shiny and then the hairdresser will set it for you.'

'But why should I have my hair washed when it's not dirty. I had it done last week.'

'No,' the nurse persisted, 'It's three weeks since you last went to the hairdresser. Look, I've got a record of it in the hairdressing book.'

'Bah!' said Gracie. 'You could have written it in the book just now, to trick me. I'm quite satisfied with my hair the way it is, so take your book to the next customer.'

Not the kind of conversation to endear this very young carer to this very old resident. And yet, others were able to find a meeting ground.

'How are you this morning, Gracie?'

'I'm not sure how I feel. I don't feel sick or anything, I'm not in pain. I feel [pause] insulted.' Quick to allay the nurse's fears that she had suffered inappropriate or unkind comments from a staff member, Gracie continued, 'Oh, I don't mean verbally insulted. I just feel…'

'That your whole self has suffered an insult?'

'Yes, that's right. My whole being is insulted.'

'Tell me what makes you feel you have suffered such an insult.'

Gracie recounted the events of recent months when she had been forced to leave her own home and enter hospital 'for my own good'. Then, she found herself being assessed for nursing home care and, even several months after admission, she could not accept this serious 'blow' to her being. No explanations about her increasing frailty at home alone, no logic about the imminent danger to herself when she continually left the gas on or tripped over the ragged carpet, none of these reasons was adequate.

'Who made this decision?' she asked.

'Oh, the geriatrician,' replied the nurse with confidence and authority, 'He's the person specially trained to know the needs of older people.'

'Hmph,' replied Gracie, 'What would he know!'

Trying to give further credence to this professional decision-making process, the nurse added, 'They don't let just one person decide. They have a team meeting, it's called the assessment team.'

'Oh,' said Gracie with an air of sarcasm, 'So you mean I'm here on the considered judgement of a government department!'

Gracie wanted to be heard. Widowed since the age of 50 and having her two children die quite young, she had lived independently for over 50 years. It was indeed insulting to leave her beloved home and find herself among strangers.

Nor was she to be reassured by the homelike environment the nursing home promised. Having been coaxed into the lounge to listen to a visiting music group, she enquired in a loud voice, 'Who are all these people in my lounge? You said this was my home, but I didn't invite them in. Tell them to go home, or take me to my room.'

Sometimes it was hard to know how to pacify Gracie, but some staff had the knack. Knowing Gracie had a cousin of whom she was very fond, one intuitive nurse asked Gracie if she would like to speak to Annie on the phone, thinking that someone of her own family might cheer her up.

It is difficult to find a quiet place for a resident's phone call in a busy nursing home with shared rooms and few places for privacy. So, Gracie's conversation was overheard. 'That you, Annie? I just thought I'd call to see how you are? Are you sure I'm not interrupting your tea? Oh, you've just put the potatoes on? They're looking after me well here. Yes, the meals are nice, and yes, I suppose it's a relief not to have to cook for myself any more. How's Bert? Yes, that would be nice if you could come and see me. Next Tuesday? All right, my dear. I'll let you go now. Lovely to hear from you.'

Although this episode was recounted throughout the nursing home over the next few days as a breakthrough in creative communication between resident and family, there was no further evidence of any other staff taking the initiative to connect Gracie to her cousin by phone.

On another occasion it seemed as though Gracie may have wanted to discuss the issue of death and dying — surely a pertinent issue for one so old?

'How are you this morning, Gracie?'

'One step nearer heaven,' she replied.

Ready to take this cue, ripe for interpretation, the nurse encouraged Gracie to talk more descriptively, 'Do you have any fears or concerns about dying, Gracie?'

'Heavens, no,' she replied, 'It doesn't bother me at all. I suppose it will just feel like sleep.'

Several more futile attempts were made to involve Gracie in a deep and meaningful discussion about death. Surely a woman of her age would have some deep philosophical contribution towards the common research topic of death and dying? Not so. If Gracie had any deeper thoughts on the subject she was certainly not about to share them. And, as she continued to make the same reply each morning for the next two years, it was apparent she was not really talking about her imminent death! If Gracie's concern at 102 years of age was not necessarily to speak of death, neither was she wanting to talk about activities which may help her regain some of her independence. She was not interested in assisting with her own hygiene or doing anything much at all. In a world which gains meaning through activity and busy-ness, Gracie wanted to find some point to her existence.

'I feel that at 102 I'm not much use to anybody. I just feel as though I'm something to be cared for; and they do care for me very well. I think that I'm pretty good for my age but the trouble is that nobody else has lasted as long as I have and I'm not sure what the point of it all is… Do I have to do anything? You're so patient to sit here with me. Are you sure I don't have to be doing something? Can I just sit here? It's lovely of you to stop and talk to me. I feel this has been better than 40 tonics!'

This very brief conversation had the effect on Gracie of an old-fashioned 'pick-me-up' tonic; a magic potion that was life giving. Gracie was not seeking explanations, advice, instructions, directions or even deep discussion about life's meaning. Life's meaning seemed to make sense only through the close, tactile and conversational presence of another human being. In the nursing home world where so much activity is focused on instructions and tasks (washing, dressing, bathing, toileting) and so much 'conversation' is prefaced by, 'Now, Mrs Smith, I just want you to…', Gracie was seeking another way of being together with her carer. Constantly refusing to join in any of the social programs, Gracie's one source of meaning came from a two or three minute meeting when she felt the presence of another person not as a burden imposed, but as a liberating encounter.

Those who took up the challenge to meet Gracie at the point of her greatest need helped to bridge the gap between the not-so-old and the old-old.

ON REFLECTION…

What of our own frailty as carers?

Gracie's frail physical presence housing a strong, determined spirit suggests something of a role reversal between resident and carer. We were not necessarily able to meet Gracie's needs by merely attending to her physical comfort, nor by continually asking her what she wanted and why she persisted in calling out. Our inability to enter her world suggests our own limitations, even our own disability and frailty. On a physical level, all Gracie's carers were far more robust than she. Yet, in our inability to understand her needs, we showed our own frailty and inadequacy.

A mere curiosity?

Although there are more centenarians than ever before, the presence of one or two residents over 100 may still be a novelty in some nursing homes. It is important that the resident does not become a mere curiosity ('Hasn't she got marvellous skin?' 'She's still got a mind of her own!' or 'I've never seen anyone this old before.'). Care and sensitivity are also required when publicity is considered. Gracie did not want her photo published on her 102nd birthday ('Who'd want to see my ugly old face!') but for her 103rd birthday she changed her mind ('Do I look all right in this cardigan?'). Publicity can be a positive feature when the concentration is on the person in the context of their life history, rather than merely on their chronological age.

Discussing death and dying

It ought not be assumed that residents facing death necessarily wish to talk about it. Some may welcome the opportunity for a deep and meaningful discussion on the topic of death and dying while others see no need for divulging their feelings to anyone. There is no value judgement to be placed on either response. For some, death remains a remote and strange phenomenon, to be kept out of reach — into the distance of the future regardless of their age. Others may be very grateful for a carer to take up their cue when the topic is raised. Sensitivity is required to provide opportunities for such discussion, without the resident feeling any compulsion to speak about what they hold to be private matters. Residents may, of course, like any of us, change their minds. Closing the door on discussion one day may not mean the subject is closed for all time. Gracie's regular morning statement about being 'one step nearer heaven' may not usually call forth a response. However, carers need to be aware that the unexpected often happens. There may have been other occasions when Gracie would have liked further dialogue on the subject. These occasions often arise spontaneously, and when the carer is least prepared. This does not mean the carer is expected to have the answers. Responding with an open-ended question is often the most appropriate way of inviting dialogue. 'Tell me what heaven means to you, Gracie' may be the prompt required.

Being and doing

Gracie's question about whether she should be doing anything is a sharp reminder of contemporary emphasis on productivity. It is also a reminder to staff that the care they give is not focused on things to be done; care is grounded in the vulnerability of the other person. This involves being with the other person as one who watches with and stands by that person; attending and listening with openness, rather than confronting the person with a set of prescriptive questions or tasks. This focus involves the being of the carer as well as the being of the resident; an attitude conveyed by a smile, a gesture, a hug, a supporting hand. The carer is also vulnerable, not always knowing how to respond to this old-old resident; however, in taking this stance the carer bridges the gap. This kind of care is about the kind of people we are, rather than what we do.

Swimming against the tide

Some economists, rationalists, statisticians and demographers would have us believe we are being confronted by a tidal wave of ageing, which is going to ruin the economy by stretching health resources to the limit. The warning is like that for a global disaster. Others would have us believe in a utopian world where medical miracles will cure all diseases and prolong life indefinitely. Whatever the dominant tide, residents and carers may flounder in the crosscurrents or swim across the rip, swimming in to shore rather than being swept out to sea. This goal of heading for the shore, rather than being taken out beyond the horizon, will be accomplished by maintaining strong advocacy and life-saving support for those who have lived to old-old age.

Nursing home 'placement'

This term describes Gracie's feelings about being made into an object — 'like a lump of wood' — rather than a human being. One picks up an object and places it somewhere else. When Gracie spoke of being 'insulted' she seemed to be saying she had suffered blows more readily associated with instruments or weapons rather than humans. Great sensitivity is needed at the point of decision making regarding nursing home care. The ideal situation occurs when the prospective resident is able to choose their own nursing home accommodation, on the basis of first-hand comparisons. However, this is seldom the case, as the increased frailty of residents demonstrates.

When a person faces nursing home admission, great care is needed during the pre-admission process. While the predominant media perceptions of nursing homes is of 'a fate worse than death', or 'God's waiting rooms' or 'the last resort', a far more positive view can be offered to the prospective resident and their family. When this process is followed with professional confidence and pride, a spirit of hope replaces a climate of despair. Rather than being left with a 'this is the end of the road' attitude, residents and their families may have their despair reversed by an attitude which promotes a philosophy such as, 'there is life after entering a nursing home'.

Monologue or dialogue?

Gracie's monologue, her constant calling out and repeating certain phrases, such as 'Where am I? Is anybody there?', may be interpreted as a call for a partner in conversation. While some staff were content to let her continue a constant stream of words which defied logical explanation or a reasoned answer, others took her signal as a quest for dialogue. Immediately Gracie felt someone was listening, she was reassured. She was reassured to have another human being, of any age, sit beside her without making demands, willing to enter into conversation. A monologue begins and ends with the self; a dialogue suggests the story will be carried on. When a resident receives a partner in dialogue, then the gap between the ages is bridged; continuity between two people is established and the mystery of life's meaning is shared.

FURTHER READING

Arblaster G, Brooks D, Hudson R, Petty M (1990): Terminally ill patients' expectations of nurses. *The Australian Journal of Advanced Nursing* 7(3): 34–43.

Ariès P (1981): *The Hour of Our Death* (Helen Weaver, trans.). New York: Alfred A Knopf.

Becker E (1973): *The Denial of Death*. New York: The Free Press.

Benner P (1984): *From Novice to Expert: Excellence and Power in Clinical Nursing Practice*. California: Addison-Wesley Publishing Company Nursing Division.

Benner P, Wrubel J (1989): *The Primacy of Caring*. California: Addison-Wesley Publishing Company Inc.

Blytheway B (1995): *Ageism*. Buckingham: Philadelphia: Open University Press.

Cole TR, Winkler MG (eds) (1994): *The Oxford Book of Aging*. Oxford: Oxford University Press.

De Beauvoir S (1869): *A Very Easy Death* (Patrick O'Brien, trans.). Ringwood, Australia: Penguin.

Ebersole P, Hess P (1998): *Toward Healthy Aging: Human Needs and Nursing Response*. (5th edn). St Louis: Mosby.

Elias N (1985): *The Loneliness of the Dying* (Edmund Jephcott, trans.). Oxford: Basil Blackwood.

Faber H (1984): *Striking Sails: A Pastoral-Psychological View of Growing Older in Our Society* (Kenneth R Mitchell, trans.). Nashville: Abingdon Press.

Garratt S, Hamilton-Smith E (eds) (1995): *Rethinking Dementia: An Australian Approach*. Melbourne: Ausmed Publications.

Garrett G (ed.) (1991): *Healthy Ageing: Some Nursing Perspectives*. London: Wolfe Publishing Ltd.

Gibb H (1990): *Representations of Old Age: Notes towards a Critique and Revision of Ageism in Nursing Practice*. Geelong: Deakin University.

Gibson D. (1998): *Aged Care: Old Policies, New Problems.* Cambridge: Cambridge University Press.

Hudson R, Richmond J (1994): *Unique and Ordinary: Reflections on living and dying in a nursing home.* Melbourne: Ausmed Publications.

Hudson, R. (1997) 'Documented life and death in a nursing home.' In Richmond, J (Ed) *Nursing documentation: writing what we do.* Ausmed Publications: Melbourne.

Hudson R, Richmond J (1998): The Meaning of Death in Residential Aged Care. In: J. Parker & S. Aranda (eds): *Palliative Care: Explorations and Challenges.* Sydney: MacLennan & Petty, pp. 292–302).

Ignatieff M (1984): The Needs of Strangers. London: Chatto & Windus — The Hogarth Press.

Ignatieff M (1993): *Scar Tissue.* Toronto: Viking.

Johnstone M-J (1994): *Bioethics: A Nursing Perspective.* (2nd edn). Sydney: W B Saunders.

Johnstone M-J (1999): Old Age and Euthanasia. In: R. Nay & S. Garratt (eds): *Nursing Older People: Issues and Innovations.* Sydney: MacLennan & Petty, pp. 99–118.

Kanitsaki O (1999). Transcultural Issues and Innovations. In: R. Nay & S. Garratt (eds): *Nursing Older People: Issues and Innovations.* Sydney: MacLennan & Petty, pp. 78–98.

Kitwood T (1997): *Dementia Reconsidered: The Person Comes First.* Buckingham Philadelphia: Open University Press.

Kübler-Ross E (1969): *On Death and Dying.* New York: Macmillan.

Lewis C (1961): *A Grief Observed.* London: Faber and Faber.

Moody HR (1992): *Ethics in an Aging Society.* London: The Johns Hopkins University Press.

Nay R (1996): Nursing home entry: meaning making by relatives. *Australian Journal on Ageing* 15(3): 123–126.

Nay R (1997). Relatives' experiences of nursing home life: characterised by tension. *Australian Journal on Ageing* 16(1): 24–29.

Nay R, Garratt S (eds) (1999): *Nursing Older People: Issues and Innovations.* Sydney: MacLennan and Petty.

Nay R, Gorman D (1999): Sexuality in Aged Care. In: R. Nay & S. Garratt (eds): *Nursing Older People: Issues and Innovations.* Sydney: MacLennan & Petty, pp. 191–211.

Newton E (1981): *This Bed My Centre.* Melbourne: McPhee Gribble.

Nightingale, Florence(1969) *Notes on Nursing: what it is and what it is not.* New York: Dover Publications Inc.

Nouwen JM, Gaffney WJ (1976): *Aging: the Fulfilment of Life.* Garden City, New York: Image Books.

Parker J, Aranda S (eds) (1998): *Palliative Care: Explorations and Challenges.* Sydney: MacLennan and Petty.

Parker J, Gardner G (1991–1992): The silence and silencing of the nurse's voice: a reading of patient progress notes. *The Australian Journal of Advanced Nursing* 9(2): 3–9.

Paterson J, Zderad L (1988): *Humanistic Nursing.* New York: National League for Nursing.

Pearson A (1998): Nursing older people: learning from experience. *International Journal of Nursing Practice* 4(1): 1.

Pearson A, Nay R, Taylor B, Tucker C, Angus J, Griffiths V, Ruber A (1996): *Relatives' Experience of Nursing Home Entry: Meanings, Practice and Discourse.* Adelaide, Australia: University of Adelaide Department of Nursing.

Ramsay P (1970): *The Patient as Person: Explorations in Medical Ethics.* London: Yale University Press.

Raphael B. (1994): *The Anatomy of Bereavement.* Northvale, NJ: Jason Aranson.

Richmond J (ed.). (1997): *Nursing Documentation: writing what we do*. Melbourne: Ausmed Publications.

Ronaldson S (ed.) (1997): *Spirituality: The Heart of Nursing*. Melbourne: Ausmed Publications.

Rumbold B (1993): Some reflections on pastoral care and ageing. *St Mark's Review* 155 (Spring, 1993) 20–25.

Sarton M (1974): *As We Are Now*. London: Victor Gollancz Ltd.

Scott-Maxwell F (1968): *The Measure of My Days*. New York: Alfred Knopf.

Stevens J (1996): Working with the elderly: do nurses care for it? *Nursing Review* 1(4): 1–4.

Stevens J, Herbert J (1997): Ageism and nursing practice in Australia. *Nursing Review* (September 1997): 17–24.

Street A (1995): *Nursing Replay: Researching Nursing Culture Together*. Melbourne: Churchill Livingstone.

INDEX

All our years,
all the memories come…

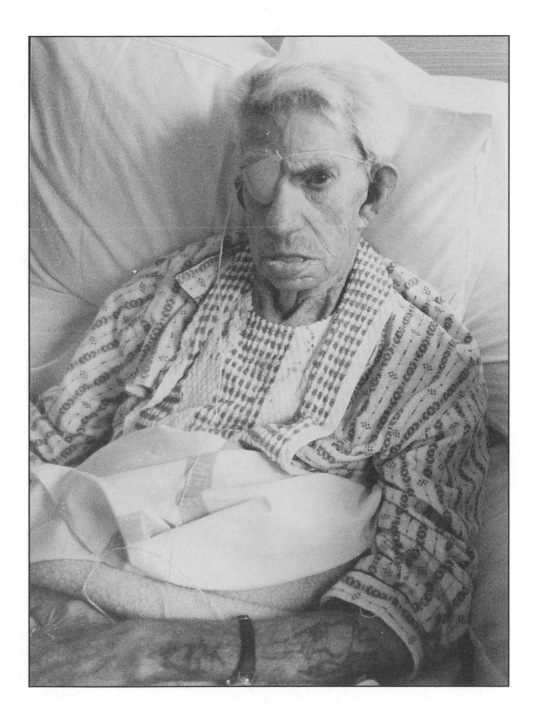

This is a funny sort of place to end your days —
and they say it is my home!
I just watch and keep my counsel,
for memories are free and I have plenty of them.

Put your hand upon my arm
and sit beside me just a moment more —
I hate to keep you from your work
but understand, my heart still beats . . .

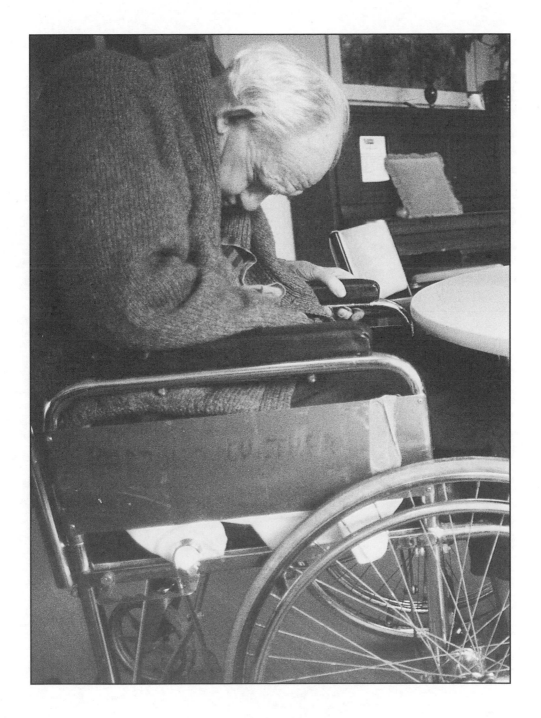

I was a farmer, nurse —
I wasn't always bent like this:
straight as the maize grew in the field,
I threw bales of hay much as you toss me . . .

For life has shown me many truths,
and though I may seem old to you
these misshapen hands were nimble once…